MARTIN LUTHER KING, JR. AND THE CIVIL RIGHTS MOVEMENT

Edited by David J. Garrow

A CARLSON PUBLISHING SERIES

The Social Vision of Martin Luther King, Jr.

Ira G. Zepp, Jr.

PREFACE BY DAVID J. GARROW

CARLSON
Publishing Inc

BROOKLYN, NEW YORK, 1989

Library of Congress Cataloging-in Publication Data

Zepp, Ira G.
   The social vision of Martin Luther King, Jr. / Ira G. Zepp, Jr.
      p.   cm. — (Martin Luther King, Jr. and the civil rights
   movement ; 18)
   Originally presented as the author's thesis (doctoral—St. Mary's
Seminary, 1971).
   Bibliography: p.
   Includes index.
   1. King, Martin Luther, Jr., 1929-1968. 2. Sociology, Christian–
–History of doctrines—20th century. 3. Race relations—Religious
aspects—Christianity—History of doctrines—20th century.
I. Title. II. Series.
E185.97.K5Z46 1989   261.8′092—dc20   89–7118
ISBN 0-926019-12-0 (alk. paper)

Typographic design: Julian Waters

Typeface: Bitstream ITC Galliard

The index to this book was created using NL Cindex, a scholarly indexing program from the Newberry Library.

For a complete listing of the volumes in this series, please see the back of this book.

Printed on acid-free, 250-year-life paper.

Manufactured in the United States of America.

For

CHARLES E. CRAIN

Professor of Religion, Western Maryland College, 1949-1978

Teacher, colleague, friend

Who seeks truth and is an example of grace

Contents

CHAPTER THREE: NONVIOLENCE

CHAPTER FOUR: CHRISTIAN REALISM

CHAPTER FIVE: PERSONALISM

CHAPTER SIX: KING'S VISION OF THE BELOVED COMMUNITY

Series Editor's Preface

Ira Zepp's 1971 doctoral dissertation on the intellectual sources of the ethical and social thought of Dr. Martin Luther King, Jr., remains, eighteen years later, the most valuable and useful study of written influences upon King yet completed. Many of Zepp's analytical insights were reflected in *Search for the Beloved Community: The Thinking of Martin Luther King, Jr.* (Judson Press, 1974; University Press of America, 1986), which he co-authored with one of King's own divinity school professors, Kenneth L. Smith, but Zepp's much more extensive dissertation is a crucial piece of analysis that each and every serious student of Martin Luther King, Jr., ought to be familiar with.

Much writing on King's intellectual sources has been either flat-footed quotation and summary, or single-theme perspectives which have erroneously sought to claim King for one particular school of thought–such as Boston University personalism–or another. In comparison with most of this work, Zepp's dissertation, like the modest Smith and Zepp 1974 volume, stands head and shoulders above the crowd in appreciating and reflecting the intellectual complexity and richness that helped produce the ethical and social thinking of Martin Luther King, Jr.

Only in the late 1980s have scholars started to appreciate more fully the extent to which Dr. King was heavily influenced both by the oral sermonic traditions of the southern black Baptist church in which he grew up, and by the liberal, white Protestant preaching tradition, exemplified by New York's Riverside Church pastors Harry Emerson Fosdick and Robert McCracken, to which King was exposed by means of published collections of sermons which he studied carefully throughout his formative years. The ongoing work of scholars such as Keith Miller will increasingly shed more and more light on these heretofore under– or unappreciated sermonic influences on the preaching and writing of Dr. King, but Ira Zepp's impressive study will still remain one of the most complete and useful analyses of Martin Luther King, Jr.'s intellectual roots ever written, no matter how extensive the shelf-full of works on Dr. King becomes in subsequent years. No King scholar should be without a carefully-perused copy of this book, and I'm extremely pleased that Carlson Publishing's eighteen volume series, *Martin Luther King, Jr. and the Civil Rights Movement*, is able to bring it to the attention of those scholars and libraries that will benefit from its ready availability.

David J. Garrow

Preface
1989

Soon after Martin Luther King, Jr., was assassinated, I had to submit a dissertation proposal for the doctor of philosophy to the faculty of the Ecumenical Institute of St. Mary's Seminary and University. Since my concentration in graduate studies was in theology and ethics, and since I admired the witness and work of the recently slain civil rights leader, I knew I wanted to do something on Martin King. That was twenty years ago.

I had read his books by this time and was taken by the autobiographical reflections of his intellectual journey in *Stride Toward Freedom* (Chapter 6) and in *Strength to Love* (Chapter 17). In those chapters, King referred happily and gratefully to the foundation of intellectually respectable religion he found in his mentors at Morehouse College. He then notes how he continued at Crozer Theological Seminary "a serious intellectual quest for a method to eliminate social evil." Then at Boston University, he discovered that personal idealism was "my basic philosophical position." It seemed to me that these chapters were fields that needed mining.

It was also clear to me that the "Beloved Community" was a central metaphor that pervaded his writing and speaking from Montgomery to Memphis. So I proposed to research the intellectual sources of King's ethical thought with a particular interest in his understanding of the Beloved Community. My intention was to provide an expansive intellectual, historical, and theological contextualization of King's seminary and graduate school years.

In many ways, the dissertation is a period piece. Therein lies its value and its deficiencies. It is limited by historical perspective, the data available at the time, and my own hermeneutical stance. Nevertheless, it has been decided, in the interest of historical integrity, to publish the dissertation virtually as it was written, "warts and all."

Two of the "warts" need to be addressed immediately. The dissertation was written before Martin King or I was conscious of sexist language. In 1970, inclusive language had not made its way into academic writing nor into the patterns of everyday speech. I apologize for this anachronism in the book.

In addition, my research took advantage of only the published articles and books by and about King available as of 1970. Some unpublished material such as early manuscripts of his addresses and sermons, letters, notes, and interviews were in the Boston Collection and I spent considerable time there in 1969.

But unavailable at that time was similar, immensely significant and indispensable material from 1963-1968, which is now housed in the King Archives at the Martin Luther King, Jr. Center for Social Change in Atlanta. This exhaustive collection of hand-written sermons, audio-tapes of King's speeches, sermons, and interviews provide us with the authentic message of King. The archives has only recently been made accessible to King scholars.

The methodology of the dissertation and a good deal of its research data found its way into a book I co-authored with Dr. Kenneth L. Smith, one of King's teachers at Crozer and now Dean of Colgate Rochester/Bexley Hall/Crozer Theological School in Rochester, New York. It was published by Judson Press in 1974 and was entitled *Search for the Beloved Community: The Thinking of Martin Luther King, Jr.*.[1]

I would like to respond briefly to some criticisms of the dissertation and suggest what might be its enduring contribution.

1. The main criticism of the dissertation has been its narrow understanding of "intellectual" and/or its perceived assumption that the only intellectual sources of King's thought were his graduate school courses. Those courses were one influence; they were, of course, not the only ones. The rich tradition of his family and the black church were ignored. Although this weakness of the dissertation was recognized on the first page and a disclaimer was made to that effect, the criticism is well taken.

I am indebted to James Cone for his persistence in declaring that King cannot be understood by simply appealing to the "perspectives of white theologians." King was a product of the black church and was fundamentally influenced by the rhetoric and content of the black religious tradition and its preaching.

Fortunately, this imbalance is being redressed in Cone's own writing, as well as in the work of Vincent Harding, William Watley, and David Garrow, among others.[2] However, we are still waiting for a systematic and definitive study of the black church's influence on Martin King.

2. John Ansbro, in his study of King's thought,[3] comments on the apparent disparity between the conclusions of the dissertation and *Search for the Beloved Community*. It has to do with whether King believed in the historical actualization of the Beloved Community. Ansbro says

> "Zepp should not have abandoned his earlier interpretation, which was based mainly on King's dependence on Niebuhr. At the conclusion of his dissertation Zepp had stated that perhaps King's dream, as King understood it, remained a dream which should be the object of our striving but which would never be totally 'realized in history'."[4]

First of all, there is ample room for honest disagreement among King interpreters whether or not he thought the Beloved Community would be fully realized in history. King, himself, gave signals to support one or both positions. Secondly, I did not actually "abandon my earlier interpretation." Upon further reflection I understood more clearly the eschatological nature of King's vision of the Beloved Community. It is "already" and "not yet" as King said, but that vision also is a magnet attracting us to more completely fulfill its ideals of love and justice. King saw glimpses of this in the civil rights movement and its presence in to whatever degree society was integrated and free of racism and bigotry. I now see King as more dialectical in his understanding of the actualization of the Beloved Community than in the original dissertation.

3. David Garrow has helped King scholars immeasurably by revealing the discovery that a good deal of what appears under King's name was not written by him. His books, especially *Stride Toward Freedom, Where Do We Go From Here: Chaos or Community?, Why We Can't Wait* and many of his articles were edited, if not written, by such friends as Stanley Levison, Harris Wofford, and Bayard Rustin.[5] Nevertheless, this ghost-writing was always in the spirit of King and he would certainly have finally approved the finished product.

My dissertation research accidentally uncovered that King frequently quoted (without attribution) passages of varying length from writers and theologians. For whatever reason, credit was not given to such authors as Walter Rauschenbusch, Anders Nygren, Paul Ramsey, Paul Tillich, and Harris Wofford.[6]

I assumed in 1970 that King was too busy with all his national and international travel, hundreds of speeches annually, and his pastoral work, to be careful about footnoting his quotations. I never thought it was a deliberate attempt to mislead the reader. But what this means is that a very careful analysis in the vein of "redaction criticism" is needed to determine what in King's published writings is his own and what is his writers. Unless and until that is determined, the only trustworthy and reliable source for King scholarship is the material by his hand and voice in the King Archives in Atlanta.

4. Finally, not withstanding the preceding caveat, perhaps the enduring value of the dissertation is its systematic delineation of the theological *milieu* which King found in his graduate school years and how he creatively brokered that intellectual heritage for his listeners and readers. We are all grateful beneficiaries of that brokerage.

While what follows is an attempt to deal with the whole spectrum of King's academic background, including his debt to the seeds sown by the sermons of George Kelsey and Benjamin Mays in the Morehouse College Chapel, there is an obvious tilt toward the various aspects of the evangelical liberal tradition he found at Crozer. On the other hand, John Ansbro, writing a more thematic rather than historical study, emphasizes the personalistic tradition at Boston University.

All the above, plus more, will be necessary to provide the entire picture of King's academic training and its influence on his life and thought. This book is just one small part of that ongoing project.

The new era of King research begun by the work of David Garrow, James Cone, and Frederick L. Downing[7] and made possible by the library of unpublished material at the King Archives in Atlanta, means that King scholarship will continue to flourish. It will vindicate King as a first rate theologian. We know he was a first-rate preacher and civil rights worker.

Ira G. Zepp, Jr.
Western Maryland College
Westminster, Maryland

January 1989

Introduction

A. *The Purpose of the Study*

The purpose of this study is to analyze systematically the decisive intellectual influences on the thought of Martin Luther King, Jr. and to attempt to show how they affected his understanding of the "beloved community."

First of all, our specific interest will be *intellectual* sources. There are, naturally, other influences on King's attitudes and activity. Among the more important would certainly be his family background, the religion of the black church, and the friends he made.

Of course, it would be impossible to draw a firm line between intellectual influences and those of his family, religion and personal relationships. But King inherited, by way of his educational journey, discernable ideas prevalent in twentieth century theology and philosophy. In every case, he reflected seriously upon them and made them his own. It is with these significant ideological traditions that we are concerned in this dissertation.

Secondly, we are dealing primarily with King's ethical thought. We are not essentially interested in King as a theologian, an interpreter of the Bible, or as an analyst of history, although each of these aspects enter into our study.

Our goal is to indicate how his major intellectual influences inform his own ethical formulations or, in other words, how they enable King to relate the Christian faith to social structures. Although by profession he was a Baptist clergyman, he was by intellectual training and inclination a social ethicist. It is the latter to which we will be particularly sensitive.

Thirdly, we are, for the most part, using as resource material his published writings. Exceptions to this method are reliance upon several key interviews with King's teachers and references to some manuscripts of speeches found in the Boston Collection. In fact, however, almost all of the material in King's sermons and addresses finds its way into articles which in turn eventually appear as part of one of his five published books. We are attempting to trace these intellectual influences through his extant writings.

Finally, we are interested in showing how these various significant influences help King to articulate his vision of the beloved community. The ultimate concern of King's life and thought was the creation of a human community devoid of the barriers of class, color, and privilege. It is a community reminiscent of the Hebrew's messianic era and the Christian's Kingdom of God. All King's striving, especially his practice of nonviolence, was to help bring mankind closer to the realization of this community.

B. *The Reason for the Study*

King, himself, in the two versions of "Pilgrimage to Nonviolence" (Chapter Six in *Stride Toward Freedom* and Chapter Seventeen in *Strength to Love*), sketches his indebtedness to certain intellectual forces determinative for his thought.

All of King's biographers, when they record his intellectual background, rely almost completely upon these two chapters. There has been no research beyond a chapter in each biography, which reflects, as we have said, what King already stated in a cursory way. Furthermore, with the exception of William Robert Miller, not one of the biographers has been a theologian or philosopher. This has limited the depth and boundaries of interpretation and analysis, for we are, indeed, dealing with the disciplines of theology and philosophy.

So there has not been an exhaustive treatment dealing with the effect of King's intellectual sources on his thought. To what extent did Walter Rauschenbusch inform King's social vision? King said that Rauschenbusch left an "indelible imprint" upon his mind. Can this be documented in fact? What is the relationship between King's articulation of nonviolence and that of Mahatma Gandhi's? What were the lessons King learned from studying Reinhold Niebuhr? Was King's liberalism fundamentally modified in any way by his contact with Niebuhr? Can it be demonstrated that personalism was King's philosophical position, as he claims it was? We will try to answer these questions by extensively and carefully investigating what King has said in his books and articles.

At times the influences will be relatively obvious. In other cases, the intellectual influences will be more subtle and by implication. That is so because King never wrote a systematic treatise outlining in logical order his idea of God, church, and society. He wrote sermons, tracts for the times, and his own interpretation of the social revolution in America which began in 1955.

Another reason for the study is to place King in a broader intellectual framework. The popular conception of King is that of a nonviolent civil rights leader, the American Gandhi. However, his primary intellectual endeavor was to relate the Church to the world, with nonviolence being the strategy to implement that relationship. Therefore, nonviolence was only one of the prominent ideas given attention by King. As our study will reveal, King was involved, at a rather deep level, with a variety of ideas, each of which had their special influence on his life.

We view King as being primarily committed to the social dimension of life. He could not think in anti-social or unsocial terms. T. S. Eliot's "We have no life, if we have not life together" would not have been lost on King.

From time to time in his writings, he speaks of becoming "more and more interested in social ethics," of worship at its best being a "social experience," of the "social gospel" being the true witness of a Christian life, of our nation lacking a "social vision," of the purpose of education enabling us to become "an instrument of social advancement," of all his formal training equipping him with a "positive social philosophy," of his "serious intellectual quest for a method to eliminate social evil."

Therefore, it is natural for King to think in terms of community, of human interrelatedness, of persons being fulfilled in relationship to other persons.

It is also natural for King, because of this genuine social orientation, to be deeply committed to the vision of the beloved community.

C. *The Method of Study*

This is primarily a research paper, although criticism and analysis appear with some frequency.

3

As we discuss the influences of the social gospel, nonviolence, Christian realism, and personalism on King's thought, we find ourselves dealing with significant traditions of intellectual history in the past one hundred years.

First of all, we will outline in some detail the unique and central ideas of each tradition that has been influential on King. This will involve us in a brief discussion of background material for each influence, especially as it bears particularly on King.

Each influence will be discussed in some depth, so as to allow us to place King in a broad intellectual context and also to enable us to see how these various influences find their way into his mind.

Then, secondly, King's response to and reflections upon the tradition will be presented in some detail. In all cases, while a given area is under discussion, brief references and footnotes will point to its presence in King. But intermittently or at the end of each chapter there will be sustained attempts to show how King's written material has been directly and indirectly affected by the tradition, how he modified it, and how he interpreted it. In general, we will endeavor to see how King fits into this intellectual history and what his relationship is to these major theological and philosophical themes.

ONE

Martin Luther King
and
Liberalism

A. *Introduction*

To understand Martin Luther King, Jr., intellectually and ideologically, one must understand the liberal theological movement in the United States, primarily as it found expression in the social gospel and in personalism.

Although he was reared in the conservative, simplistic piety of Baptist Protestantism, King was soon influenced irrevocably by theological liberalism. The liberalizing began in Morehouse with George Kelsey's Bible course and Benjamin Mays's interest in Rauschenbusch, waxed strong at Crozer under evangelical liberal George W. Davis and Niebuhrian Kenneth Smith, and matured at Boston University under the personalism of Edgar S. Brightman and Harold DeWolf.

King's self-acknowledged debt to liberalism appears most candidly in two term papers written during his doctoral studies at Boston and in the second version of "Pilgrimage to Nonviolence" found in *Strength to Love.*

> Most of my criticism stems from the fact that I have been greatly influenced by liberal theology, maintaining a healthy respect for reason and a strong belief in the immanence as well as the transcendence of God.[1]

> My liberal leaning may root back to the great imprint that many liberal theologians have left upon me and to my ever present desire to be optimistic about human nature.[2]

> Liberalism provided me with an intellectual satisfaction that I had never found in fundamentalism . . . there are aspects of liberalism that I hope to cherish always; its devotion to the search for truth, its insistence on an open and analytical mind, and its refusal to abandon the best lights of reason. The

contribution of liberalism to the philological-historical criticism of biblical literature has been of immeasurable value and should be defended with religious and scientific passion.[3]

B. *Sources of American Religious Liberalism*

American religious liberalism arose as a reaction to a rigid nineteenth-century Calvinism. The latter was America's real theological heritage by way of Puritanism and it emphasized orthodoxy in doctrine and the verbal inspiration of the Bible.

Liberalism was an attempt on the part of many Christian theologians to come to grips with the impact of Darwin's theory of evolution, the advance of the natural sciences, and an emerging technology. The obscurantism of much of contemporary Christianity left it ill-prepared to deal with the captivating inroads science was making in the late nineteenth and early twentieth centuries. Hence in much of liberalism there is an appeal on the one hand to reason (an accommodation to the scientific method) and on the other hand to religious experience (a reaction to doctrinal orthodoxy).

Liberalism also was a product of the rapidly growing appreciation of history in the last century. The historical approach to an understanding of church doctrine and historical criticism of the scriptures placed both dogma and Bible in a perspective that virtually disallowed the belief in divine dictation of the Old and New Testaments and the sanctity of the creeds and confessions. The history of the Bible, the life of Jesus, church history, and the history of Christian doctrine became important disciplines.

C. *Religious Liberalism in General*

Outlines of the basic elements of religious liberalism have been provided by several recent theologians. Two of the most significant are Kenneth Cauthen[4] and Henry P. Van Dusen.[5] A more recent survey has been prepared by Lloyd J. Averill.[6]

Cauthen classifies the main themes of liberalism as follows:

–emphasis on religious experience
–concern of God for all of life
–strong ethical orientation
–rights of reason and moral feeling

-taking seriously the humanity of Jesus
-emphasis on the dynamic nature of history
-the liberal spirit–open and tolerant[7]

Van Dusen's understanding of the essential nature of religious liberalism is briefer, but just as comprehensive.

-authority of Christian experience
-centrality of Jesus Christ
-loyalty to the historic faith
-moral and social compassion[8]

Both Cauthen and Van Dusen emphasize two overriding themes in liberalism–the sense of the continuity of all of life and a related belief in the immanence of God. Actually, liberalism turns on these two fundamental convictions.

King's thought is a combination of all these motifs. The main theological and intellectual themes found in his writings are liberal themes. For instance, his stress on the fatherhood of God and the brotherhood of man, the ethicizing of religion, optimism about man and history, emphasis on the human Jesus, his tolerance toward a pluralism of world religions, and an appeal to religious experience all reflect his liberal training.

D. *Evangelical Liberalism*

There are two main streams of liberal thought in American Christianity. They have been often denoted as evangelical liberalism (or some would say, religious liberalism) and modernistic liberalism (or humanistic or naturalistic liberalism).

Cauthen lists the following as evangelical liberals: William Adams Brown, Harry E. Fosdick, Walter Rauschenbusch, Albert Knudson, and E. W. Lyman. As modernistic liberals he classifies Shailer Matthews, Douglas C. MacIntosh, and Henry N. Wieman. It so happens that all of these men had direct or indirect influence on King.

Evangelical liberalism was an attempt on the part of some devout and sensitive Christians to make the historic faith of the church intellectually acceptable to modern man–an attempt to retain the essence of the Gospel without straining unnecessarily the credulity of contemporary man.

7

Van Dusen said that "authentic evangelical liberalism" was a desire

> to declare a conviction, at once credible to the mind of today and yet in
> unmistakable and unchallengeable continuity with *true* Christian faith, i.e.,
> the faith of Jesus of Nazareth.[9]

Cauthen suggests two sub-types of evangelical liberalism: the ethical-social
liberal and the metaphysical liberal.[10] We shall see how Rauschenbusch,
representing the former, and Edgar Brightman, representing the latter, came
to have a direct bearing on King's thought. King was, however, an
immediate heir of evangelical liberalism as it was expressed in the life and
teachings of George W. Davis, his major professor at Crozer Theological
Seminary.

E.   *The Influence of George W. Davis*

That King was a liberal in ideology and spirit is generally known. But that
the thought of George W. Davis was the initial and permanent liberal
influence on King's life is not generally known.

In a letter to Davis, King wrote:

> I must admit that my theological and philosophical studies with you have
> been of tremendous help to me in my present studies. In the most decisive
> moments, I find your influence creeping forth.[11]

No biographer of King has taken this into serious consideration. Neither
Louis Lomax, Lerone Bennett, William Robert Miller, Robert Bleiweiss, nor
Coretta herself even mention George W. Davis. Nor do Lionel Lokos and
John Williams in their critical reflections on King's life.

Lawrence Reddick captures King's sense of indebtedness to Davis and the
high regard in which Davis was held by King in a brief reference to an
interview Reddick had with King concerning his Crozer experience. "He was
a marvelous teacher," says Martin, "conversant with the trends of modern
culture and yet sincerely religious. He was warm and Christian. It was easy
to get close to him."[12] David Lewis, who has the most perceptive and
exhaustive biography thus far, only mentions Davis twice and both times
with reference to Davis's interest in Gandhi.[13] King, himself, does not help
matters. There is no mention of Davis in his published writings.

But there is no question, upon reviewing his Crozer courses and the content of Davis's articles published in the *Crozer Quarterly*, that it was from Davis that King inherited the best in evangelical liberalism–from Schleiermacher to Ritschl to Rauschenbusch to Brightman. Davis was the key man in King's theological formulations and it was through Davis that the new world view of liberalism (both the social-ethical and metaphysical emphasis) was sympathetically and carefully opened for King.

It is impossible to understand the theology and ethics of King and their intellectual roots without a knowledge of George W. Davis and the place he occupied on the Crozer faculty from 1940-1950.[14]

F. *The Liberalism of George W. Davis*

Before outlining the theological orientation of Davis, let us examine how so much of liberalism focused in him.[15] Davis was a northern Baptist (American Baptist Convention) with liberal theological and social views. Perhaps these were inherited from his father who was active in the trade union movement in the steel mills of Pittsburgh. After graduating from the University of Pittsburgh and deciding upon the ministry for his vocation, he attended Colgate-Rochester Divinity School. It is important to remember that Walter Rauschenbusch and William Newton Clarke both had recently taught there and the evangelical-social gospel tradition was a strong one during Davis's student days.

From Colgate-Rochester, he went to Yale where he received his Ph.D., studying under D. C. MacIntosh, whose empirical theology and pacifist leanings greatly influenced Davis.

When Davis arrived at Crozer in 1938 (then located in Chester, Pennsylvania) and through King's tenure there, it was known as the "little University of Chicago."[16] The faculty was thorough-going in its liberalism with the primary emphasis upon the historical and the critical. This emphasis was led by E. E. Aubrey (who had come to Crozer from the University of Chicago) and Morton S. Enslin, both of whom might be called modernistic/humanistic liberals.

Over against this version of liberalism was George W. Davis's evangelical liberalism–a healing synthesis of the ethical and the metaphysical.

It should be noted that the Crisis Theology, as it was known in Europe, and Neo-Orthodoxy, as it was generally known in America, which had begun to gain strength in major theological faculties in this country during the

9

forties, was virtually ignored at Crozer. The names of Barth, Brunner, Tillich, and the Niebuhrs were relatively unknown and, if mentioned, were caricatured as sophisticated fundamentalists.[17]

As we shall see, Davis became more critical of the superficial liberalism and more open to the new theology. But, in the main, until Kenneth Smith came to Crozer in 1950 (King's senior year), bringing with him the Niebuhrian version of Neo-Orthodoxy, Crozer was solidly rooted in a liberalism which dated, in its American formulation, to the early part of the twentieth century. It was this liberalism that King studied at Crozer and primarily with Davis.

The textbooks required in Davis's courses reveal his background and theological point of view. His course in Systematic Theology entitled "Christian Theology Today" was a study of

> the nature and method of theology; the Christian conception of God; man, his nature, need and destiny; the religious significance of Jesus of Nazareth and His part in salvation; the place and task of the Church as the carrier of Christian faith and experience.[18]

The texts used regularly for this year long course were William Newton Clarke's *An Outline of Christian Theology* published in 1898, and William Adams Brown's *Christian Theology in Outline*, published in 1906.[19] They were classical texts in the liberal tradition and both Clarke and Brown had served as theological mentors to a whole generation of evangelical liberals like Davis.

Walter M. Horton complimented Clarke and Brown as having "no real successors as systematic liberal theologians."[20] Averill has more references to these two men (with the exception of Walter Rauschenbusch) than to any other figure in his study of the American liberal tradition.

These texts are closely argued systematic treatises taking Jesus, scripture, history, and reason with utmost seriousness. The main influences traced in these books are Schleiermacher and Ritschl. Cauthen calls Brown a neo-Ritschlian and found Clarke's emphasis on the appeal to religious experience strikingly similar to Schleiermacher.[21]

G. *Representative and Relevant References in Clarke*

Students were assigned to outline the texts carefully and it is appropriate briefly to point to some passages that were influential for King. Undoubtedly, since Davis's lectures followed the books closely,[22] these same themes must have been emphasized in class lectures and they reappear vividly in Davis's own writings.

The first two sentences of Clarke's book indicate the typical liberal approach to the task of theology. "Theology is preceded by religion, as botany by the life of the plant. Religion is the reality of which theology is the study."[23] Theology really is the "fruit of religion, and religion is a life,"[24] rather than an elucidation of God's revelation in Christ.

It is this openness, however, that allows Clarke to say:

> in all the great non-Christian religions there are expressions of holy aspiration, or of love and adoration toward a good God, that are worthy utterances of religion, and closely akin to Christianity.[25]

Clarke is also interested in history as God's medium of revelation. "Not in writing, but in living history" God reveals himself. To this Clarke adds:

> To Israel throughout its history God revealed himself not mainly in words, and still less in writing, but in action. The prophets did indeed speak of him, and speak from him, but they also pointed to him as God manifest in his doings–a God present and acting, and known by his acts.[26]

The concept of a moral law at work in history is also found in Clarke.

> The 'power, not ourselves, that makes for righteousness' is no dream, but a glorious reality. Something is going forward in individual life, and in the movement of mankind at large, that men did not devise–something so truly in the nature of purpose as to be surely the work of mind, something that accords in character with the character of God.[27]

Clarke's understanding of God, "God as personal spirit, perfectly good, and motivated by holy love, and ordering all" finds expression in Davis and King. More pertinently, Clarke stresses that the personal nature of God points to his self-consciousness and self-direction. We have no better word than personal to describe God. "God may be more than we can mean by personal, but he is not less."[28]

The ethical and practical strain of liberalism appears in Clarke.

> . . . it is also true that Christianity will not be well understood except from within; for it is not merely a system–it is a life . . . a Christian is one who is attuned to the will of God.[29]

As we shall see, these themes of Clarke appear in Davis and reappear in King.

H. *King's Courses From Davis*

During his first year at Crozer, King took two elective courses from Davis. They were "Great Theologians" and "Mysticism." Rauschenbusch was one of the great theologians investigated in the former course. This is why in "Pilgrimage to Nonviolence" King said, having just mentioned his entering Crozer, "I came early to Walter Rauschenbusch's *Christianity and the Social Crisis*."[30] In the second version of "Pilgrimage to Nonviolence," he is less clear. "In the early 1950's I read Walter Rauschenbusch's *Christianity and the Social Crisis*."[31] The truth of the matter is that he encountered Rauschenbusch for the first time during his first year at Crozer in 1948-1949.

As a senior, King took Davis's course, "Philosophy of Religion," and the main text was E. A. Burtt's *Types of Religious Philosophy*, with MacIntosh's *Theology as an Empirical Science* and Brightman's *A Philosophy of Religion* as supplemental texts.

For our purposes, it is necessary to note that Brightman, who strongly influenced Davis, was well known by King at Crozer before he went to Boston. Not only was Brightman important to Davis, he was held in high esteem by the Crozer community. The affection and regard with which Crozer held Brightman is reflected in a statement by Enslin as he introduces him to *Crozer Quarterly* readers as "a frequent and ever-welcome contributor."[32]

For a course, entitled "Psychology of Religious Personality," which King took his senior year, he did his first serious reading of Gandhi. Although Gandhi was a familiar name at Crozer (a collection of Gandhi material was placed in the Bucknell Library at Crozer by Davis), the catalyst for King was an address by Dr. Mordecai Johnson in the spring of 1950. Dr. Johnson had just been around the world and to India and was so convincing in his presentation of nonviolence that King decided to read further. Dr. Johnson's "message was so profound and electrifying that I left the meeting and bought half a dozen books on Gandhi's life and work."[33]

Smith has seen the paper King wrote for Davis on the thought of Gandhi and recalls that, among others, the books King used for his Gandhi research at that time were:

–Gandhi's Autobiography: *The Story of My Experiments With Truth*
–Romain Rolland's *Mahatma Gandhi: The Man Who Became One With the Universe*
–Richard Gregg's *The Power of Nonviolence*
–C. F. Andrews's *Mahatma Gandhi's Ideas* and
  Mahatma Gandhi: His Own Story
–F. B. Fischer's *That Strange Little Brown Man, Gandhi*[34]

Davis was also a pacifist and an advocate of nonviolence as a means of social change. His own pacifist orientation is reflected in a quotation from the World Council of Churches Executive Committee unanimously declaring that in an atomic age, war has become "a perversion; it is against the moral order by which man is bound; it is a sin against God."[35]

All in all, King took thirty-four credit hours with Davis. The courses were in the areas of systematic and historical theology, philosophy and psychology of religion, and comparative religion.

I. *A Brief Survey of Davis's Theological Position*

A fair and accurate way to summarize Davis's thought is found in his last article in the *Crozer Quarterly* entitled "Liberalism and a Theology of Depth."[36] This article represents the mature Davis seriously grappling with the impact of neo-orthodoxy, primarily Barthianism, and appropriating the positive aspects into his own system. There seems to be here an indication that Davis is moving toward the more historic understanding of Christian faith.

In the article, Davis appears somewhat defensive and apologetic concerning liberalism's failures and inadequacies. He asserts at the outset that Christianity is a religion of depth.

By depth, in the sense in which it is here employed, we mean that Christianity breaks through the surface phenomena of existence, penetrating the mere events of history, the face of nature, and the physical life of man to bring an apprehension of what controls history, what glorifies the face of nature, and what motivates man as a spiritual entity.[37]

Idealism, the philosophical framework which helped theological liberalism articulate its world view, enables Davis to get behind what appears and to discover the hidden meaning of existence.

Davis sees three levels of Christianity: the *surface*, dealing with the externals of religion–ceremony, ritual, churches, books, etc.; the *sub-surface*, dealing with the life of Jesus, church history, uniqueness of denominational expression, etc.; and the *depth* phenomena of Christianity which consists of

> the roots out of which the book, the church, the history, the doctrines, and distinctive life of Jesus came. What made these possible and clothed them with reality in the first place?[38]

Davis suggests that liberalism has been preoccupied with the surface and sub-surface of Christianity to the virtual exclusion of the depth which was responsible for Christian faith, but he does not disavow the liberal's right to be critical nor is he ungrateful for all liberalism has done.

However, he does bring under severe judgment what he calls "the growing weakness of liberalism" because

> it failed to grasp the Bible as a whole, an apprehension which is impossible without an appreciation of the depths which it constantly plumbs. Failing to descend to the depths, many a liberal Christian satisfied himself with disturbing himself and his fellow Christians through calling attention to the multiple problems of date, authorship, interpolation, contradictory statements, outgrown ideas, rearrangement of the text, discrepancies, cultural coloration, historical setting, and the hope of the author. Doing that piecemeal with book after book of the Bible, too many liberals exhausted themselves to the point where they had not sufficient intellectual strength left to wrestle with the question of depth.[39]

Here, Davis is describing a scholar like Morton Scott Enslin, his New Testament colleague, who disturbed so many theological students into unbelief by his unrelenting historical criticism of the Bible. The above quotation indicates Davis's concern to maintain a balance between criticism and the gospel–an approach that enabled many students, including King, brought up in the fundamentalist tradition, to maintain an intellectually respectable and yet deeply personal faith in God.

In this article Davis pleads for the liberalism he knows and loves to "expose" all the facts of Christianity and to go beneath the biblical criticism, historical perspective, and adjustment to contemporary thought and culture to ferret out those depths which made Christianity possible in the first place and which render it a live option today.[40]

The indispensable element needed for a revitalized liberalism is a depth theology–one which takes into consideration "all the facts of Christian history, community, and experience."

Davis offers precisely such a theology and delineates four basic elements that would constitute the depth phenomena of Christian faith.

1. The moral foundations of Reality–"life does not have moral foundations because of the spiritual nature of ultimate reality."[41]
2. Spiritual control of the universal process implied by moral foundations.[42]
3. Specific action–"the depth is particularly related to Jesus Christ."[43]
4. Continuing divine concern and human opportunity–"the testimony of the Holy Spirit."[44]

For Davis all four of these could be summed up in his primary conviction that the foundations of Reality are moral. Davis's notion of history, view of God, understanding of man, sense of community, and the ethical basis of faith are bound up in this basic assertion. We will spell this out thematically by referring to Davis's published writings.

1. The Moral Order[45]

Davis's articles abound with direct and indirect references to a moral law which supports our world just as physical laws do. Besides the article just under discussion, another one, "God and History,"[46] will serve to illustrate how central the concept of moral foundations is for Davis. Some sample references are:

'Though the mills of God grind slowly, yet they grind exceeding small.' The realization of God's intention for the race may be slow of fruition; nonetheless it ripens.[47]

. . . there is yet a tide in the affairs of men which steadily buffets (the torrents of selfish individualism) as they burst into the sea of our common life.[48]

. . . there is a moral order which is fundamental and eternal, and which is relevant to the corporate life of men and the ordering of human society. If mankind is to escape chaos and recurrent war, social and political institutions must be brought into conformity with this moral order.[49]

The religious meaning for Davis of the above quotations is that the universe, in fact, is "under spiritual control." The ancient faith that the stars in their courses fought against Sisera is "the modern Christian faith also."

2. History

Absolutely integral to his understanding of the Moral Order is the belief that God acts in history. The contention that there is a "divine purpose in history" has always been made by religious man. Says Davis, "His is no irrational conclusion."[50]

That God "works within the structure of the universe and the processes of history" is another way of describing what Davis means by "spiritual control" and it is the latter which sharply divides the Greek philosophical view of history from the Judeo-Christian. This "control" allows Biblical faith to see history directed toward a goal rather than repeating itself in endless cycles; it allowed the prophets to see God in "The turbulent, sweating, dust-obscured battle of human life"[51] rather than in meditation and mystic solitude. The fruit of nineteenth century liberal appreciation of historiography found expression in Davis's conclusion.

> For the Jew history was no movement through recurrent cycles, as it was for the ancient Greek and Roman; it was rather progress towards a world-shaking consummation. God was in the process, giving dynamic direction to events.[52]

Another aspect of Davis's view of history is the historical character of divine revelation. This is an idea which he apparently takes with more seriousness as he himself grows, teaches, and studies. In 1943 he wrote:

> The Biblical philosophy of history is one which intimately associates God with earthly events . . . historic events do not just happen. They are done by God.[53]

In 1951, he goes even further and the following indicates to the writer that he is moving toward the more classical understanding of Christian faith, or at least to a reconstructed type of liberalism. Here Davis states that one of the depths we must strike is that in Jesus we perceive the eternal in the timely, the infinite in the finite, the divine in the human . . . God's thought culminated in the historic event of the person, life, crucifixion, and resurrection of Jesus of Nazareth. Without that divine event, Christianity could not be. It means in truth that the source of the Christian religion lies in God rather than in man.[54]

It appears that Davis is here consciously or unconsciously influenced by the paradox so pivotal in crisis theology and adopts a stance toward reason not usually held by liberals. This is evidenced by the continuation of his argument in which he refers to Soren Kierkegaard's "scandal of particularity" with obvious agreement. He prefaces the Kierkegaardian reference with the observation that we cannot really know the essence of God. Then he continues.

All I can do is to suggest what God may be in his essence and to suggest that the loving spirit which I believe is characteristic of God finds decisive expression in Jesus of Nazareth. From there on the Christian religion is a venture of faith, believing that which is really above human reason, yes, beyond the highest human thought. A century ago, the Danish philosopher-theologian, Soren Kierkegaard, termed this presence of God in Jesus Christ the 'absolute paradox' or the paradox of God in time. He claimed that the human mind could not fathom this fact. If it was to be accepted, God himself must provide the faith through which alone it could be apprehended. And so it is. To find the love of God, for instance, in a cross.[55]

It is important to recall that while Davis was grappling with the paradoxical nature of Christian faith, King was his student. As a result, King may have been helped to bridge the gap from liberalism to Reinhold Niebuhr with more ease than had not Davis's own thinking been in a state of ferment at that time. But Davis's concern for "both/and" rather than either liberalism or neo-orthodoxy also greatly influenced King.[56]

3. *Value of the Personal*

Without entering into a detailed discussion of personalism (which will appear later), we must mention how significant the category of the personal was for Davis. He was surely influenced by the personalist school of Bowne and Brightman and as a theologian grounded his conviction about the personal nature of the human in Christian faith. He agreed with those who were convinced that the greatest emancipating force in the early centuries of our era was Jesus's discovery that human life is personal.

17

In the light of God's love for men, revealed to many in the life and sacrifice of Jesus of Nazareth, each man became a being of infinite worth.[57]

This is one of Jesus's great contributions: the worth which he ascribed to the human person, the value which Jesus placed upon personality, and that the true nature of human life is personal.

By personal, Davis did not mean individualism or the differences which distinguish one person from another, but rather "that potential quality of life which separates *homo sapiens* from all other forms of creation and, indeed, lifts him above them."[58]

Davis, like many liberals, centered the belief in the personal nature of man in a prior belief about the fatherhood of God. God is a loving father; we, his children, are objects of his compassion and concern. This establishes man as "supremely worthful" and "inherently valuable." So the force and greatness of Christianity is its contention that "the ultimate category of human life lies in the personal."

We have seen how Davis was indebted to personalism. The following quotation reflects the interweaving of elements central to that philosophical position, namely, moral order, purpose in history, and value of personality.

> . . . God's intention in history is, in part, to produce free personalities. 'The stars in their courses' fight against all who would dominate the human spirit and beat it into humiliating subjection. It matters not whether such a tyrannical spirit is found in a father, an employer of labor, a minister of religion, or an Adolf Hitler. In the long run the tides of history will overtake his kind and destroy him. Such a person fights not alone against his child, his workman, his parishioner, or humanity, he fights as well against God at work in this unquenchable tendency of the ages.[59]

These themes echo repeatedly in the writings of Martin Luther King, Jr.

4. *Life as Social*

Another major emphasis on Davis was the social character of life and that this is the goal toward which we are being directed.

> One of the most obvious facts about man is that he is a social animal . . . the desire of God is that mankind creatively achieve an increasingly social life . . . the logic of history favors increasing sociality.[60]

In the article, "God and History," Davis outlines three shifts he has discerned in history. The first is from the external to the inner (from rite and ceremony to inner attitude); the second is from the impersonal to the personal (from treating people as things to treating them as persons); and the third shift, the culmination of the other two, is from the individual to the social (from individualism to a love that is inclusive and which unites all kinds of people).

Davis continues by stating that history is tending to the creation of what Archbishop Temple called, "The Commonwealth of Value." And Davis then betrays the effect Rauschenbusch had on him when he says:

> In this movement we witness the slow realization of God's intention in history. Completed, it will usher in God's kingdom on earth. Then shall be inaugurated that age of which the prophet Jeremiah has God speak saying, 'No longer need they teach one another to know the Lord; all of them, high and low alike, shall know me, says the Lord, for I will forgive their wrongdoing and remember their sin no more.'[61]

It is only within the social that the individual's character can evolve. Human character does not grow and develop among groups where individualism is the life style.

> It is much more likely to grow in democratic cooperative, and Christian societies, where men are constantly exhorted to manifest regard for the personal rights and opportunities of others.[62]

Davis makes a careful distinction between individuality within fellowship and an individualism against fellowship. The spirit of all mature religions is social, but this should not stifle individuality or suffocate the personal. There is, in the area of the "social," healthy interrelationships and interdependence. "I am my brother's keeper and my brother is my keeper."[63] As Davis interprets this third major shift in history, he concludes that God intends human life to achieve solidarity.

> The structure of man and of the universe is set against all rank individualism, which ever seeks to feather only its own nest. Against that the very stars fight.[64]

It is inevitable that Davis would make mention of the importance of universal human community. He recalls that Jesus never allowed his contemporary Jews to believe that Israel was the final loyalty. Since the purpose of God extends to all human life, no genuine community could be

19

achieved by absolutizing the nation, tribe, or race. If we refuse to conform to this third shift in history, if we fail to see that "narrow social loyalties lead to fratricidal strife," we may

> be pushed by necessity, rather than led by aspiration, as God would have preferred, into that larger worldwide society towards consummation of which the signs of history unmistakably point.[65]

And when Davis, on another occasion, claims that "mankind is now under a ceaseless pressure to get together into larger units of cooperative life or perish," and "We know now that we must live together or perish. If we will not have one world, we may have no world,"[66] he presages some of the main themes in King, notably his oft-made comment that the choice is not "between violence and nonviolence, but nonviolence and nonexistence."[67]

5. *The Ethical Nature of Faith*

In one of his earlier essays, "The Ethical Nature of Salvation," Davis stressed what was an essential element in evangelical liberalism, namely, the moral and ethical nature of Christian faith. He is concerned to balance the supernatural aspects of salvation with the ethical, which has been so overshadowed by the former.

Repentance, which leads a man into a moral communion and fellowship with God, is a step into "the very heart of the religion of Jesus. He makes the goal of human character likeness in moral quality to God himself."[68] Jesus asked his disciples to be like the Father, i.e., to be perfect, and to become morally like God is to enter into complete fellowship with him or to experience what Jesus meant by salvation.

This, for Davis, is how Jesus understood sonship. If a man becomes like God in his ethical orientation (in the qualities of love and forgiveness), he becomes a son of God.

> Too frequently the Christian religion has thought of sonship with God simply as a matter of our humanity; that is, as based upon natural creation. Jesus did not think so. Sonship for him was a relation which a man achieves only by becoming morally like the Father. His words are explicit: 'Love your enemies . . . that ye may be sons.'[69]

After Davis, in the above essay, reviews the New Testament records, including Jesus, early Jewish Christians, Paul, and John, he says that there is a definite ethical foundation to Christian salvation which God cannot remove. It is from this foundation that the Christian's ineradicable interest in the good life stems. The extent to which the ethical is seen as the goal and test of one's faith is in a concluding remark by Davis.

> While no Christian will discount what God has done for us in the Galilean, he should not overlook the fact that God expects a moral adjustment to his holy life. On no other basis is a moral fellowship possible between God and man. And nothing less than such moral fellowship is what Christians ultimately mean by salvation.[70]

What we are contending is that Davis, representing the distillation of liberal thought and the irenic spirit of the liberal mind, introduced King to the major motifs of his own thought. King would continue to develop, broaden, and criticize them, but they were found first in a clearly articulated and intellectually acceptable form in George W. Davis.

TWO

The Social Gospel

A. Background Influences

Walter Rauschenbusch, the social gospel's most eloquent spokesman, was the product of the best in German pietism. The pietistic movement in Germany during the eighteenth century was a reaction to the sterility of Protestant orthodoxy with its stress on adherence to creeds and to a church structure devoid of personal fellowship and mutual caring. This reaction was in the name of personal religious experience and an ethical life consonant with that experience. This phenomenon was most pronounced in the Moravian movement which produced one of the seminal theologians of the nineteenth century, Friedrich Schleiermacher.

Hugh Ross Mackintosh[1] has suggested that pietism's concern with new life focused attention on the subjective dimension of a person's religious life, while orthodoxy, with its concern for justification before God, was preoccupied with the objective act of God in Christ. It is natural that Orthodoxy would stress right *belief*, while pietism would emphasize right *morality*. That is why it is often concluded that pietism was more ethical than theological in its orientation.[2]

Pietism, with its twin concerns for individual personal religious experience and a new moral life as evidence of that experience, is a forerunner of what we know as Protestant liberalism.

And Pietism produced two significant theologians–each representing an emphasis of the pietistic movement–Schleiermacher, the experiential and Ritschl, the ethical. This is not to imply that Schleiermacher was unconcerned about the ethical side of faith or that Ritschl was indifferent to the importance of the religiously experiential, but that each of them, in his own way, stressed one aspect of the pietist heritage. Schleiermacher retained an appreciation of Kant's philosophical pietism and rejected his rationalism, while Ritschl retained an appreciation of Kant's ethical concern and rejected both Kant's speculation (rationalism) and Schleiermacher's focus on inner feeling. Ritschl had a deep suspicion of pietism and subjectivism in religion and recalled Protestantism to a biblical appreciation of history.

23

One can contend that Rauschenbusch was a happy combination of the dual aspect of this heritage. He saw the necessity of holding the ethical and the experiential in balance. These were also the concerns of George W. Davis and Martin Luther King, Jr.[3]

1. Albrecht Ritschl

The strongest influence on Rauschenbusch was Ritschl and the Ritschlian school, especially as it was represented by Adolf von Harnack. Through Harnack and Rauschenbusch, Ritschl became the primary source of American liberalism.

> Ritschl was the most influential theologian of the late nineteenth century, and the principal teacher of American liberals.[4]

Ritschl viewed Christianity as an ellipse with two foci–one focal point was what he termed "redemption through Christ" (the religious focus) and the other was the Kingdom of God (the moral and social focus).[5] These two organically related interests are foci around which Christianity revolves as an ellipse. Ritschl reacted sharply against the subjectivism and latent mysticism of Schleiermacher and found solid ground in history, which was for him the Person of Jesus Christ, as opposed to Schleiermacher who "broadly speaking . . . found the starting point of theology in what happens within the believing soul, not in historic fact."[6]

The focal point denoted "Kingdom of God" enabled Ritschl to concentrate on the historical nature of faith, the practical and ethical nature of Christianity–all three of these were extremely important to Rauschenbusch and furnished the theological basis for his social understanding of Christianity.

Both foci–Christ's redemption and Kingdom of God–point unmistakably for Ritschl to history, which is his central concern. For him, this was a more reliable footing than Hegel's and Kant's metaphysics and Schleiermacher's subjectivism and he arrives at this as a result of the Biblical, especially the Old Testament, appreciation of history.

Ritschl's concern for history became one of liberalism's main tenets. By stressing the historical revelation of Christianity over the God-consciousness of Schleiermacher, Ritschl raised the ethical to a central place, gave the historical Jesus a position hitherto not held, and in his follower, Harnack, for which this was a major position, the Church was emphasized as an historical community. Lloyd Averill summarizes Ritschl's influence on liberalism.

> The rejection of metaphysics as a legitimate theological enterprise and the preference of experiential and experimental over the speculative, while found in Schleiermacher, received even·more energetic and forceful statement in Ritschl.[7]

It is necessary here to point out the difference between Ritschl and Schleiermacher in terms of religious experience. For Ritschl, the experience had moral content, while for Schleiermacher it was rather an isolated feeling of dependence, a God-consciousness. Averill himself concludes:

> This prominence given to experience was supported in different ways by both Schleiermacher and Ritschl. The former located genuine religion in the universal and distinctively religious experience of absolute dependence, and the latter insisted on both the possibility and the necessity that Jesus become a part of the believer's own historical environment–which is to say, a part of his own personal experience–before genuine communion with God could take place.[8]

"The historicism, which was to be a mark of the liberal movement"[9] was a complement to Ritschl's anti-metaphysical bias. In the Foreword to *Christianizing the Social Order*, Rauschenbusch comments that "historical studies . . . are my professional duty and my intellectual satisfaction." And in *Foundations*, a Baptist theological quarterly, Rauschenbusch says, "History above all gives us roundness and maturity and richness . . . only a man saturated with history has a right to be heard."[10]

> The centrality Ritschl gave to the Kingdom of God, his definition of the Kingdom in terms of the moral organization of the human community according to the will of God, and his correlative view of that social solidarism which spawns the kingdom of evil were widely adopted and are seen with special clarity in the work of Rauschenbusch.[11]

Ritschl's definition of the Kingdom of God as "the moral organization of humanity through love-prompted action"[12] is very similar to Rauschenbusch's "The Reign of God came to mean the organized fellowship of humanity acting under the impulse of love."[13]

Ritschl's understanding of sin as the product of selfishness and ignorance gave the liberals one of their most frequently used definitions.

25

Rauschenbusch adopts the former as his understanding of sin because he is too theologically sensitive to say sin is simply ignorance.

> Theology with remarkable unanimity has discerned that sin is essentially selfishness. This is an ethical and social definition, and is proof of the unquenchable social spirit of Christianity.[14]

Another significant influence on Ritschl was Hermann Lotze.[15] The latter's appeal to Ritschl was natural. Lotze was primarily a metaphysician, but he would not permit

> metaphysics, as a science of being, a right of existence independent of ethics. Man is a creature not of reason alone but of feeling, and the emotional demands of his nature have to be met. Because of this, *values* arise–moral, aesthetic, religious. Indeed we cannot properly speak of ultimate "reality" except in terms of ultimate "value."[16]

It was this insight of Lotze that enabled Ritschl to formulate his conviction that theological statements are "judgments of value."[17] As regards Lotze, Ritschl kept his concern for value and his implied emphasis on ethics, while dismissing Lotze's metaphysical orientation.

Lotze is an important and key figure in the liberal tradition as it is expressed in King. Why do we find statements about the "ultimate value of the human person" both in the social gospel and personalism? There is an obvious debt to Kant, but Lotze was the predominant influence on Ritschl, and thereby on Rauschenbusch, as well as being one of the main influences on Borden Parker Bowne, who founded the personalist tradition at Boston University. To both of these traditions, emphasizing the value of human personality, King fell heir.

Rauschenbusch and William Adams Brown were both studying in Berlin in 1891 and Harnack, probably the most faithful disciple of the Ritschlian school, had just come to Berlin to teach. It was inevitable, then, that Ritschlian themes would become an integral part of the American Protestant liberal theological scene.[18]

Since King read Rauschenbusch carefully and used William Adams Brown as a text in theology, one can see how important Ritschl's thought, if only indirectly and secondhand, would be to King.

Rauschenbusch's debt to Ritschl is quite clear in *Theology of the Social Gospel*, as he pays tribute to Ritschl's emphasis on solidarity. Rauschenbusch's chief regret about Protestant thought is its individualism, brought about, he feels, because of excessive reactions in the Reformation to the monolithic power of the medieval Church. But in the nineteenth century, Rauschenbusch sees a breakthrough to a "new solidaristic strain" in theology.

He recalls that Schleiermacher in his later and maturer works, especially *The Christian Faith*, is less individualistic than in his former writings and reflects seriously upon the organic connection between personal and communal life. Rauschenbusch documents this by a long quotation in which Schleiermacher discusses the "universal racial sin of humanity,"–what Rauschenbusch would call the Kingdom of Evil.[19]

Rauschenbusch, calling Ritschl the "most vigorous and influential theological intellect in Germany since Schleiermacher," says that Ritschl

> abandoned the doctrine of original sin but substituted the solidaristic conception of the Kingdom of Evil. He held that salvation is embodied in a community which has experienced salvation; the faith of the individual is part of the faith of the church. The Church and not the individual is the object of justification; the assurance of forgiveness for the individual is based on his union with the church.[20]

It is this solidarity and organic interrelationship of life which, for Ritschl, is really Schleiermacher's "epoch-making contribution to theology" and not his espousal of subjective religion. Rauschenbusch quotes from Ritschl with obvious approval.

> The consciousness of solidarity is one of the fundamental conditions of religion, without which it can neither be rightly understood nor rightly lived.[21]

Upon another occasion in *Theology of a Social Gospel*, Rauschenbusch claims that Ritschl has done more than anyone else to put the "ethical conception of Christianity contained in the idea of the Kingdom of God to the front of German theology."[22]

Rauschenbusch attributes the rise in the interest of social ideas, especially in Ritschl, to an "explanation of ideas derived from Hebrew religion." As we shall see, Rauschenbusch placed great importance on the prophets as sources of the social gospel.

> Ritschl built his essential ideas of the Kingdom of Evil and the Kingdom of God on Schleiermacher's work, and stressed the teaching of Luther that our service to God consists not in religious performances, but in the faithful work we do in our secular calling. The practical importance of these elements of

27

Ritschl's theology is proved by the strong social spirit pervading the younger Ritschlian school . . .[23]

Ritschl's emphasis on the Kingdom of God, the place of history in theological understanding, and the ethicizing of Christianity had great influences on Rauschenbusch.

B. *The Social Gospel*

1. *Introduction*

The Social Gospel was the theological formulation responsive to the needs of American society between the Civil War and World War I. It was the American expression of a worldwide concern on the part of the churches to relate Christianity to social structures resulting from the Industrial Revolution.

Prior to the Civil War, American Protestantism, reflecting the frontier, rural culture, was primarily revivalistic and individualistic in orientation. A person's relationship to God was of paramount importance and his relationship to social evils was incidental. A trend away from this individualistic piety began in the abolitionist movement, in which many clergymen participated.

Following the war between the States, several socio-economic phenomena emerged to force the church to rethink its position and to shift its emphasis from individual morality to social morality. Among these were a rapidly expanding industrial economy, the increasing power of capitalism, a multiplying technology, and the growth of urban centers. These, of course, brought attendant problems–child labor, exploitation of the worker, competitiveness, and monopolies.

Since this emerging mass-urban-industrial society was *the* determining factor on the lives of individual men and women, many churchmen thought they should be dealing directly with this determining force. So Handy says that the major contention and lasting impression on American church life was "that Christian churches must recognize and deal responsibly with social and economic questions."[24]

C. H. Hopkins, in his authoritative account of the development of the Social Gospel, *The Rise of the Social Gospel in American Protestantism, 1865-1915*, states that a minority of Protestant leaders saw the very genius of Christianity contradicted by the assumptions of the new capitalism. Their attempts to reorient the historic faith of America to an industrial society comprised the social gospel.[25]

2. The Central Themes of the Social Gospel

The main ideas of the social gospel reflect many of the major motifs of Protestant liberalism, generally.[26]

–a stress on the immanence of God, which was a theological response to the impact of Darwinian evolution. God is in and through the processes of life, not a transcendent, "wholly other" Deity, as taught by orthodox Christianity.

–a confidence that the social teachings of Jesus could provide reliable guides for both individual and social life. This was of a piece with the newly acquired knowledge of the historical Jesus. Books such as Shailer Matthews' *The Social Teachings of Jesus*, George Peabody's *Jesus Christ and the Social Question*, Walter Rauschenbusch's *The Social Principles of Jesus*, and even George Sheldon's *In His Steps*, were quite popular.

–organic view of society. This for Hopkins was a logical implication of the immanence of God.[27] Since God is in all of human and natural life, all of life is interrelated. There is a solidaristic view of life, to use Ritschl's phrase.

–a conviction that at the center of Jesus's teachings was the Kingdom of God. The latter was a historical possibility if man worked hard enough to eliminate social injustice. "The universal reign of love and justice"[28] was a popular definition of the Kingdom of God or as George Herron had it "The church is a means to an end–the Kingdom of God–a just social order."[29]

–a firm faith in progress. This was, however, not inevitable, for it was achieved by man's willing response to the initiative of God. This betrays an optimistic view of human nature and assumes that man is willing and able to choose "social good over private advantage."[30]

–belief that institutional and social structures could be "Christianized," i.e., brought under the dominance of Christ's love. "Christ came, therefore, to save individual subjects but also to harmonize their social relations–in other words to save society."[31] The process whereby institutions would be saved indicates the optimism of man, belief in progress, and confidence that individual salvation would issue in social salvation. Social regeneration is to come about through the dissemination of the spirit of reverence for personality throughout society. Beginning with individuals, it will proceed to groups and institutions,

29

pervading them with the Christ spirit of brotherliness. It is an evolutionary process.[32]

The latter element is what Handy calls a "conservative" type of social Christianity. Representatives of this position believed that social change would be affected by individuals changing. On the other hand, there was an extreme group who might be called Christian socialists, who would desire the overthrow of existing institutions. A kind of *via media*, however, was suggested by Henry May, called "Progressive Social Christianity," more moderate and reformatory in character. This is the Social Gospel of Rauschenbusch.[33]

Hopkins cites two strands of the social gospel in Protestantism–the more rational, sometimes humanistic approach of the Unitarians, Congregationalists, and Episcopalians, and the more evangelical and pietistic approach of Baptists, Methodists, and other separatist bodies. This group was noted for

> an ideology looking toward a kingdom of God raised on earth by consecrated groups of individuals, whereas the former tradition inclined to apply the 'Christian law' of love to the transactions of society.[34]

The "progressive social Christianity" and the evangelical brand of the pietists answer to what earlier we called evangelical liberalism of the social-ethical variety and the aspect of social gospel King met at Crozer.

3. The Social Gospel of Walter Rauschenbusch

Rauschenbusch holds an indispensable place the Social Gospel movement. Two brief statements reveal his central importance.

> Above the clamor of many voices the classic statement of American social Christianity is that of Walter Rauschenbusch, whose works were undoubtedly the most significant religious publications in the United States, if not in the English language in the first two decades of the new century.[35]

> "Rauschenbusch was the most celebrated exponent" of the Social Gospel.[36]

Rauschenbusch was reared in an individualist-oriented pietism of a German Lutheran family turned Baptist. Through the crucible of his first parish in Hell's Kitchen in New York, 1886-96, he realized the inadequacy of the individualistic approach to his parishioners' urban problems and developed a deep appreciation for the power of social structures which determine the lives of people.

This forced Rauschenbusch to study again the Bible and Christian tradition. In this re-examination he found by way of the prophets, Jesus, and the early church a profound concern for the social dimension of life. Rauschenbusch never made the individual and social an either/or. He felt they were a necessary Biblical both/and. He stressed consistently that the "religious" is primary (and by "religious" he means one's God-relationship), but that its goal and test is the social. This was a healthy combination in Rauschenbusch and not the imbalance which occurred in many of his followers. Rauschenbusch was at this point a sound evangelical liberal with a social-ethical bias.

Handy suggests that Rauschenbusch found the Biblical basis for his social gospel in

the doctrine of the kingdom of God, which brought together his evangelical concern for individuals and his social vision of a redeemed society.[37]

It is significant that one of the greatest debts King acknowledges to anyone is the tribute he pays Rauschenbusch. It is found almost word for word in both versions of "Pilgrimage to Nonviolence" and it is the only major theme found in both versions. Even references to Boston University and his mentors there are not found in the second version. Though the latter was in a "How My Mind Has Changed" series for *The Christian Century* the emphasis on Rauschenbusch continues. It indicates how deeply influenced King was by Rauschenbusch and his ideas. It was a decisive influence, and the rest of his thought and activity are to be seen in the framework he derived from the impact of the social gospel. King says

Not until I entered Crozer Theological Seminary in 1948, however, did I begin a serious intellectual quest for a method to eliminate social evil. Although my major interest was in the fields of theology and philosophy, I spent a great deal of time reading the works of the great social philosophers. I came early to Walter Rauschenbusch's *Christianity and the Social Crisis,* which left an indelible impression on my thinking by giving me a theological basis for the social concern which had already grown up in me as a result of earlier experiences. Of course, there were points at which I differed with Rauschenbusch. I felt that he had fallen victim to the nineteenth century 'cult of inevitable progress' which led him to a superficial optimism concerning man's nature. Moreover, he came perilously close to identifying the Kingdom

31

of God with a particular social and economic system–a tendency which should never befall the Church. But in spite of these shortcomings Rauschenbusch had done a great service for the Christian Church by insisting that the gospel deals with the whole man, not only his soul but his body; not only his spiritual well-being but his material well-being. It has been my conviction ever since reading Rauschenbusch that any religion which professes to be concerned about the souls of men and is not concerned about the social and economic conditions that scar the soul is a spiritually moribund religion only waiting for the day to be buried. It well has been said: "A religion that ends with the individual ends."[38]

This observation reveals the abiding and determinative influence of Rauschenbusch on King. We will proceed to examine this in detail.

The two Rauschenbusch sources which will concern us most are *Theology for the Social Gospel*[39] and *Christianity and the Social Crisis*.[40] These are his most influential and important books.[41] These two books were also the most significant for King, with the latter being the most determinative, according to King's own admission. In the development of the social gospel's influence on King, we will be concentrating on the contents of these two books.

Rauschenbusch's literary work was an *apologia* for the necessary relationship between Christianity and social issues. His overriding concern was "How does the Biblical message relate to social structures of the human community?"

The seriousness with which Rauschenbusch took his task is revealed in a few short, but telling, statements from *Christianity and the Social Crisis* and *Theology For the Social Gospel*

"We need either a revival of social religion or the deluge."[42]

"(The) magnetic pole of all our thought" is "the solution of the social problems."[43]

". . . the moral power generated by the Christian religion is available for the task of social regeneration."[44]

"His (Jesus's) healing power was for social help, for the alleviation of human suffering."[45]

". . . social wrongs were the real obstacles to the coming of the Kingdom of God."[46]

"It (social gospel) concentrates religious interest on the great ethical problems of social life."[47]

"The social gospel registers the fact that for the first time in history the spirit of Christianity has had a chance to form a working partnership with real social and psychological sciences."[48]

An excellent summary of Rauschenbusch's argument is found in the beginning of the last chapter in *Christianity and the Social Crisis.*

We rest our case. We have seen that in the prophetic religion of the Old Testament and in the aims of Jesus Christ the reconstruction of the whole of human life in accordance with the will of God and under the motive power of religion was the ruling purpose. Primitive Christianity, while under the fresh impulse of Jesus, was filled with social forces. In its later history the reconstructive capacities of Christianity were paralyzed by alien influences, but through the evolution of the Christian spirit on the Church it has now arrived at a stage in its development where it is fit and free for its largest social mission.[49]

An operating principle for Rauschenbusch was the priority of the Hebraic over the Hellenic. This priority he undoubtedly obtained from Harnack. In *Theology For the Social Gospel*, Rauschenbusch claims that we cannot avoid the

central proposition of Harnack's *History of Dogma,* that the development of Catholic dogma was the process of the Hellenization of Christianity; in other words, that the alien influences streamed into the religion of Jesus Christ and created a theology which he never taught nor intended.[50]

For Rauschenbusch, therefore, the social gospel was not an "alien influence," but integral to the Hebraic view of life. The latter orientation, adopted by Rauschenbusch, led him to a concern for the "bodily" nature of reality which inevitably led him to his emphasis on ethics. It is natural, also, that Rauschenbusch would have as his central category the ideal of human community or Kingdom of God. For him, this meant that Biblical faith was revolutionary and this-worldly.

On the other hand, he rejected the Greek emphasis on the soul which often led to preoccupation with ceremonies to enable one to obtain eternal life. Rauschenbusch concluded that this approach was ascetic and other-worldly. This distinction, admittedly somewhat simplistic, was very central to Rauschenbusch.

This distinction of Rauschenbusch may be simply schematized in the following way

Hebrew–
  body–ethics–Kingdom (community)–revolutionary–this-worldly

Greek–
  soul–ceremony–Eternal Life (individual)–ascetic–other-worldly

Or as Rauschenbusch puts it, "The hope of eternal life . . . was the desire to escape from the world and be done with it. The kingdom was a revolutionary idea, eternal life was an ascetic idea."[51] The ascetic force in religion lifts men out of their social relations instead of bringing them into normal relations.[52]

Before we discuss at length the themes of Rauschenbusch which were influential on King, we will briefly review as essential background Rauschenbush's theological understanding of God, sin, and salvation.

a. *God*

Rauschenbusch disavowed the traditional division in theology between Latin and Greek, Protestant and Catholic, and said that a more basic division is between a *despotic* and *democratic* theology. "From a Christian point of view that is a more decisive distinction."[53]

In his chapter on God in *Theology For the Social Gospel*, Rauschenbusch very forcefully states that Jesus's use of "Father" for God democratized the conception of God and moved God out of the coercive political frame and "transferred it to the realm of family life, the chief embodiment of solidarity and love. He not only saved humanity; he saved God."[54]

Of course, "Father" is still a symbolic way of speaking of ultimate reality, and Rauschenbusch did not stress the importance of the content often poured into "Father." He was uncritical of the overly-anthropomorphic meaning we could attach to the concept "Father." This was probably due to a certain optimism Rauschenbusch had about man.

Rauschenbusch finds some deficiency at this point even in the Reformation, which did not completely restore the Christian conception of God. Luther may have been democratic in his understanding of the God-man relationship, but he (along with Calvin) was not personally in sympathy with democracy in the political sphere.

Luther's cooperation with the Princes in the subjugation of the peasants and Calvin's concern for a theocracy headed by the Elect indicated to Rauschenbusch that they were still within an autocratic, if not despotic, frame of mind, politically.

Rauschenbusch felt that the real Reformation was what has been called the "Left-Wing" of the Reformation, represented by the Anabaptist movement. The social gospel, in the main, arose in the free churches which can trace their lineage to the radical left of the Reformation. So, says Rauschenbusch, "The social gospel is God's predestined agent to continue what the Reformation began."[55]

The democratized God is the "common basis of all our life." Each individual personality, although distinguishable, is rooted in the eternal life of God.

> The all-pervading life of God is the ground of the spiritual oneness of the race and of our hope for its closer fellowship in the future.[56]

It is this idea which solidifies our human consciousness, which makes mankind organically one, and for Rauschenbusch this is the essence of religion. It is also the basis by which he supports a solidaristic view of humanity (Ritschl) and the brotherhood of man under the Fatherhood of God (Harnack). The democratized God (the Christian God for Rauschenbusch) is by nature a "breaker of barriers."

> All who have a distinctively Christian experience of God are committed to the expansion of human fellowship and to the overthrow of barriers.[57]

The God who "breaks barriers" is also for Rauschenbusch the "all-embracing source and exponent of the common life and good of mankind."[58] It is precisely such an observation as this that enables Rauschenbusch to relate his understanding of God to the aim of the social gospel. He attempts to show that, in ridding the conception of God of historic accretions of despotism, in protecting God from the indictment contained in the unjust suffering of great social groups, for which man is responsible, and realizing that God is the ground of social unity, freedom, justice, and solidarity, the common good of mankind and the aims of the social gospel are possible.[59] In fact, when we submit to God, we are submitting to the supremacy of the common good.[60]

b. Sin

Here, again, Rauschenbusch is consistent in his contention that theology often reflects political climate. Theological understanding of sin has been formulated against the background of *monarchical* institutions. The first duty of a subject in a monarchy is *to bow to the royal will*. He may be utterly dehumanizing in his social and family relationships, but if he crosses the king, that is quite another matter. So

> when theological definitions speak of rebellion against God as the common characteristic of all sin, it reminds one of the readiness of despotic governments to treat every offense as treason.[61]

It is understandable, then, that Rauschenbusch would conclude with Ritschl that *"sin is essentially selfishness."* This definition is integrally related to the social gospel–the only notion of sin appropriate to this view of Christianity. "The sinful mind, then, is the unsocial and anti-social mind."[62]

For Rauschenbusch, the "element of selfishness emerges as the character of sin matures."[63] "Sin, being selfish, is covetous and grasping. It favors institutions and laws which permit unrestricted exploitation and accumulation."[64] Sin defined as selfishness is an *"ethical and social definition,* and is proof of the unquenchable social spirit of Christianity."[65] "The definition of sin as selfishness furnishes an excellent theological basis for a social conception of sin and salvation."[66] Sin as selfishness is juxtaposed to the religious ideal of society. "Sin selfishly takes from others their opportunities for self-realization in order to increase its own opportunities abnormally."[67]

This social definition of sin as selfishness is more essentially Christian, says Rauschenbusch, than the dualistic conception of the Greek father, "who thought of sin as fundamentally sensuousness and materiality, and saw the chief consequences of the fall in the present reign of death rather than in the reign of selfishness."[68] This is true enough, but Rauschenbusch is conspicuously silent when it comes to sin as pride, *hybris*, self-elevation–a classical Christian understanding. His own emphasis on sin as selfishness may not be radical enough, although it is an essential ingredient in the social understanding of sin.

Rauschenbusch does admit to three forms of sin–sensuousness, selfishness, and godlessness–in ascending and expanding stages. These various stages represent "sin against our higher self, against the good of men, and against the universal good."[69]   But in reality, the latter two are synonymous. The conflict between the selfish Ego and the common good of humanity is expressed in religious terms as the conflict between self and God.[70] So when Rauschenbusch does speak of rebelling against God, it is inseparable from exploiting or violating our neighbor.

> We rebel against God and repudiate his will when we set our profit and ambition above the welfare of our fellows and above the Kingdom of God which binds them together.[71]

The climax of sin is not found in heresy or private sins, but in social groups

> who have turned the patrimony of a nation into the private property of a small class, or have left the peasant laborers cowed, degraded, demoralized, and without rights in the land. When we find such in history, or in present-day life, we shall know we have struck real rebellion against God on the higher levels of sin.[72]

This is true for Rauschenbusch, because he is convinced that sin is never a private transaction between the sinner and God. "Humanity always crowds the audience room when God holds court."[73]   There is an inseparability, an identity (Rauschenbusch does not make much of a distinction) between our God-relationship and our neighbor-relationship. When we love and serve our fellowman, we are loving and serving God. "We rarely sin against God alone."[74]

It is this solidarity of life that enables Rauschenbusch to support the doctrine of original sin. In fact, he takes pleasure in doing so, because "it is one of the few attempts of individualistic theology to get a solidaristic view of its field of work."[75]

Original Sin is a relevant doctrine for social Christianity because it presupposes the *unity of the human race*–a unity which is the "basis and the carrier for the transmission and universality of sin." This doctrine of sin is a way of describing a social reality, namely, that *"one generation corrupts the next."* Sinful behavior of adults is not transmitted through the genes, "but by *being socialized.*" Original Sin "runs down the generations not only by biological propagation, but also by social assimilation."[76] Rauschenbusch illustrates this by a reference to racial attitudes in America.

> When Negroes are hunted from a northern city like beasts, or when a southern city degrades the whole nation by turning the savage inhumanity of a mob into a public festivity, we are continuing to sin because our fathers created the condition of sin by the African slave trade and by the unearned wealth they fathered from slave labor for generations.[77]

Since all of human life is interrelated and interwoven and since laws and institutions are social means of infection, breeding new evils each generation, we begin to see the "solidaristic and organic conceptions of the power and reality of evil in the world." This is what the social gospel means by the Kingdom of Evil.

> The social gospel is the only influence which can renew the idea of the Kingdom of Evil in modern minds, because it alone has an adequate sense of solidarity and a sufficient grasp of the historical and social realities of sin.[78]

It is for Rauschenbusch a matter of common sense that sin is "lodged in social customs and institutions" and is thus absorbed by the individual from his social group.

c. *Salvation*

"If sin is selfishness, salvation must be a change which *turns a man from self to God and humanity*."[79] At a very basic level, then, salvation is the move from a self-centered life to a life centered on God and man, a life of love coordinated with the life of our neighbors in obedient response to the loving impulses of God. This would result in service to our fellowman. Or as Rauschenbusch very succinctly puts it, "*Salvation is the voluntary socializing of the soul.*"[80]

While Rauschenbusch does not disparage the necessity for personal salvation, he sees it as definitely a one-sided view which the social gospel seeks to correct. A salvation strictly concerned with the soul and its personal interests "is an imperfect and only partly effective salvation." This is especially true if one assumes the truth of his exposition of the superpersonal nature of sin and of the Kingdom of Evil.

Since the social gospel stresses the importance and power of superpersonal forces in the community, the individualistic approach to sin and salvation is deficient. The latter approach, because it does not understand the sinful nature of the social order (society), is not resourceful in evoking "faith in the will and power of God to redeem the permanent institutions of human society. . . ."[81]

Now the novelty in the social gospel, which is really "the old message of salvation, enlarged and intensified,"[82] is the confidence and clarity with which it "sets forth the necessity and the possibility of redeeming the historical life of humanity from the social wrongs which now pervade it. . . ."[83]

When Rauschenbusch speaks of saving the superpersonal forces in society, he means that they should be brought under the law of Christ. As with individuals who upon repentance and conversion submit to the law of Christ, so institutions upon their repentance and conversion must be Christianized. In the case of professions and organizations, this means specifically the relinquishing of monopoly power and the incomes derived from legalized extortion and bringing them under the law of service. In the instance of governments and political oligarchies, whether it be an absolute monarch or a capitalistic semi-democracy, it means the submission to real democracy. "Therewith they step out of the Kingdom of Evil into the Kingdom of God."[84]

These theological presuppositions help us understand Rauschenbusch's work and they inform all the religio-social positions he adopts.

d. *The Prophetic Model of Social Religion*

It could be said that all of Rauschenbusch's writings are really footnotes to his chapter on the prophets in *Christianity and the Social Crisis* entitled "The Historical Roots of Christianity: The Hebrew Prophets." This chapter is one of the most perceptive in all literature dealing with the nature and the function of the Biblical prophet.

All of the major themes we will discuss in his articulation of the social gospel are found in fetal form in this discussion of the prophets. One can imagine King, a twenty-year-old seminary student, reading this evangelical, zealous account of Rauschenbusch's heroes of religion. His own appreciation of the prophets and his prophetic view of history undoubtedly can be traced to these pages in Rauschenbusch.

Rauschenbusch contends that Jesus is squarely in the Old Testament prophetic tradition and that Christianity is a direct heir of the prophetic appreciation for the social dimension of life.[85] When Christianity has attempted to influence social and political life, it betrays its indebtedness to the Old Testament, whose social ideas have constituted "permanent forces making for democracy and social justice."

> Thus a study of the prophets is not only an interesting part in the history of social movements but it is indispensable for any full comprehension of the social influences exerted by historical Christianity, and for any true comprehension of the mind of Jesus Christ.[86]

Christianity is heir to the prophetic message most directly through the Jewish-Christian communities which comprise the radical social wing of the early church. The Jewish Christians were responsible for the prevalence of social thought in the Synoptic Gospels, and the Epistle of James represents this same prophetic spirit with its emphasis on practical religion.

Rauschenbusch called James the "most democratic book of the New Testament."[87] Very often in Judaism the poor and the godly were identified–the Old Testament frequently speaks of the wicked rich man and the blessed poor man. This is a reflection of exalting the lowly and humbling the mighty, as seen in the Magnificat.[88]

e. *The Prophetic Principle*

The prophetic principle is one of dialectical yes and no to all historical relativity. Only qualified allegiance can be given to God. A prophet cannot put his stamp of approval on anything as it is.

> Some sense of antagonism between the will of God and the present order of things is necessary to ignite the spirit of the prophet.[89]

Since for Christianity the world is good and bad, made by God, but now controlled by sin

> if a man wants to be a Christian, he must stand over against things as they are and condemn them in the name of that higher conception of life which Jesus revealed. If a man is satisfied with things as they are, he belongs to the other side.[90]

One must add to this tension between "what ought to be" and "what is" a combination of religious fervor, a democratic spirit, strong social feeling, and free utterance to produce genuine prophecy.[91]

This combination produced the Hebrew prophets and many other radical movements in Christianity. All those bodies were of the same type, recalling the pristine Christianity of the first century. As Rauschenbusch describes this type, one can see the relationship between radical tension with one's society and the prophetic mentality.

> Strong fraternal feeling, simplicity and democracy of organization, more or less communistic ideas about property, an attitude of passive obedience or conscientious objection toward the coercive and militaristic governments of the time, opposition to the selfish and oppressive Church, a genuine faith in the practicability of the ethics of Jesus, and, as the secret power in it all, belief in an inner experience of regeneration and an inner light which interprets the outer word of God. These radical bodies did not produce as many great individuals as we might have expected because their intellectual leaders were always killed off or silenced. But their communities were prophetic. They have been the forerunners of the modern world.[92]

To a preacher who wishes to deal seriously with social questions, Rauschenbusch has his own version of "Thus saith the Lord" to suggest. He will not be able to escape the charge of partiality, and the wider our social cleavage, the more difficult will it be to satisfy both sides.

> Nor is it his business to try trimming and straddling. He must seek to hew as straight as the moral law. Let others voice special interests; the minister of Jesus Christ must voice the mind of Jesus Christ. His strength will lie in the high impartiality of moral insight and love to all.[93]

f.   *Religion and Ethics*

Integral to the prophetic understanding of life was the inseparability of religion and ethics.

> The prophets were the heralds of the fundamental truth that religion and ethics are inseparable, and that ethical conduct is the supreme and sufficient religious act.[94]

If one believes in the social gospel, one may choose any method of developing the spiritual life, provided it has an ethical outcome.

> The social gospel takes up the message of the Hebrew prophets, that ritual and emotional religion is harmful unless it results in righteousness.[95]

For the Hebrew prophet, righteousness was what God demanded, a right life was the appropriate act of worship, and the righting of social wrongs the goal of the religious man.

Christianity, in its original purity, claims Rauschenbusch, reflected the prophetic conviction that the service of God was sought in ethical conduct and not in ceremonial ritual. In fact, Christianity was even more a religion of absolute spirituality, "insisting simply on right relations to men as the true expression of religion." If Christianity could have retained this original thrust, if it could have remained purely ethical and spiritual, i.e., prophetic, "it would have been an almost inconceivable leap forward in social and religious evolution."[96]

Rauschenbusch's own bias toward and personal commitment to the prophetic world-view makes him very suspicious of mysticism.[97] His fear is based on the facility with which man can avoid responsibility for his neighbor and take refuge in God. His charge against mysticism is that "the mystic way to holiness is not through humanity but above it."[98]

For Rauschenbusch, there would be no "immediate" relationship to God or ecstatic union with him that did not at the same time incorporate the dimension of the human and the ethical. This is why he often said that the social gospel, while not denigrating personal salvation, provided significant tests for it.

g. *Religion as Social*

In his attempt to revive the oldest gospel of all, the social gospel, Rauschenbusch consistently shows that life, being social, means that religion, fundamentally, must have a social dimension. This dimension is the norm by which religion is judged.

He is aided in this conclusion again by the Hebrew prophets. The community of Israel produced the prophets. They were not religious individuals, separated from a traditional covenant community. Prophets are not produced by an "individualistically oriented religion." The latter may breed "priests, missionaries, pastors, and scholars, but few prophets."[99] On another occasion, Rauschenbusch claimed that "individualistic evangelicalism, while rich in men of piety and evangelistic fervor, has been singularly poor in the prophetic gift."[100]

"A wider social outlook" is necessary for the occurrence of the prophetic gift. Even men of our age who have a sense of the prophetic vision and the power of language have almost always had "the social enthusiasm and faith in the reconstructive power of Christianity."[101]

The prophet, produced by a broad social outlook, is himself a man of social vision. He sees the Word of God as coming to the community and therefore is in the business of translating that Word into social meaning and language.

Even his experience of God is not the usual solitary type in which the individual was preoccupied with his own salvation or his own peace of mind. This experience was one with a conscious outlook toward humanity.

> When Moses saw the glory of God in the flaming bush and learned the ineffable name of the Eternal, it was not the salvation of Moses which was in question but the salvation of his people from the bondage of Egypt.[102]

Rauschenbusch is more explicit on this point. He says that in the Old Testament accounts of how men received their prophetic mission, none of them struggled

> for his personal salvation as later Christian saints have done. His woe did not come through fear of personal damnation, but through his sense of solidarity with his people and through social feeling; his hope and comfort was not for himself alone but for his nation.[103]

By fusing Christian spirit and social consciousness, the social gospel creates a type of religious experience corresponding to the prophetic type.[104] The prophetic "plan of redemption" was always a social, communal, solidaristic redemption for the entire nature. Furthermore, claims Rauschenbusch, the morality insisted on by the prophets was

> not merely the private morality of the home, but the public morality on which national life is founded. They said less about the pure heart for the individual than of just institutions for the nation.[105]

Since the prophets dealt with Israel as a whole, and not separately with each individual Israelite, and since their eye was on social morality, the evils most condemned by them in the name of Yahweh were injustice and oppression. Rauschenbusch quotes Professor Kautzsch

> Since Amos it was the alpha and omega of prophetic preaching to insist on right and justice, to warn against the oppression of the poor and helpless.[106]

Rauschenbusch sees Jesus's "fundamental sympathies," as the Old Testament prophets', with the poor and oppressed.

Rauschenbusch's passion and power of argument reaches unparalleled heights in his support of the above contention and this persuasive rhetoric certainly was not lost on King. In Rauschenbusch's own life and thought there was a strong egalitarian strain and a decided concern for the poor classes[107] and women[108], and the championing of the cause of the disadvantaged, which was for him the central Biblical concern. Note the following passages:

> If any one holds that religion is essentially ritual and sacramental, or that it is purely personal; or that God is on the side of the rich; or that social interest is likely to lead preachers astray; he must prove his case with his eye on the Hebrew prophets, and the burden of proof is with him.[109]

> The dominant trait of their (the prophets') moral feeling reacted on their theology, so that it became one of the fundamental attributes of their God that he was the husband of the widow, the father of the orphans, and the protector of the stranger. . . . His modern brother is the proletarian immigrant of our cities, who also has no share in the modern means of production and no political power to protect his interests. When the prophets conceived Jehovah as the special vindicator of these voiceless classes, it was another way of saying that it is the chief duty in religious morality to stand for the right of the helpless.[110]

> We offer free pardon to individuals and rarely mention social wrongs. We have seen that the prophets demanded right moral conduct as the sole test and fruit of religion, and that the morality which they had in mind was not the private morality of detached pious souls but the social morality of the nation. This they preached, and they backed their preaching by active participation in public action and discussion.[111]

Rauschenbusch says that if the prophets were limited to our religious individualism, the unique Old Testament contribution of "ethical monotheism" would have never emerged.

> Our philosophical and economic individualism has affected our religious thought so deeply that we hardly comprehend the prophetic view of an organic national life and of material sin and salvation.[112]

h. *Rauschenbusch's Further Reflections on the Prophets*

1. *Present Justice*

Rauschenbusch properly observed that religions with a heavy stress on a life beyond this one can afford to postpone indefinitely the resolution of inequities. In the hereafter everything will be balanced. Yet in Hebrew prophetic theology with an undeveloped view of the future life and with "no adjourned assizes for the individual," God must prove his justice here or never. If the righteous suffered and the unrighteous prospered, "the moral order of the universe was under indictment." Christianity, in fact, with its strong belief in a future life, has neutralized demands for social justice in the present.[113]

Because of this emphasis on the present life, the prophet insisted on present social righteousness. This concern for the present is the biblical basis for the NOW of the civil rights movement. Postponement of justice is a denial of justice.[114]

2. *Prophets Without Honor*

Rauschenbusch has keen insight into the human facility (frailty?!) to idolize prophetic witness in the past and be threatened by it in the present.

> A later day can always study with complacency the attack made on the vested interests in a previous epoch, and the championship of eternal principles always seems divine to a generation that is not hurt by them. . . . It is always posterity which builds their sepulchres and garnishes their tombs.[115]

All prophets suffer the burden of being ahead of their time and not living to see their ideas realized. They are usually implemented by men who basically disagree with them. For example, the priests and scribes finally end up integrating ethical monotheism into Israel's religious life, but in doing so that ideal was appreciably refracted. Rauschenbusch's comment is a stroke of genius.

> That is the Divine Comedy of history. The Tories carry out the liberal programmes. It is a beneficent scheme by which the joy of life is evened up. The "practical men" and conservatives have the pleasure of feeling that they are the only ones who can really make reforms work. The prophetic minds have the satisfaction of knowing that the world must come their way whether

it will or not, because they are on the way to justice, and justice is on the way to God.[116]

3. The False Prophet

Another example of Rauschenbusch's insight into the prophetic stance is his understanding of the false prophets. He reminds us that they were not preachers of an idolatrous faith, much less were they liars.

> They were the mouthpiece of the average popular opinion and they drew their inspiration from the self-satisfied patriotism which seemed so very identical with trust in Jehovah and his sanctuary. They were apparently the great majority of the prophetic order; the prophets of our Bible were the exceptional men. The "false prophet" corresponded to those modern preachers who act as eulogists of existing conditions, not because they desire to deceive the people, but because they are really so charmed with things as they are and have never had a vision from God to shake their illusion. The logic of events proved to be on the side of those great Hebrews who asserted that black is really black, even if you call it white, and that a wall built with untempered mortar and built out of plumb is likely to topple. Because history backed their predictions, they are now in the Bible and revered as inspired.[117]

Rauschenbusch had great optimism about the prophetic role. He felt that in his own time the priest was dying and the prophet was entering his heritage, "provided the prophet himself is still alive with his ancient message of an ethical and social service to God."[118] And the very last words of *Theology For the Social Gospel*: "The era of prophetic and democratic Christianity has just begun. This concerns the social gospel, for the social gospel is the voice of prophecy in modern life."[119] One of the key passages which illustrates the influence of Rauschenbusch and the social gospel on King is

> A Christian regeneration must have an outlook toward humanity and result in a higher social consciousness. The saint of the future will need not only a theocentric mysticism which enables him to realize God, but an anthropocentric mysticism which enables him to realize his fellow-man in God.[120]

i. King and the Prophetic Influence

With the exception of the Sermon on the Mount, the prophets influenced King more than any other part of scripture. Sometimes by direct quotation,[121] but mostly by tone and implication, the prophetic message is found in his speeches and writings. King felt that in discussing the role of the ministry today, we must

> ultimately emphasize the need for prophecy. Although not every minister can be a prophet, some must be prepared courageously to accept the suffering that comes from the high calling of insisting on righteousness. May the problem of race in America soon make hearts burn so that prophets will rise up, saying, "Thus saith the Lord," and cry out as Amos did, ". . . let justice roll down like waters, and righteousness like an ever-flowing stream."[122]

King had the prophetic sense to determine authenticity from unreality. He knew the difference between false and true peace. The Montgomery boycott uncovered the uneasy peace existing beneath a surface of order and tranquility. When he was criticized for the disruption between the races caused by the boycott, he speculated that this is what Jesus must have meant when he said

> "I have not come to bring peace, but a sword." Certainly Jesus did not mean that he came to bring a physical sword. He seems to have been saying in substance: "I have not come to bring this old negative peace with its deadening passivity. I have come to lash out against such a peace. Whenever I come, a conflict is precipitated between the old and the new. Whenever I come, a division sets in between justice and injustice. I have come to bring a positive peace which is the presence of justice, love, yea, even the Kingdom of God.[123]

When he was being tried in court in September, 1958, King made a statement which illustrates the prophetic influence in his life. He tells the judge that he cannot pay the fine and will readily accept the alternative offered by the court and do so without malice.

> My action is motivated by the impelling voice of conscience and a desire to follow truth and the will of God wherever they lead . . . I also make this decision because of my deep concern for the injustice and indignities that my people continue to experience. . .[124]

King often called for a true revolution of values based on the Beatitudes and Isaiah 40–a "leveling down hills and leveling up the valleys."[125] This revolution is weighted strongly toward justice. It is in the name of justice.[126]

King also, in true prophetic style, is averse to blind conformity. The church he finds is a largely conformist institution which has often served to crystallize, conserve, and even bless the patterns of majority opinion. The erstwhile sanction by the church of slavery, racial segregation, war, and economic exploitation is testimony to the fact that the church has hearkened more to the authority of the world than to the authority of God. Called to be the moral guardian of the community, the church at times has preserved that which is immoral and unethical. Called to combat social evils, it has remained silent behind stained-glass windows. Called to lead men on the highway of brotherhood and to summon them to rise above the narrow confines of race and class, it has enunciated and practiced racial exclusiveness.[127]

j. Rauschenbusch and History

Rauschenbusch, as a result of the nineteenth century interest in history, especially as found in Ritschl, was himself profoundly concerned for the historical. Not unrelated to Rauschenbusch's interest was that he taught church history at Rochester-Colgate Divinity School.

Max Stackhouse says, "The fundamental category of Rauschenbusch's thought is history."[128] The same anti-mystical, anti-metaphysical bias found in Ritschl is easily detected in Rauschenbusch.

> When God revealed himself, it was not by communicating abstract propositions or systems of doctrine. The fundamental fact in the Christian revelation was that the Word became flesh. Therewith, Truth became History . . . The future of Christian theology lies in the comprehension of Christianity in history.[129]

Stackhouse believes that Rauschenbusch found evangelicals too personalistic, Calvinists too doctrinal, liberals too concerned with the relation of theology and scientific theories, and found no available theology with a radical sense of future transformation and fulfillment. That is why Rauschenbusch leaned so heavily toward socialism–it was a movement speaking in eschatological-social terms. The Kingdom of God, the result of Rauschenbusch's search for an adequate theological base, "functions as the interpretive concept by which (he) exegetes history."[130]

Again Stackhouse suggests that for Rauschenbusch the medium is the message, and the medium is history.[131] Or, in Rauschenbusch's own words, "History is a revelation of God's will. God thinks in action, and speaks in events."[132]

A Christian discussion of the past and future must be religious, i.e., "filled with the consciousness of God in human affairs. God is in history. He has the initiative. Where others see blind forces working dumb agony, we must see moral will working toward redemption and education."[133]

The method of the *religionsgeschichtliche Schule* impressed Rauschenbusch. He saw the historical study of religion as a serious and progressive effort to "interpret individuals by their social contacts," and heartily approved of the "great work of biblical criticism" which placed every biblical book in its "exact historical environment as preliminary to understanding its religious message." The historical context of an author included the "religious drifts and desires and beliefs of his age, to which he more or less consciously reacted."[134] In even higher praise, Rauschenbusch says, "The historical method has already done what the social gospel might wish it to do."[135]

This concern of Rauschenbusch is traced in the development of *Christianity and the Social Crisis*, which begins with three indispensable chapters, all historical in character–Hebrew prophets, Jesus, and the early church. A true grasp of past history is sorely needed if we are "to forecast the future correctly and act wisely in the present."[136] He actually sees the social gospel movement as helping to create the modern study of history.

Where we used to see a panorama of wars and strutting kings and court harlots, we now see the struggle of the people to wrest a living from nature and to shake off their oppressors. The French Revolution was the birth of modern democracy, and also of the modern school of history.[137]

In a significant address given in 1914, entitled "The Value and Use of History," Rauschenbusch relates history and social ideas.

History . . . is interested in the permanent and organized life of great groups of men, and cares for individuals only when they are the exponents or creators of organized, collective life. Only in history do we learn to think in social categories and to see the continuity of social forces and movements. So history gives us a feeling for the life of the community and a realization of its immense power in shaping the life of all its members.[138]

History teaches us to distinguish the significant and insignificant, the great and small, the failure and the success.

For instance, it ought to help us choose between democracy and monarchy, between a society founded on equality of opportunity and one founded on special privilege.[139]

A view of history will determine how one practically acts,e.g., the premillenial view of history is a real obstacle to social welfare interest. The prophets, on the other hand, appealed to history and desired amelioration now. The historical and the prophetic are interwoven.

k. *King and History*

Throughout King's writings and activities one finds a keen sense of history and a profound awareness of God's involvement in the historical process. King firmly believed that God was at work in this universe.

> He is not outside the world looking on with a sort of cold indifference. Here in all the roads of life, he is striving in our striving. Like an ever-loving Father, he is working through history for the salvation of his children. As we struggle to defeat the forces of evil, the God of the universe struggles with us.[140]

The Exodus event, the *sine qua non* of Israel's historical religious life, was a predominant theme in King's speeches and writings. This event, the model *par excellence* of God's involvement in history, was seen by King as an appropriate symbol for the civil rights movement. As God delivered ancient Israel from bondage to freedom, so he will bring the Negro from slavery to liberty.

In *Why We Can't Wait*, King observes that the 1965 Voting Rights Act was born in Selma, Alabama, "where a stubborn sheriff handling Negroes in the Southern tradition had stumbled against the future."[141]

King also was able to communicate to the movement that God was active in its history. He did it so well that on November 13, 1956, when the announcement came to Montgomery that the Supreme Court declared bus segregation unconstitutional, a bystander exclaimed, "God almighty has spoken from Washington, D.C."[142]

King's insistence on a moral law that works its way through history always on the side of love and justice is evidence of his belief in the importance of history and God's presence in it.[143]

l. *Rauschenbusch on Church and World*

Another significant contribution of Rauschenbusch to the understanding of social Christianity was the relationship of the Church to the world. This also was a great influence on King.

There is imbedded in the church, says Rauschenbusch, the notion that the world (society as we know it) is basically evil and for 1500 years those who wanted to live authentic Christian lives withdrew from that society. Now such asceticism is impossible for the vast majority of men. Now, there are only two other possibilities.

> The church must either condemn the world and seek to change it, or tolerate the world and conform to it. The other possibility has never yet been tried with full faith on a large scale. All the leadings of God in contemporary history and all the promptings of Christ's spirit in our hearts urge us to make the trial. On this choice is staked the future of the church.[144]

Rauschenbusch was dedicated to the possibility of the church being a change agent. He juxtaposed Christ and American culture, according to Robert Cross,[145] and "maintained that not just the moral inclinations of individuals but the central institutions of capitalistic society stood under judgment." And society being under such judgment, the church is called to "undertake the work of a Christian reconstruction of social life."[146]

Rauschenbusch was not naive concerning the past record of the church. The social effects usually attributed to the church's efforts never constituted a "reconstruction of society of a Christian basis." They were, more often than not, a "suppression of the most glaring evils in the social system of the time."[147]

The church would occasionally make public statements protesting inexcusable evil, but it would accept

> as inevitable the general social system under which the world was living at the time, and has not undertaken any thoroughgoing social reconstruction in accordance with Christian principles.[148]

Rauschenbusch was not naive regarding the relationship of converted individuals to converted society. He was aware that "indirectness of the social influence of Christianity" was accepted as a kind of dogma. "We are told that Christianity is sure to affect society but that Christianity must not seek to affect it."[149] That is, the church's vocation is to

> implant the divine life in the souls of men, and from these regenerated individuals forces of righteousness will silently radiate and evil customs and institutions will melt away without any propaganda.[150]

But, asks Rauschenbusch, would the church not be more effective if it made this its conscious determination, if it set out specifically to change certain customs?

> Why should the instinctive and unpurposed action of Christian men be more effective than a deeply rooted and intelligent purpose? Since when is a curved and circuitous line the shortest distance between two points?[151]

Consonant with this position is a respect for the power of social structures.

> Our social machinery is almost as blindly cruel as its steel machinery. . . .[152]

> The social gospel realizes the importance and power of the superpersonal forces in the community.[153]

Just as we must repent in personal religion, so in social religion there must be repentance for our social sins. Part of Rauschenbusch's realism (which antedates Reinhold Niebuhr's by a generation) is the recognition of "sin and evil deepseated in the very constitution of the present order."[154]

If the evangelical reminds the advocate of a better social order that the latter does not know the depth of sin in the human heart, those who believe in Christianity's power to improve the social order can remind the evangelical that he is far too unrealistic about entrenchment of sinful social structures and how sometimes he bows before "one of the devil's spider-webs praising it as one of the mighty works of God."[155]

Regeneration, personal and social, means that we must pass under the law of Christ. "That means a revolution of social values."[156]

Another aspect of Rauschenbusch's realism is his refusal to mutually exclude the personal and the social gospel. For him, there was one (the whole) gospel with personal *and* social implications. To men verging on a kind of baptized humanism, Rauschenbusch would say, "No comprehension of Jesus is even approximately true which fails to understand that the heart of his heart was religion" (by which Rauschenbusch meant his God-relationship).[157] To those who insisted that Christianity is best expressed by ascetic, soul-saving individualism, Rauschenbusch would say

> whoever uncouples the religious and the social life has not understood Jesus. Whoever sets any bounds for the reconstructive power of the religious life over the social relations and institutions of men, to that extent denies the faith of the Master.[158]

Rauschenbusch was careful not to be trapped in one corner or the other. He maintained a healthy balance often overlooked by his critics and his more ardent disciples, both of whom might have thought him a one-dimensional man.

> There are two great entities in human life–the human soul and the human race–and religion is to save both. The soul is to seek righteousness and eternal life; the race is to seek righteousness and the Kingdom of God. The social preacher is apt to overlook the one. But the evangelical preacher has long overlooked the other.[159]

> One of the most serious charges that can be raised against preaching on social questions is that it is unreligious. It is the business of a preacher to connect all that he thinks he says with the mind and will of God, to give the religious interpretation to all human relations and questions, and to infuse the divine sympathy and passion into all moral discussion.[160]

> Social preaching has come under suspicion because experience has shown that when a preacher begins to speak on social questions, he is apt to veer away from the established course and fly off on a tangent. The new ideas take such hold on him that all other Christian truth seems stale and outworn in comparison. His preaching becomes one-sided. He twangs on a harp of a single string, and it becomes a weariness. . . . Absorbed in public questions such men may forget to appeal to the individual soul for repentance and to comfort those in sorrow. This is a sore defect.[161]

In further articulating his understanding of the dialectical tension and ultimate unity between the personal and the social, Rauschenbusch speaks of

> two personalities to which religion holds out a hope of salvation. The little personality of man, and the great collective personality of mankind. To the individual, Christianity offers victory over sin and death, and the consummation of all good in the life to come. To mankind it offers a perfect social life, victory over all the evil that wounds and mars human intercourse and satisfaction for the hunger and thirst after justice, equality and love.[162]

At any given time in history, one or the other may be stressed. Israel and the synoptics emphasized the communal and the Greek world of the early Christian centuries and the Gospel of John stressed individual fulfillment in the longing for eternal life. "A perfect religious hope must include both: eternal life for the individual, the Kingdom of God for humanity."[163]
This again substantiates the label given to Rauschenbusch–an evangelical liberal of the ethical social variety. Rauschenbusch would never conclude that

Jesus was simply a social reformer or a teacher of morality or that fulfillment of economic and material needs would be a complete answer to anxiety and meaninglessness.

However, the real test of religion for Rauschenbusch is the social one and the latter is integrally included in any definition of it.

> The saving qualities of the church depend on the question whether it has translated the personal life of Jesus Christ into the social life of its group and then brings it to bear on the individual.[164]

m. *King on Relation of Church to World*

In no uncertain terms, King calls the Church to responsibility for and involvement in the social order. This is the church's "historic obligation." "It has always been the responsibility of the church to broaden horizons, challenge the status quo, and break the mores when necessary."[165] More pointedly, King emphatically disagrees with clergymen who believe it is not the church's role to "intervene in secular affairs."[166]

As "the voice of moral and spiritual authority on earth"[167] and as "guardian of the moral and spiritual life of the community,"[168] the church is obligated to address itself to the moral issues in society. The three primary evils in America and world society, according to King, are racism, economic exploitation, and war.[169]

The one that dominates King's concern is racism. Throughout his writings, the church is taken to task for its irresponsibility in this area. Anyone observing the church scene in American history would have to admit "the shameful fact that it has been an accomplice in structuring racism into the architecture of American society."[170] It "sanctioned slavery" and "cast the mantle of its sanctity over the system of segregation."

On the matter of racial justice, the "church has not been true to its social mission."[171] The failure was due to silence and the church's own participation in the race-caste system by cooperating with colonialism, apartheid, and American slavery. Some of his severest language is reserved for the faithless church. Observing that the church is the "most segregated major institution in American society," he comments how

> often the church has been an echo rather than a voice, a taillight behind the Supreme Court and other secular agencies, rather than a headlight guiding men progressively and decisively to higher levels of understanding.[172]

It has too often blessed a status quo that needed to be blasted, and reassured a social order that needed to be reformed. So the church must acknowledge its guilt, its weak and vacillating witness. . .[173]

The church has come dangerously close to committing the unpardonable sin–of so consistently living the lie of segregation–it has "lost the capacity to distinguish between good and evil."[174] "If the church does not recapture its prophetic zeal, it will become an irrelevant social club without moral or spiritual authority."[175]

It will be one of the tragedies of Christian history if future historians record that at the height of the twentieth century the church was one of the greatest bulwarks of white supremacy.[176]

It was King's conviction that the church should "move out into the arena of social action."[177] The church must first regain its institutional integrity by purging itself of all segregation within its body and then the church must become

increasingly active in social action outside its doors. It must seek to keep channels of communication open between the Negro and white community. It must take an active stand against the injustice that Negroes confront in housing, education, police protection, and city and state courts. It must exert its influence in the area of economic justice.[178]

If it lives out such professions, people will knock at the church door and find the "bread of social justice, the bread of peace."[179] Whenever the church is so witnessing, it has been a powerful influence for good. King recalls the early Christians, rejoicing to suffer for their faith, not merely being thermometers "that recorded the ideas and principles of popular opinion," but thermostats "that transformed the mores of society."[180] King recalls also that the early Christians were arrested for "disturbing the peace" and for being "outside agitators." A community loathed to see them enter its gates. But they were a committed "colony of heaven," obeying God and not man. Their dedicated efforts brought about social change–eradication of infanticide and gladiatorial contests. "Small in number, they were big in commitment."[181]

King conceived of the church's role, not as master or servant of the state, "but rather the conscience of the state. It must be the guide and the critic of the state, and never its tool."[182] It is absolutely essential for King that the church recapture its prophetic zeal, its participation actively in the struggles for peace, economic and racial justice, and be known as a "great fellowship of love."

King calls upon the churches to recognize the urgent necessity of taking an unequivocal stand on the crucial problem of race, "America's greatest moral dilemma." The passion and depth of his conviction that the church could and should be involved in social issues is found in the following:

> If we are to remain true to the gospel of Jesus Christ, we cannot rest until segregation and discrimination are banished from every area of American life.[183]

1. Silence of the Church

Strictures are placed against the silence of clergymen and churches. When King comments on the disturbance accompanying James Meredith's admission to the University of Mississippi, he says

> And where was the cry of the Lord's prophets? . . . Surely the abysmal silence of the church and the clergy cannot pass without its due reckoning. . . . When I review the painful memory of the last week at Oxford and cannot recall a single voice, "crying in the wilderness," the questions are still the same: "What kind of people worship there? Who is their God?"[184]

When King compares the contemporary church to the first century church he observes how different things are. So often the contemporary church

> is an archdefender of the status quo. Far from being disturbed by the presence of the church, the power structure of the average community is consoled by the church's silent–and often vocal sanction of things as they are.[185]

King concedes that there have been exceptions to this silence, in the form of individual witnesses by clergymen and rabbis and "sublime statements of the major denominations," but at the local level too many ministers are silent.

> It may well be that the greatest tragedy of this period of social transition is not the glaring noisiness of the so-called bad people, but the appalling silence of the so-called good people. It may be that our generation will have to repent not only for the diabolical actions and vitriolic words of the children of darkness, but also for the crippling fears and tragic apathy of the children of light.[186]

King was always pleased when clergymen attended meetings designed to change segregation laws and to improve race relations. He makes a special point in *Stride Toward Freedom* to say that the largest number present at the first community gathering after Rosa Parks's arrest was from the Christian ministry.

> Having left so many civic meetings in the past sadly disappointed by the dearth of minister participating, I was filled with joy when I entered the church and found so many of them there.[187]

He was also impressed by the significant number of white churches supporting and participating in the March on Washington in 1963. "Never before had they been so full, so enthusiastically, so directly involved."[188]

King, himself, practiced what he preached about the church's relationship to society. Being somewhat embarrassed by the "silk-stocking" image of his first parish, Dexter Avenue Baptist in Montgomery, he was anxious to open the church to all classes and to provide a worship service that, at its best, "is a social experience with people of all levels of life."[189]

The alert and socially sensitive young pastor then proceeded to set up a social program at Dexter Avenue which would be an expression of his concern with such problems as voter registration.

> . . . One of the first committees that I set up in my church was designed to keep the congregation intelligently informed on the social, political, and economic situations. The duties of the Social and Political Action Committee were, among others, to keep before the congregation the importance of the NAACP and the necessity of being registered voters, and–during state and national elections–to sponsor forums and mass meetings to discuss the major issues.[190]

Soon after his arrival in Montgomery as pastor, he became active in several local committees of community interest as evidence further of his concern to relate the church to the world. He became a member of the local branch of the NAACP, Alabama Council on Human Relations, and other citizen committees.[191]

2. *The Whole Gospel–Body/Soul in King*

Behind this obvious strong belief that the church has a responsibility for the social needs of the world is a profound theological position suggesting the unity of body and soul and the unity of the individual and society. This, of course, eventuates in the unity of religion and ethics and it is there that the influence of Rauschenbusch and the social gospel is most strongly felt. King, like Rauschenbusch, wanted desperately to maintain a balance, to stress that Christianity is a "two-way road."

> On the one side, it seeks to change the souls of men and thereby unite them with God; on the other, it seeks to change the environmental conditions of men so that the soul will have a chance after it is changed.[192]

Although King does not use the categories of Hebraic/Hellenic, he does contrast other-worldly and Biblical and says that churches committing themselves to a complete other-worldly religion make "a strange un-biblical distinction between body and soul, between the sacred and the secular."[193] This is reminiscent of Rauschenbusch's concern that "alien influences" (Hellenism) had distorted our Hebrew roots and aided in this false dichotomizing of reality.

Whereas the Hebrew world-view sees life "whole" and good, the Hellenic (i.e., Platonic, which was most influential on Christianity) sees it divided, with earth, history, and the body essentially evil. This division is seen in the pietistic comments of Dr. Frazier, a Methodist minister in one of the early mass meetings in Montgomery. He was scandalized that the boycott was being led by a group of ministers.

> "The job of the minister," he said, "is to lead the souls of men to God, not to bring about confusion by getting tangled up in transitory social problems."[194]

King responded with what was the essential theological rationale for his involvement in social issues as a Christian minister.

> I can see no conflict between our devotion to Jesus Christ and our present action. In fact, I see a necessary relationship. If one is truly devoted to the religion of Jesus he will seek to rid the earth of social evils. The gospel is social as well as personal.[195]

King was aware that the reluctance of Negro ministers to become aggressive in social action was based on the same one-sided theology of Dr. Frazier. They, too, sincerely believed that ministers were not supposed to get mixed up in such earthly, temporal matters as social and economic improvement; they were to "preach the gospel" and keep men's minds centered in "the heavenly."[196]

King's reaction here is similar to the above concern for balance.

But religion true to its nature must also be concerned about man's social conditions. Religion deals with both earth and heaven, both time and eternity. Religion operates not only on the vertical plane but also on the horizontal.[197]

3. *Importance of the Personal*

To make certain he was not misunderstood, King took time to emphasize the importance of the vertical dimension of faith.

Any religion that is earthbound sells its birthright for a mess of naturalistic pottage. Religion, at its best, deals not only with man's preliminary concerns but with his inescapable ultimate concerns. When religion overlooks this basic fact it is reduced to a mere ethical system in which eternity is absorbed into time and God is relegated to a sort of meaningless figment of the human imagination.[198]

He was greatly distraught that we have "guided missiles and misguided men," that we "minimize the internal of our lives and maximize the external."

We will not find peace in our generation until we learn that a "man's life consisteth not in the abundance of the things which he possesseth," but in those inner treasures of the spirit which "no thief approacheth, neither moth corrupteth."[199]

Both personal character and social justice need to be supported by spiritual means and without a spiritual and moral awakening, we will destroy ourselves.

Our generation cannot escape the question of our Lord: What shall it profit a man, if he gain the whole world of externals–airplanes, electric lights, automobiles, and color television–and lost the internal–his own soul?[200]

In one of his most famous sermons, "The Three Dimensions of a Complete Life," the last and presumably most important dimension is one of height or "that upward reach toward something distinctly greater than humanity." We must get beyond the combination of length (developing your inner powers) and breadth (concern for others) to height (giving our allegiance to that eternal Being who is the source and ground of all reality). We cannot stop with the first two. If we do, "we seek to live without a sky."[201]

It is apparent that King appreciated the individual and personal side of religious life. The latter is a reflection of what Rauschenbusch meant by the "God-relation" and what Tillich meant by "ultimate concern."

4. Concern for Structural Change

But King also desired to emphasize the social and corporate. "By ignoring the need for social reform, religion is divorced from the mainstream of human life."[202] That a minister would preach the "true gospel" and not talk about social issues is a

> blueprint for a dangerously irrelevant church. By disregarding the fact that the gospel deals with man's body as well as his soul, such a one-sided emphasis creates a tragic dichotomy between the sacred and the secular. To be worthy of its New Testament origin, the church must seek to transform both individual lives and the social situation that brings to many people anguish of spirit and cruel bondage.[203]

Rauschenbusch could not have been more adamant than King in insisting that social conditions be "saved," or as we say today, humanized. King's sensitivity to the conditions that breed Marxism are seen also in the following reference.

> Any religion that professes to be concerned with the souls of men and is not concerned with the slums that damn them, the economic conditions that strangle them, and the social conditions that cripple them is a dry-as-dust religion. Such a religion is the kind the Marxists like to see–an opiate of the people.[204]

To the ministers of Birmingham, King

> stressed the need for a social gospel to supplement the gospel of individual salvation. I suggested that only a "dry-as-dust" religion prompts a minister to extol the glories of heaven while ignoring the social conditions that cause men an earthly hell.[205]

> As Christians, we must think not only about "mansions in the sky," but also about the slums and ghettoes that cripple the human soul, not merely about streets in heaven "flowing with milk and honey," but also about the millions

of people in the world who go to bed hungry at night. Any religion that professes concern regarding the souls of men and fails to be concerned by social conditions that corrupt and economic conditions that cripple the soul, is a do-nothing religion, in need of a new blood. Such a religion fails to realize that man is an animal having physical and material needs.[206]

One of the lessons the Negro church had to learn and an emphasis very early in King's career was the social implications of faith.

> . . . the church is not living up to its full responsibilities if it merely preaches an other-worldly gospel devoid of practical social connotations. It must concern itself, as Jesus did, with the economic and social problems of this world.[207]

Perhaps the most graphic influence of Rauschenbusch's concern to Christianize the social order in King is found in the latter's discussion of the Jericho Road. We must be willing to do more than play the Good Samaritan along life's roadside.

> One day the whole Jericho Road must be transformed so that men and women will not be beaten and robbed as they make their journey through life. True compassion is more than flinging a coin at a beggar, it understands that an edifice which produces beggars needs restructuring.[208]

n. *Rauschenbusch on Kingdom of God and Human Community*

Essential to understanding Rauschenbusch and his influence on King is a knowledge of his views of the Kingdom of God. It was his central, all-pervading theme. It is at the literal and symbolic heart of his major theological work, *Theology For the Social Gospel*. It was Rauschenbusch's contention that theology must not simply make room for the doctrine of the Kingdom of God, "but give it a central place and revise all other doctrines so that they will articulate organically with it."[209]

Rauschenbusch's concern for the Kingdom allowed him to speak often about the nature of the Christian community. Both these concepts were the heritage from Ritschl and the latter's concern for the Kingdom and a solidaristic view of life. As Rauschenbusch is discussed, we can see a definite relationship between his articulation of the human and Christian community and King's "beloved community."

Rauschenbusch's emphasis on the corporate and the communal reflects his prior concern that all life is basically social, that human life is organically interrelated. He asserted that religion, along with all other great human impulses, "demands social expression."[210]

When he discusses the individualistic orientation Israel's religious life took during persecution and exile, he still advocates that

> If the religious value of the individual was being discovered, why should the religious value of the community be forgotten. . . . Personal religion was chiefly a means to an end; the end was social.[211]

The incurably social nature of man and of Christianity is illustrated vividly for Rauschenbusch in that even when religions desire to escape from society, they end up building a true social life of their own. "Every monastery proposed to be an ideal community."[212]

Rauschenbusch sees a distinction between what usually passes as religion (an individualistic definition, "The life of God in the soul of man) and Christianity in which there is an emphasis on the life of God in the fellowship of man. In Christianity "the mystic experience was socialized."[213]

Rauschenbusch's earliest formulation of his understanding of the Kingdom of God was not available to King. It was in an unpublished book entitled *The Righteousness of the Kingdom*, recently discovered by Max Stackhouse. His basic ideas do not change; they are simply developed and refined in his classic statement in Chapter 13 of *Theology For the Social Gospel*.

In *The Righteousness of the Kingdom*, Rauschenbusch sees the roots of Jesus's understanding of the Kingdom in the Hebrew motifs of covenant and theocracy. The Jewish ideal of life is "righteous community ordered by divine laws. . . ."[214] Just as in Ritschl, Christianity revolved around two foci, the redemption of the individual by Christ and the Kingdom of God, so in Rauschenbusch the Kingdom of God has a twofold aim

> the regeneration of every individual to divine sonship and eternal life, and the victory of the spirit of Christ over the spirit of this world in every form of human society and corresponding alteration in all the institutions formed by human society. These two are simultaneous aims.[215]

Rauschenbusch never fundamentally changed this position. In 1917 in *Theology For the Social Gospel* he would say:

> the establishment of a community of righteousness in mankind is just as much a saving act of God as the salvation of an individual from his natural selfishness and moral inability.[216]

It is important, on the one hand, to correct a distorted interpretation of Rauschenbusch (namely, that he advocated "building the Kingdom" by man's efforts), and on the other to see the dialectical tension between God's activity and man's willing response. Nothing could be clearer than his first definitive statement on the Kingdom in *Theology For the Social Gospel.*

> The Kingdom of God is divine in its origin, progress, and consummation. It was initiated by Jesus Christ, in whom the prophetic spirit came to its consummation, it is sustained by the Holy Spirit, and it will be brought to its fulfillment by the power of God in his own time. . . .[217]

The Kingdom is the result of God's initiative, his working in human history.

But, in reality, this is only half of Rauschenbusch's position. Men are not to wait for God to send or complete the Kingdom. The factor that enables the Kingdom to grow and be realized is the willing response of men to cooperate with the labor of God. It is divine in origin, but man's responsive effort is indispensable for its continuance. Or as Rauschenbusch says, "The Kingdom is for each of us the supreme task and the supreme gift of God."[218] He can even be more explicit.

> We are standing at the turning of the ways. We are actors in a great historical drama. It rests upon us to decide if a new era is to dawn in the transformation of the world into the Kingdom of God or if Western civilization is to descend to the graveyard of dead civilizations and God will have to try once again.[219]

But a passage such as the following, however, does give evidence to Rauschenbusch's critics that he tends to identify man's efforts with construction of the Kingdom.

> . . . every increase in mercy, every obedience to justice, every added brightness of truth would be an extension of the reign of God in humanity, an incoming of the Kingdom of God.[220]

But in his own understanding there is a polarity of God's initiative (religion) and man's response (ethics). Rauschenbusch himself would rather talk of the inseparability of the Kingdom of God and ethics. When the Kingdom of God is minimized in Christian theology and we lose contact with the synoptic thought of Jesus (the revolutionary prophet of ethical righteousness) as did happen in the Pauline, Latin, Augustinian, Lutheran strand of Christianity, we also lose contact with the ethical principles of Jesus.

The distinctive ethical principles of Jesus were the direct outgrowth of his conception of the Kingdom of God. When the latter disappeared from theology, the former disappeared from ethics.[221]

All the teaching of Jesus and all his thinking centered about the hope of the Kingdom of God. His moral teachings get their meaning only when viewed from the center.[222]

The doctrine of the Kingdom of God is

absolutely necessary to establish that organic union between religion and morality, between theology and ethics, which is one of the characteristics of the Christian religion. When our moral actions are consciously related to the Kingdom of God they gain religious quality.[223]

We will further develop Rauschenbusch's understanding of the Kingdom with the following sub-themes.

1. *Relation of Kingdom to Church*

This is a strategic theological relation for Rauschenbusch. The two ways are always in tension, always related, always distinguished, and the church is second in priority to the Kingdom of God.

Perhaps the best and most succinct way Rauschenbusch puts the relation is, "the church is primarily a fellowship for worship; the Kingdom is a fellowship of righteousness."[224] Here Rauschenbusch is in effect juxtaposing the ceremonial and priestly to the ethical and prophetic with an obvious preference for the latter.

The Kingdom of God breeds prophets; the Church breeds priests and theologians. The Church runs to tradition and dogma (the past); the Kingdom of God rejoices in forecasts and boundless horizons (the future and eschatology).[225]

One must understand Rauschenbusch's appreciation of eschatology (see Chapter 18 in *Theology For the Social Gospel*) which is distinguished from a future life, "pie in the sky," palliative for social disorder here. We can then understand why he states that when the Kingdom of God is lacking in theology, the salvation of the individual is seen in its relation to the Church and to the future life, but not in its relation to the task of saving the social order.[226]

The church is seen in a secondary place and its primary role is an instrumental one, i.e., it helps make possible the realization of the Kingdom. All the activities of the church, its institutional structure, and its theology must be judged by their effectiveness in creating the Kingdom of God. "Since the Kingdom is the supreme end of God, it must be the purpose for which the church exists."[227] While admitting that "religion demands social expression" and that all human groupings need structures and organization to perpetuate themselves and their ideas, Rauschenbusch claims that

> the mischief begins when the church makes herself the end. She does not exist for her own sake; she is simply a working organization to create the Christian life in individuals and the Kingdom of God in human society.[228]

The church is always tempted to usurp the place of the Kingdom of God and substitute itself for the Kingdom and "thereby put the advancement of a tangible and very human organization in the place of the moral uplifting of humanity."[229] Whenever in history the Kingdom has been less than the dominating religious reality, the church rapidly moved in as the highest good.

When this occurred, as we intimated earlier, there was an ethical lapse, a loss of the revolutionary stance, and an appearance of the conservative social influence typical of an institution, increasing "the weight of the other stationery forces in society."[230]

When there is lacking the centrality and priority of the Kingdom, support for democratic movements and social justice is wanting. As well, the secular life of man is depreciated at the expense of church life–"religious value is taken out of the activities of the common man."[231]

From Rauschenbusch's point of view, there would be no saving power inherent in the Church–in its priesthood, character, or doctrine. The saving power of the church

> rests on the presence of the Kingdom of God within her. The church grows old; the Kingdom is ever young. The church is perpetuation of the past; the Kingdom is the power of the coming age. Unless the church is vitalized by the ever nascent forces of the Kingdom within her, she deadens instead of begetting.[232]

This is true for Rauschenbusch because he sees the church as one social institution along side of others—the family, industry, State. And the church, *qua* institution, is bound to the society that creates it and that it represents. But the Kingdom is not bound to the society, not "confined within the limits of the church," rather the Kingdom is all the institutions, including the church, realizing itself through them all. "It embraces the whole of human life. It is the Christian transfiguration of the social order."[233]

The church is judged by the Kingdom ideal, which is *Christianized social life*, a community of righteousness. When the church seeks its own life, when like all other social agents with power, she is tempted to use it for herself, when "organizing ability which might have reconstituted social life" was expended on the organization,[234] then the Kingdom ideal will serve as a corrective to and conscience of the church. The ideals of love, brotherhood, justice, righteousness are above the church and that by which the church is tested and judged.

Since the Kingdom of God is the "true human society," and since Jesus's ethical teachings portray what would create the true society, the test of Christ for any custom, law, or institution is "does it draw men together or divide them?"[235] Or, as King would say, "does it make for 'community or chaos.'"

2. Rauschenbusch and Kingdom of God as Transformed Society

Repeatedly, in the writings of Rauschenbusch, the Kingdom of God is synonymous with a transformed and regenerated society. In his first book, *The Righteousness of the Kingdom*, he says

> By the power of the spirit dwelling in it (the community of spiritual men founded by Christ which was the germ of the Kingdom), it was to overcome the spirit dominant in this world and thus penetrate and transform the world.[236]

In *Christianity and the Social Crisis*, the essential purpose of Christianity (and the purpose of Rauschenbusch's own life and thought as well) is stated with clarity. It is

> to transform human society into the Kingdom of God by regenerating all human relations and reconstituting them in accordance with the will of God.[237]

As we mentioned earlier, Rauschenbusch claimed that Christianity rested historically on the prophetic religion of Israel. It was the aim of the Hebrew prophets to "constitute the social and political life of their nation in accordance with the will of God." Jesus, being in the prophetic tradition, very naturally founded the Kingdom of God, which "involved a thorough regeneration and reconstitution of social life." And primitive Christianity, bearer of this tradition, yearned for that new era in which would be realized, "social life on a new moral basis."[238]

For Rauschenbusch the Kingdom of God was radical in its collective nature.

> The Kingdom of God is still a collective conception, involving the whole social life of man. It is not a matter of saving human atoms, but of saving the social organism.[239]

Human individuals were never to be viewed apart from human society; the gregarious and socializing tendency in man was never to be neglected. To do otherwise would be to engage in a fundamental heresy and curtail the work of spiritual forces working for the establishment of a righteous society.

And the Kingdom of God as a "social and collective hope" was for this earth as compared, for instance, to eternal life, an individualistic hope which was not for this earth. The Kingdom was to thrust men into their "normal relations," i.e., their social relations here and now.[240]

This leads us to Rauschenbusch's most famous definition of the Kingdom, now almost a classic within the social gospel framework–"The Kingdom of God is humanity organized according to the will of God."[241] This reflects the covenantal and theocratic elements we discussed earlier, found in the first attempt to delineate his understanding of the Kingdom. He says the same thing in other words and this suggests how important it is to Rauschenbusch. "The Reign of God came to mean the organized fellowship of humanity acting under the impulse of love."[242] And "(Jesus's) attitude to life was the direct product of his twofold belief, in the Father who is love and the Kingdom of God, which is righteousness."[243]

Rauschenbusch often uses Kingdom of God and true human society and righteous community interchangeably and each point to a "fellowship of justice, equality and love."[244]

It would seem that humanity organized "according to the will of God" and "acting under the impulse of love" is a parallelism. For Rauschenbusch, at some length, spells out this classic definition precisely in terms of love.[245]

67

This implies what Christ revealed–that life and personality are of divine worth. The will of God as expressed through the Kingdom of God, "tends toward a social order which will best guarantee to all personalities their freest and highest development." And since love is the supreme law of Christ, the Kingdom of God implies a "progressive reign of love in human affairs and a tendency toward the unity of mankind" without denying human individuality and freedom.

The highest expression of love for Rauschenbusch (his understanding of *agape*, although he does not use the word) is the "free surrender of what is truly our own life, property and rights." This concept moves Rauschenbusch into the "socialist" camp, for it really means "the redemption of society from private property in the natural resources of the earth, and from any condition in industry which makes monopoly profits possible."[246]

This love also finds concrete expression in service to others. When discussing the Kingdom of God as a "realm of love," Rauschenbusch says this must mean it is also a "commonwealth of cooperative labor, for how can we actively love others without serving their needs by our abilities."[247]

So for Rauschenbusch the marks of the Kingdom of God are "the worth of personality, freedom, growth, love, solidarity, service."[248]

This summary definition serves well as a transition to another aspect of the Kingdom for Rauschenbusch which had determining influence on King, namely, the Kingdom as inclusive human community. The transformed society is an open society. The inclusiveness of the Kingdom is a reflection of and participation in the Christian God, who has been a

> breaker of barriers from the first. All who have a distinctively Christian experience of God are committed to the expansion of human fellowship and to the overthrow of barriers.[249]

Jesus's contemporaries understood the Kingdom as a Jewish affair and its presence would depend on proper religious observance. His revolutionary conception, however, was that the Kingdom was a "human affair and would rest on right human relations."[250]

Since the Kingdom of God is not bounded by the Church, it includes all human relations and ultimately transcends divisions of profession, nationality, religion, etc. Wherever primitive Christianity went, "we see a new society nucleating."[251]

When the early Christians emerged as an historical force, there were two dominant religious options available, the Gentile and Jewish, and a deep separation existed between them.

> Christianity added a third genus, and Christians were profoundly convinced that they were to assimilate and transform all others into a higher unity.[252]

Raushenbusch, a little later, explains in detail.

> Most social organizations follow natural lines of cleavage. Blood kinship, tribal sympathies, neighborhood, financial profit, social protection or advancement—these are some of the forces that bind men together. Christianity cut across these natural and conventional lines. It wore down the existing barriers with irresistible force and brought men together by a new principle of stratification. Jews were wrenched loose from the firm hold of their race and religion. Greeks from their culture and pleasures; and both joined on a footing of equality.[253]

Rauschenbusch saw a real need to restore to Christianity the millennial hope, which had largely been omitted from mainstream Christianity. He did not wish to engage in setting time and place, but he did want to justify the substance of its claim. It was the Christian ideal of a social life under the law of Christ, in which peace, justice, and a glorious blossoming of human life is present.

> Our chief interest in any millennium is the desire for a social order in which the worth and freedom of every least human being will be honored and protected; in which the brotherhood of man will be expressed in the common possession of the economic resources of society; and in which the spiritual good of humanity will be set high above the private profit interests of all materialistic groups. We hope for such an order for humanity as we hope for heaven for ourselves.[254]

3. Means to Achieve Community

Jesus, like all prophets before him and since, hoped for and contributed to the amelioration of the national, social, and religious life around him. But the methods he would use to achieve the transformed community of righteousness were love and nonviolence. By rejecting all violent means to transform society, he "transferred the inevitable conflict from the field of battle to the antagonism of mind against mind and of heart against lack of heart."[255]

Comments, such as the following from Rauschenbusch, surely affected King and found their place in his writings.

> The fundamental virtue in the ethics of Jesus was love, because love is the society-making quality. Human life originates in love. It is love that holds together the basal human organization, the family. The physical expression of all love and friendship is the desire to get together and be together. Love creates fellowship.[256]

Rauschenbusch placed high priority on the maintenance of the loving community and in one significant passage appeals to Jesus's statements from the Sermon on the Mount.

> If a man has offended us, that fact is not to break up our fraternity, but we must forgive and forgive and forgive, and always stand ready to repair the torn tissues of friendship. If we remember that we have offended and our brother is not alienated from us, we are to drop everything, though it be the sacrifice we are just offering in the temple, and go and recreate fellowship. If a man hates us or persecutes and reviles us, we must refuse to let fraternity be ruined, and must woo him back with love and blessings. If he smites us in the face, we must turn the other cheek instead of doubling the barrier by returning the blow. These are not hard and fast laws or detached rules of conduct. If they are used as such they become unworkable and ridiculous. They are simply the most emphatic expression of the determination that the fraternal relation which binds men together must not be ruptured.[257]

4. Kingdom Present and Future

For Rauschenbusch the Kingdom is present and future. It is an "historical force . . . a vital and organizing energy now at work in humanity"[258] ". . . the energy of God realizing itself in human life."[259] But its "future lies among the mysteries of God." For us the Kingdom of God is "always coming, always pressing in on the present, always big with possibility."[260]

Just as an individual Christian is "already" but "not yet," so the Kingdom is always in the making. Human society serves as raw material for Christian society. When the Spirit of Christ has hallowed all the natural relations of men and given them a divine significance and value, then the Kingdom will have arrived. But it will probably never be realized in any present moment. It is a process which is never completed in history. "The Kingdom of God is always but coming."[261]

Rauschenbusch attempts to avoid the charge of being naive and utopian and does neutralize his optimism about the historical possibilities of the Kingdom with the following realistic observation.

> In asking for faith in the possibility of a new social order, we ask for no Utopian delusion. We know well that there is not perfection for man in this life: there is only growth toward perfection. . . . We make it a duty to seek what is unattainable. We have the same paradox in the perfectibility of society. We shall never have a perfect social life, yet we must seek it with faith.[262]

The Rauschenbusch themes in Kingdom of God and human community and their relationship to and influence on King will be discussed in the last chapter, which deals with King's idea of the "Beloved Community."

THREE

Nonviolence

A. *Background and Context*

Martin Luther King is probably best known as the leader of the Christian nonviolence movement in America. He and history (the *Zeitgeist*, as he called it) met to create what Thomas Merton has termed

> one of the most positive and successful expressions of Christian social action that has been seen anywhere in the twentieth century. It is certainly the greatest example of Christian faith in action in the social history of the United States.[1]

However, nonviolence dominated his life and activity more than it did his thought and writing. In terms of the latter, nonviolence appears as *one* of the several important intellectual and ethical strands of his thought–among the latter are the church's relation to the world, a dialectic of optimism/realism about man's nature and history, the emphasis on the universal moral law, and the notion of the beloved community.

On the other hand, this is not to minimize the centrality of nonviolence for the life and thought of King. History will record him as one of the ablest exponents of the nonviolent philosophy of Jesus and Gandhi. In fact, his writings, especially "Pilgrimage to Nonviolence," and "Letter from Birmingham Jail" are already appearing in anthologies on the subject of nonviolence.[2]

King was heir to a whole tradition of protest in this country, beginning with John Woolman and the Quakers, William L. Garrison and the abolitionists, and A. J. Muste and the conscientious objectors to both World Wars I and II–a movement which has been a significant, sometimes vocal minority and which has influenced our country out of all proportion to its size and prestige. King, himself, observed that "although nonviolent direct action did not originate in America, it found a natural home where it has been a revered tradition to rebel against injustice."[3]

King also appeared in a providential context of history–what could be called a *kairos*–a time filled full of meaning and opportunity as regards the nonviolent movement in America and the place of the black man in it.

When King was thirteen years old, in 1942, James Foreman, then race relations secretary for the Fellowship of Reconciliation, suggested that pacifists and nonpacifists both join forces to eliminate racial discrimination. Their operating principle would be nonviolence. In 1943, the Congress of Racial Equality was formally organized.

Many feel that CORE's espousal of nonviolence was conceived primarily as a tactic rather than as a way of life. However, it was involved in demonstrations, sit-ins, and other forms of protest long before Montgomery. CORE was later to become an integral part of the Civil Rights movement and is presently concerned to support black economic programs and black control of institutions in communities where black people are in a majority.

Asa Philip Randolph, called the American Gandhi before King, attempted a peaceful march on Washington in 1941 to protest segregation in government operated defense factories and in the armed services. President Roosevelt undercut his motivation when he issued an Executive Order on June 25, 1941, barring discrimination in war industries. The march was cancelled.[4] Randolph did remain, however, a prominent figure in the later struggle for human rights. He was the Master of Ceremonies at the March on Washington in August of 1963.

Dr. Benjamin Mays, president of Morehouse College when King was a student there and a loyal friend throughout the latter's career, had visited India in 1937 and interviewed Gandhi.[5]

There were several literary contacts King made during his Morehouse and Crozer years that would have moved an open and impressionable man. He relates that he was deeply impressed with Thoreau's "Essay on Civil Disobedience." The rugged individualism evidenced by Thoreau's rigid adherence to his conscience, his fundamental notion of noncooperation with an evil system, and the right to break a law that is immoral, all strongly appealed to a young man who was looking for an intellectually satisfying and practically effective instrument to alleviate the roots of injustice.

Surely, one of the most important elements in his reading and study, which appeared from time to time, was the proposed place of the Negro in a nonviolent movement.

Reinhold Niebuhr, in *Moral Man and Immoral Society*, published in 1932, a book to which King was greatly indebted, mentions the place of the Negro and the nonviolent movement in the future of American society. This astounding bit of prophecy is contained in Niebuhr's discussion of Gandhi's use of nonviolence.

> The emancipation of the Negro race in America probably waits upon the adequate development of this kind of social and political strategy. It is hopeless for the Negro to expect complete emancipation from the menial social and economic position into which the white man has forced him, merely by trusting in the moral sense of the white man. It is equally hopeless to attempt emancipation through violent rebellion.[6]

Tolstoy, who figured as one of the most influential men in Gandhi's thought, wrote the introduction to a Russian biography of William L. Garrison, in which he lauds the abolitionist as a colleague and brother. The introduction is entitled, "On the Negro Question."[7]

Gandhi, on several occasions, suggested that the Negro may have an important role to play in the social change of American society. Lerone Bennett, Jr., in his King biography, states that to a group of visiting American Negroes, Gandhi said in 1935, "Perhaps it will be through the Negro that the unadulterated message of nonviolence will be delivered to the world."[8]

American Negroes were often asked by Gandhi about the plight of the black person in this country. His identification with them was swift and genuine, for he believed that any civilization is "to be judged by its treatment of minorities." And in an August 21, 1924 issue of *Young India*, Gandhi observed that the American Negroes' task is more difficult than the Indians'.

> But they have some very fine workers among them. All they need is opportunity. I know that if they have caught the spirit of the Indian movement (the spirit of nonviolence) their progress must be rapid.[9]

King's years at Boston University would have increased this conviction. There he met Walter Muelder and Allen Knight Chalmers. Although he had classes from neither of them, he was greatly moved by their dedicated pacifism, a pacifism that was active and practical and not just theoretical.[10] Muelder says that King's coming to Boston University for graduate study was based upon, among other good reasons, the reputation Boston had in the Negro intellectual community as open to and encouraging Negro students.[11] Chalmers had also a national reputation for his concern for the black young men involved in the Scottsboro Case of the thirties. Chalmers was active in the Fellowship of Reconciliation and identified with several other pacifist organizations.

Howard Thurman, Dean of the Chapel at Boston while King was a student there and a well-known Negro pacifist, had visited Gandhi in 1935 and had several conversations with him. Bennett says that King read and re-read Thurman's *Jesus and the Disinherited* after the Montgomery boycott began. The following passage by Thurman is reflected in several of King's speeches during the Montgomery campaign.

> The religion of Jesus says to the disinherited: "Love your enemy. Take the initiative in seeking ways by which you can have the experience of a common sharing of mutual worth and value. It may be hazardous, but you must do it." For the Negro it means that he must see the individual white man in the context of a common humanity. The fact that a particular individual is white, and therefore may be regarded in some over-all sense as the racial enemy, must be faced; and opportunity must be provided, found, or created for freeing such an individual from his "white necessity." From this point on, the relationship becomes like any primary one.[12]

In his *Autobiography*, Gandhi once said, "Service of the poor has been my heart's desire, and it has always thrown me amongst the poor and enabled me to identify myself with them."[13] King's decision on whether to accept academic positions in the north or south or influential pulpits in the north or to work with his disinherited brothers in the south was helped by these associations.[14]

Bayard Rustin, who became a close friend and advisor to King, was on the editorial board of the pacifist journal *Liberation*, and was also a close student of Gandhi. Rustin was one of the most brilliant tacticians of nonviolence in the movement, helping King plan the Washington March of 1963.

Richard Gregg's book, *The Power of Nonviolence*, now virtually a classic among students and advocates of nonviolence, had a great impact on King. Gregg spent about four years in India from 1925 to 1929, including seven months at Gandhi's Sarbarmati ashram, and, according to his account, made a careful study of all the written material he could find on Gandhi. The book was first published in 1935, revised in 1944, and dedicated to Gandhi.

After subsequent visits to India and in response to the growing civil rights movement in the South, Gregg issued a second revised edition in 1959 for which King wrote a very appreciative foreword. It was Gregg's understanding of nonviolence as "moral jui-jitsu" that most influenced King, as we shall see later.

In the early fifties there was also increasing pressure brought to bear from several sides to use the Gandhian method to bring the Negroes to first class citizenship in this country. In 1951, Rammanohar Lohia, a colleague of Gandhi's, visited the United States and advised Negroes and whites to employ civil disobedience and nonviolent tactics to erase unjust racial policies. He was not taken very seriously. President Johnson of Fisk University probably reflected the sentiment of most black people when he responded that "we are too weak a minority and here we have the law and the Constitution on our side, unlike the situation you faced in India."[15]

Even as late as November, 1955, Harris Wofford, a lawyer, suggested that those concerned for civil rights and an integrated society should try Gandhi's ways, but he was not met with enthusiasm.[16]

Perhaps the pivotal event in King's youth which turned him in the direction of Gandhi was an address by Mordecai Johnson at Fellowship House in Philadelphia during King's second year at Crozer. King had already heard the absolute pacifist line of A. J. Muste at Crozer and was not convinced. His response to Muste was Niebuhrian. In *Stride Toward Freedom*, he relates this response in the following way.

> I felt that while war could never be a positive or absolute good, it could serve as a negative good in the sense of preventing the spread and growth of an evil force. War, horrible as it is, might be preferable to surrender to a totalitarian system–Nazi, Fascism, or Communist.[17]

But Johnson's presentation of Gandhi was something else. Perhaps it was the Howard University President's charisma and his deeply held belief or King's own receptivity at the time or, more likely, a combination of all three that motivated King to purchase several books[18] on and about Gandhi and read them voraciously. The following fall, he wrote a term paper on Gandhi for Davis's "Psychology of Religious Personalities" course.

He admits being "moved" by Gandhi's Salt March to the Sea and that the concept of *Satyagraha* was "profoundly significant to me."[19] The latter notion implied holding firmly to truth and love. This finally convinced King that love need not be sentimental nor for weaklings, nor just applicable to individual relationships. Gandhi persuaded him that whole communities, nations, and indeed, masses of people, could practice the "turn the other cheek" philosophy of the Sermon on the Mount–a philosophy, along with "loving your enemies," King had heretofore relegated to one-to-one relationships. The Crozer senior felt that

Gandhi was probably the first person in history to lift the love ethic of Jesus above mere interaction between individuals to a powerful and effective social force on a large scale. For Gandhi love was a potent instrument for social and collective transformation. It was in this Gandhian emphasis on love and nonviolence that I discovered the method for social reform that I had been seeking for so many months.[20]

And then, King makes a summary statement that at the same time reveals some seriousness of ethical probing and a judgment upon his own understanding of Christian ethics.

The intellectual and moral satisfaction that I failed to gain from the utilitarianism of Bentham and Mill, the revolutionary methods of Marx and Lenin, the social-contract theory of Hobbes, the "back to nature" optimism of Rousseau, and the superman philosophy of Nietzsche I found in the nonviolent resistance philosophy of Gandhi. I came to feel that this was the only morally and practically sound method open to oppressed people in their struggle for freedom.[21]

King's "satisfaction" is really with Gandhi's method and program. Later on he concedes that the content of the movement is essentially Christian, particularly Jesus's teachings in the Sermon on the Mount and his teaching of love.

But it is obvious that Gandhi's appeal to King was the social one. As we have contended, King's primary orientation was in the direction of society, its structures, its evil, its power.

Gandhi confesses that he absorbed himself entirely "in the service of the community" and had made the "religion of service my own."[22] For Gandhi, this was a way to self-realization and the realization of God, but it was this relationship to others that dominated his life. He once said, "I value individual freedom, but you must not forget that man is essentially a social being."[23] Bondurant emphasizes the social consciousness of Gandhi.

Virtue was for Gandhi essentially social . . . the Gandhian insistence upon selfless service to society, upon duty to the community as the more important correlation of right, and the final concept of a social well-being.[24]

Gandhi was vitally concerned, for instance, about the following social issues: indentured labor of Indians in South Africa, the "Jim Crow"-like discrimination in South Africa against Indians, slave wages, taxes, the pass system, social protection of lepers, child widows, illiteracy, child marriages, village sanitation, untouchability. To these pressing problems of the Indian, he brought his profound moral and spiritual message.

It was this curious mixture of basic social involvement and an almost otherworldly faith that forced Gandhi to reflect in South Africa, "Men say I am a saint losing myself in politics. The fact is that I am a politician trying my hardest to be a saint."[25] But Fischer has the most accurate analysis of Gandhi at this point and indicates the similarity between Gandhi and King in the area of social gospel.

> The important fact is that in politics Gandhi always cleaved to religion and moral consideration, and as a saint he never thought his place was in a cave or cloister but rather in the hurly-burly of the popular struggle for rights and right. Gandhi's religion cannot be divorced from his politics. His religion made him political. His politics were religious.[26]

The refusal to separate the individual and the social, the spiritual and the secular, the ethical and the religious, God and man, struck a responsive chord in King who had for two years been molded by Rauschenbusch's theology of the social gospel.

However, at this stage of his development, King's relationship to Gandhi was an intellectual, cerebral one.[27] Nonviolence, along with many other viewpoints, were put into the back of his mind, to become socially relevant later. He was not committed to it as an effective method for social change, much less as a personal way of life.

It seems that Gandhi's influence grew on King as he grew more involved in the movement for civil rights. When the Montgomery bus boycott began, there was no ready-made rationale for nonresistance, from Gandhi or anywhere. All King, his clerical confreres, and the black laymen were conscious of doing was living out the love-ethic presented by Jesus in Matthew 5. For them, the phrase "Christian love," not nonviolence or noncooperation or *Satyagraha*, accurately labeled their actions.

About a week after the boycott started, King recalls, a white woman, Miss Juliette Morgan, wrote a letter to the *Montgomery Advertiser* commenting on the similarity between the activity in Montgomery and Gandhi's movement in India, especially the Salt March. "People who had never heard of the little brown saint of India were now saying his name with an air of familiarity."[28]

What King had earlier intellectually apprehended, that the "Christian doctrine of love operating through the Gandhian method of nonviolence was one of the most potent weapons available to the Negro in his struggle for freedom" had been driven home with such force that King adopted "nonviolent resistance as the technique of the movement, while love stood as the regulating ideal. In other words, Christ furnished the spirit and motivation, while Gandhi furnished the method."[29]

And in six months' time, by May 17, 1956, King was beginning to articulate the rudimentary principles of Christian nonviolence that would stay with him throughout his life. The themes would be refined and altered to suit different occasions, but essentially they remained central to King's understanding.

These early attempts to define the movement ideologically are best illustrated by his address entitled, "A Realistic Look at the Question of Progress in the Area of Race Relations," given to NAACP Legal Defense and Educational Fund in New York May 17, 1956.[30]

> Wherever we find segregation we must have the fortitude to passively resist it. We must not think in terms of retaliatory violence. To attempt to use the method of violence in our struggle would be both impractical and immoral. Violence creates many more problems than it solves. There is a voice crying through the vista of time saying, "He who lives by the sword shall perish by the sword." History is replete with the bleached bones of nations who failed to follow this truth. So we must not seek to fight our battles for freedom with weapons of arms. The method must be that of nonviolent resistance, using love as the regulating ideal. . . . The method is not new. A little brown man in India tried it. . . . He decided to confront physical force with soul force.[31]

It was his trip to India in 1959 that thoroughly convinced King of Gandhi's position. It had, personally, a great "impact" on him. He was glad to talk with the Mahatma's relatives and to see that the result of that long nonviolent struggle in India had produced very little bitterness. He not only left India "more convinced than ever before that nonviolent resistance is the most potent weapon available to oppressed peoples in their struggle for freedom" but impressed with the mutual respect and friendship present between Britain and India. He concluded with an observation that was determinative for his thought.

> The way of acquiescence leads to moral and spiritual suicide. The way of violence leads to bitterness in the survivors and brutality in the destroyers. But, the way of nonviolence leads to redemption and the creation of the beloved community.[32]

This same theme is found in *Stride Toward Freedom*, but one suspects that now it is an existential, deeply personal conviction–a way of life, a principled commitment–that enabled King to deal effectively with conflict in personal and social relationships.[33]

B. *Influences on Gandhi*

Gandhi was probably not decisively influenced by any non-Indian source. He was supported and encouraged by other men and his own ideas were often confirmed by them, but he was essentially Indian. All his basic ideas can be found in Indian religious tradition. "The more we study Mahatma Gandhi's own life and teaching the more certain it becomes that the Hindi religion has been the greatest of all influences shaping his ideas and actions."[34]

1. *The Bhagavad Gita*

Gandhi first read the *Gita* in English while a student in London. He was ashamed that he had waited until he was twenty years old to read the most popular Scripture of his religion. So impressed was he that he translated it from the Sanskrit into his native Gujarati.

He speaks of returning to it again and again in the midst of difficulty and attributes his ability to endure tragedy and sorrow without them affecting his life drastically to the teaching of the *Gita*.[35] It was for Gandhi "an infallible guide of conduct."[36]

There is an irony in Gandhi's devotion to the *Gita*. The purpose of the book is to communicate Krishna's persuasion of Arjuna to fight. The first chapter contains Arjuna's resistance to do this and his words are strikingly similar to some passages in the Sermon on the Mount.

We have heard, Krishna
hell awaits the families which discard *dharma*.
What a terrible sin it is to kill brothers,
And cast covetous eyes on their land!
Let the sons of Dhritarashtra kill me
I will not protest.
Better be killed than kill.[37]

But the rest of the story is Krishna's clever arguments in favor of war and his defense of Arjuna's caste obligation to engage in violence. Gandhi, realizing this, rejects the literal, orthodox interpretation of the *Gita*, which justifies violence and conceives of the story as a kind of allegory. He concludes that

> under the guise of physical warfare, it described the duel that perpetually went on in the hearts of mankind, and that physical warfare was brought in merely to make the destruction of the internal duel more alluring.[38]

What probably influenced Gandhi most in the *Gita* were the early references to *ahimsa*, Arjuna's final sense of duty, and the many passages having to do with renunciation and the attainment of spiritual perfection. The latter verses could be abstracted from the context of encouraged warfare and be used for one's personal edification. Gandhi said that "renunciation is the highest form of religion."[39] This element in the *Gita* and the Sermon on the Mount appealed to him.

2. *Ruskin*

John Ruskin was a nineteenth century English political economist who in 1862 wrote a small book named *Unto This Last*. Ruskin takes the title of the book from a statement of Jesus in the Parable of the Laborers in the Vineyard, "I will give unto this last, even as unto thee." (Matt. 20:14)

Gandhi discusses the impact of Ruskin's book on him in a section of his *Autobiography* revealingly titled "The Magic Spell of a Book." After reading it through for the first time, Gandhi vowed to "change his life in accordance with the ideals of the book." He claims that of all the books he read since his formal study, Ruskin's "brought about an instantaneous and practical transformation in my life." He subsequently translated it into Gujarati with the appropriate title *Sarvodaya* (the welfare of all).

Gandhi felt that he discovered in Ruskin some of his own firm beliefs and that is why he was taken with its message. In fact, this was generally true of Gandhi; he usually was influenced by sources that confirmed his own previously held opinions.

It was undoubtedly Ruskin's strong egalitarian emphasis that appealed to Gandhi. Ruskin was concerned to avoid the exploitation of the poor,[40] to stress the equality of all vocations, especially if there is an element of sacrifice involved,[41] and to advocate a socialist attitude toward wealth and property.[42]

The teachings of *Unto This Last* I understood to be:

1. That the good of the individual is contained in the good of all.
2. That a lawyer's work has the same value as the barber's inasmuch as all have the same right of earning their livelihood from their work.
3. That a life of labor, i.e., the life of the tiller of the soil and the handicraftsman is the life worth living.

The first of these I knew. The second I had dimly realized. The third had never occurred to me. *Unto This Last* made it clear as daylight for me that the second and third were contained in the first. I arose with the dawn, ready to reduce these principles to practice.[43]

3. *Tolstoy*

It was Tolstoy's *The Kingdom of God is Within You* which "overwhelmed" Gandhi and "left an abiding impression on me."[44] He found in Tolstoy a kindred spirit struggling for the same ends. For Gandhi, Tolstoy represented "independent thinking," "profound morality," and "truthfulness."

Tolstoy's absolutist, perfectionist stand toward the ideals in the Sermon on the Mount struck a responsive chord in Gandhi. There was no question for Tolstoy that the Christian was expected to reflect literally these standards in his own life. He was obsessed with the distance between what Christ said and how Christians lived.

He recalls hearing of an Indian Christian coming to Europe soon after his conversion and being astonished by the contradictions he witnessed in a Christian society.

> We have but to look at our life from the standpoint of the Indian, who understood Christianity in its true significance, without any concessions or adaptations, and to behold the barbarous cruelties with which our life is filled, in order to be horrified at the contradictions in the midst of which we live, without noticing them.[45]

It was this high idealism plus Tolstoy's eschewing of ecclesiasticism (rites, sacraments, etc.), his avowal of a personal relationship to God as all-determining, and his willing identification with the suffering peasants that moved Gandhi to be an admirer of him. Gandhi's community in South Africa, for those willing to experiment with truth, was called Tolstoy Farm.

Actually, Tolstoy was more rigid in his adherence to nonviolence than Gandhi. The Russian novelist was a Christian anarchist who was radical in his noncooperative stand against the government. Nonviolence for Tolstoy was a literal position. There was to be no use of force whatsoever.

> A Christian enters into no dispute with his neighbor, he neither attacks nor uses violence; on the contrary, he suffers himself, without resistance, and by his very attitude toward evil not only sets himself free, but helps to free the world at large from all outward authority.[46]

Tolstoy, apparently, did not see in nonviolent resistance a method for positive social action. But from reading Tolstoy Gandhi was to see "the infinite possibilities of universal love."[47]

4. *Thoreau*

Gandhi borrowed a copy of Thoreau's "Civil Disobedience" from a South African prison library and found there, again, confirmation of ideas already fermenting in his mind. This "masterly treatise" was a deep influence on Gandhi.[48]

Gandhi was under the impression that the phrase "civil disobedience" was first used by Thoreau. He did not know that the lecture was originally given under the title "The Rights and Duties of the Individual in Relation to Government" and first appeared as "Civil Disobedience" when it was posthumously published in a volume of his entitled *A Yankee in Canada*.[49]

Gandhi was indebted to Thoreau for his personal example–one man willing to follow his conscience, break what he considered an unjust law, stand alone against the state, and accept the consequences. Thoreau's defiance and the quality of his commitment, summed up in "For it matters not how small the beginning may seem to be, what is once well done is done forever,"[50] meant much to Gandhi in his early years in the South African struggle.

But the influence of Thoreau on Gandhi has probably been exaggerated. He makes no mention of Thoreau in his *Autobiography*. And Thoreau, himself, had read widely in Hindu philosophy, including the *Gita*. Emerson, Thoreau's closest friend, and other American Transcendentalists, were influenced by Indian Scriptures. So, as Fischer says,

> Thoreau, the New England rebel, borrowed from distant India and repaid the debt by throwing ideas into the world pool of thought; ripples reached the Indian lawyer-politician in South Africa.[51]

Gandhi also placed Thoreau in a critical perspective. He sensed that Thoreau was probably not an "out and out champion of nonviolence" and that the only law he seemed concerned to break was the tax law. For Gandhi, civil disobedience in South Africa concerned a whole range of immoral laws.

And, finally, Gandhi denied a direct Thoreauvian influence on his thought in a letter to Mr. P. Koddando Rao in 1935.

> The statement that I had devised my idea of civil disobedience from the writings of Thoreau is wrong. The resistance to authority in South Africa was well advanced before I got the essay of Thoreau on civil disobedience.[52]

As a result of reading Thoreau he did change the name of his movement from Passive Resistance to Civil Disobedience for his English friends. He later used the phrase Civil Resistance which he felt better conveyed the full meaning of his activity. Thoreau's essay served as a catalyst for Gandhi and he modified it to suit his own purpose.

5. *Sermon on the Mount*

After struggling with the Old Testament without benefit, Gandhi says the New Testament "produced a different impression, especially the Sermon on the Mount, which went straight to my heart."[53] He was particularly enamored of the theme "returning good for evil." He said that the verse "resist not evil; but whosoever shall smite thee on thy right cheek, turn to him the other also," overjoyed him. It reminded him of the Gujarati verse advocating the same teaching.

> For a bowl of water give a goodly mean . . .
> But the truly noble know all men as one,
> And return with gladness good for evil done.[54]

This became Gandhi's guiding principle and the source of his many experiments with truth.

He was further impressed with Jesus's nonviolent style of life and his ultimate allegiance to Truth which led him to his suffering and crucifixion. For Gandhi, Jesus was a true *Satyagrahi*.

As we mentioned at the beginning of this discussion, Gandhi was deeply rooted in his Indian heritage. And regarding western influences and the New Testament, Merton is probably correct when he says that through acquaintance with these writings, "Gandhi rediscovered his own tradition and his Hindu *dharma*."[55]

This brief survey of influences on Gandhi also reveals the broad range of indirect influences to which King was heir by his association with Gandhi.

C. *Major Themes in Gandhi's Understanding of Nonviolence That Were Influential on King*

In English, the word nonviolence includes many aspects of resistance. As Lynd points out, it can include at least three overlapping but distinct elements.

1. Refusal to retaliate (pacifism, nonresistance, passive resistance)
2. Acting out of conviction by overt behavior (direct action, demonstration)
3. Deliberate breaking of the law for sake of conscience (civil disobedience).[56]

In and through these elements runs the thread of love which is the agent for basic social change.

When King and Gandhi use nonviolence, they include all of these aspects. Nonviolence is the best English translation of a meaning-laden Sanskrit word, *Satyagraha*, which Gandhi devised to express his movement in South Africa.

1. *Satyagraha*

Satyagraha actually was being practiced before it was defined. For several years prior to 1906, Gandhi had been involved in a noncooperation movement in South Africa. He had been using the English "passive resistance" to describe his activities and that seemed sufficient for his Indian co-workers, but the narrow, restricted definition given the phrase by westerners, especially Europeans, forced Gandhi to question the adequacy of the phrase. They understood "passive resistance" to be an instrument only for the weak who, in fact, probably hated their oppressors. And if the weak ever became strong (i.e., had weapons), they would turn to violence.

B. Kumarappa points out the dilemma this understanding of the phrase caused Gandhi. It simply did not describe the full meaning of what he meant and was doing.

> The passive resister or the one who adopts nonviolence as policy . . . is really not nonviolent, for he would be violent if he could, and is nonviolent only

because he does not for the time being have the means or the capacity for violence. It is a far cry, therefore, from passive resistance to Satyagraha.[57]

It was obvious to Gandhi that a new word was necessary to describe more accurately what the Indians were doing in South Africa. He was unable to come up with a word himself and asked the readers of his literary organ there, *Indian Opinion*, to suggest some name. In response to this contest, his second cousin, Maganlal Gandhi, submitted the word *Sadagraha* (firmness in a good cause). This won the prize, but Gandhi, encouraged by his cousin's insight, altered slightly the word to *Satyagraha*, firmness in the truth, or holding fast to truth, or truth force. It came generally to mean any effort based on truth and nonviolence.

The two indispensable elements in *Satyagraha* are truth (*Satya*) and non-injury (*ahimsa*). These elements comprise two of the four main vows taken by every *Satyagrahi*: Truth, Ahimsa, Chastity, Non-Possession. These were not unknown concepts in Hindu religion, but, "into these traditional precepts Gandhi introduced considerations unfamiliar to Indian tradition and reminiscent of the rationalist, humanist tradition of the West."[58]

a. *Religious Basis of Satyagraha*

Even though at times Gandhi would refer to God as impersonal Truth, or a principle of Life, most of the time God was what we would denote "personally real." Gandhi referred to God often as speaking to him, calling him, guiding him.

His own devotional life of prayer and meditation and his intellectual articulation of the *Satyagraha* movement both emphasize the importance of the dimension of God. In fact, the true *Satyagrahi* has no power he can call his own. "All the power he may seem to possess is from and of God. . . . Without the help of God he is lame, blind, groping."[59] As he (the *Satyagrahi*) practices faithfully self-purification and self-sacrifice, "God will assist him."

Once Gandhi was asked if a communist or a socialist (presumably atheists) could be a *Satyagrahi*. His response was:

> I am afraid not. For a *Satyagrahi* has no other stay but God and he who has any other stay or depends on any other help cannot offer *Satyagraha*. He may be a passive-resister, non-cooperator and so on, but not a true *Satyagrahi*.[60]

He then hastens to add that God is called by many names and he was tolerant of all of them, but belief in a Supreme Being of some form was "indispensable."

The practical value of such a belief was related to the probably inordinate suffering the *Satyagrahi* would have to undergo. Most human beings were not equipped to endure such humiliation and pain.

> To bear all kinds of tortures without a murmur of resentment is impossible for a human being without the strength that comes from God. Only in His strength we are strong.[61]

God was "the Voice within" and so it was necessary that *Satyagraha* presuppose the "living presence and guidance of God." This Inner Voice was the seat of moral authority for Gandhi. This "Voice" was a definite reality, for Truth in God and the "essence of religion is morality."[62] A statement that best sums up Gandhi's religious and personal life is:

> What I want to achieve–what I have been striving and pining to achieve these thirty years–is self-realization, to see God face to face, to attain *Moksha*. I live and move and have my being in pursuit of this goal.[63]

This certainly is what he meant by "I am a politician trying to become a saint."

Prayer, fasting and other acts of self-purification equipped him to be a good *Satyagrahi* which in turn enabled him to be a powerful agent for social change. *Satyagraha* was a total way of life–a way of handling all conflicts; personal, interpersonal, and social. It was rooted in a dimension of the spiritual life of Gandhi, the devout aspirant of perfect Hinduism.

b. *Truth*

This is the first vow and the most important content to Gandhi's understanding of nonviolent resistance (*Satyagraha*). There is a profound ontology associated with the etymology of the word. *Satya* (truth) is derived from *Sat*, which means "being." This means that *Sat*, Truth, are also labels for the reality called God. "In fact, it is more correct to say that Truth is God than to say that God is Truth."[64] We may still, on a lower plane, refer to God as King or Almighty, but "*Sat* or *Satya* is the only correct and fully significant name for God."[65] It is the most inclusive and comprehensive term available to us. To press the ontology, Gandhi says:

> In "God is Truth," *is* certainly does not mean "equal to" nor does it merely mean "is truthful." Truth is not a mere attribute of God, but He is That. He is nothing if He is not that. Truth in Sanskrit means *Sat*. *Sat* means *Is*. Therefore Truth is implied in *Is*. God is, nothing else is. Therefore the more truthful we are, the nearer we are to God. We *are* only to the extent that we are truthful.[66]

Ontology and ethics meet in Gandhi when he asks his followers to be truthful in thought, speech, and action. Pursuing truth, being truthful is a participation in God. As we have noted, Gandhi allowed for many definitions of God, because there are countless manifestations of God.

> They (the manifestations) overwhelm me with wonder and awe and for a moment stun me. But I worship God as Truth only. I have not yet found Him, but I am seeking after Him.[67]

Since Truth is associated with the Ultimately Real, Truth is also Soul or Spirit. So, *Satyagraha* can be known as Soul-Force.[68]

Truth-force would exclude, by definition, the use of violence, "because man is not capable of knowing the absolute truth, and therefore, not competent to punish."[69] The only "objective" standard available to us, by which we can test truth, is the human one, i.e., the fulfillment of human wants and needs. So Bondurant observes, "The proper means for discovering truth in those terms cannot, then, result in human harm or frustrate rather than fulfill human needs."[70]

It appears that Truth in Gandhi is very similar to *Justice* in King. For instance, the "truth" which was the basis of the *Vykom Satyagraha*, that to which they held fast, was the right of every human being to walk the public road through the village and by the Temple without reference to caste. "Truth" in the famous Salt March in 1930 was the basic right of Indians to have free access to their own salt and to manufacture it as they saw fit. Behind this and many other *Satyagraha* campaigns was the larger right of a people to self-government.[71]

These inalienable rights bespeak the ultimate source of Right and the ultimate nature of Truth. So the *Satyagrahi* can confidently hold fast. He is, as King often said, on the side of the moral cosmos.

So, to a query, "Will you explain *Satyagraha*?" Gandhi simply replied, "It is a movement intended to replace methods of violence and a movement based entirely upon Truth."[72]

c. *Ahimsa*

This is the cardinal tenet of the Jain religion, a Hindu reform movement of the sixth century B.C. and very prominent in Gandhi's home state of Gujarat. His mother, in particular, was influenced by Jainism. *Ahimsa* is related to Truth, but not identified with it. The relationship is one of means to end, i.e., without *Ahimsa* it is impossible to seek and to find Truth.

> *Ahimsa* and Truth are so intertwined that it is practically impossible to disentangle and separate them. They are like the two sides of a coin, or rather of a smooth unstapled metallic disc. Who can say, which is the obverse, and which is the reverse? Nevertheless *ahimsa* is the means; Truth is the end.[73]

Although Truth is unattainable and undefinable, *ahimsa* is more within our reach and if practiced diligently and ceaselessly striven after, we will approximate the realization of Truth.

Because of *ahimsa*'s close relation to Truth, the search for the latter must be nonviolent. *Ahimsa* literally means non-injury, non-killing and often is translated nonviolence. There is a negative ring to the word–the *A* meaning "no" and *Himsa* meaning "injury." But for Gandhi, this literal understanding is crude. Not to kill or harm any living thing is admittedly a part of *ahimsa*. However, this is its "least expression" according to Gandhi.

> The principle of *ahimsa* is hurt by every evil thought, by undue haste, by lying, by hatred, by wishing ill to anybody.[74]

Again, Gandhi states that *ahimsa*

> is not merely a negative state of harmlessness but it is a positive state of love, of doing good even to the evil-doer.[75]

This "state of love" Gandhi makes clear is not indulgent and placid. The followers of *ahimsa* will not help the evildoer to continue in his evil by tolerating it passively as he will not violently attempt to change him. To love him means you will actively resist him, dissociate yourself from him, even though it offends him mentally or physically.[76]

d. *Ahimsa and Agape*

Gandhi is quite clear in his own mind that *ahimsa* answers to the Christian understanding of *agape*.

> The true rendering of the word in English is love or charity. And does not the Bible say: Love worketh no ill to his neighbor, believeth all things, hopeth all things, never faileth.[77]

> Complete nonviolence is complete absence of ill will against all that lives . . . in its active form good will toward all life. It is pure Love. I read it in the Hindu Scriptures, in the Bible, in the Koran.[78]

Besides this identification with the New Testament, his own high valuation of *ahimsa* as a quality of life points to what Christianity has meant by charity and *agape*. If "*ahimsa* becomes all-embracing, it transforms everything it touches. There is no limit to its power."[79]

> But all will be well, if it is *ahimsa* that is guiding me. For the seer who knew what he gave to the world said, "Hate dissolves in the presence of ahimsa."[80]

> The force of love is the same as the force of the soul or truth.[81]

Bondurant, one of the most reliable interpreters of Gandhi, supports his identification of *ahimsa* and love. She claims that the proximity of *ahimsa* to the Christian charity and the Greek *agape* is, throughout, apparent.[82]

William Robert Miller, on the other hand, seriously questions Gandhi's identification of *ahimsa* and *agape*. He contends that it (*ahimsa*) has no inherent positive content and that it "connotes only abstention." It does mean "highest duty," but nowhere in Hindu scriptures is it equated with love. Love, as St. Paul conceived it, is not present at all.[83]

Miller sees *ahimsa* as "requiring no harm at all to any living creature" and *agape* as "showing love by action."[84] Even though the devout Hindu may be involved in *karma yoga* (serving God through action, good works), *ahimsa* in this system is really a kind of purification vow like celibacy, dietary restrictions and the like "rather than as a way of doing good."[85]

Miller may be right as to the exact exposition of *ahimsa* in the Indian scriptures, but he certainly is not true to Gandhi. The latter, if not being authentically responsive to the traditional meaning of *ahimsa*, was right in his interpretation of the spirit of the word. Or as one critic has put it, "Gandhi's insistence on positive, dynamic love brought a new quality into Hindu ethics."[86]

The last observation may be a more accurate conclusion. Schweitzer states that Gandhi transmuted "*ahimsa* (an essentially spiritual non-worldly attitude) to passive resistance (a practical worldly policy)."[87]

Lacy continues, in a paraphrase of Schweitzer, "Passive resistance is *ahimsa* put to the direct service of world affirmation and material activity, a 'nonviolent use of force' whose distinction from active resistance is 'only quite relative.'" Then Lacy concludes, "Yet this very metamorphosis may be Gandhiji's most creative contribution to social ethics."[88] And Bondurant concludes in a similar vein.

> The especial contribution of Gandhi was to make the concept of *ahimsa* meaningful in the social and political spheres by molding tools of nonviolent action to use as a positive force in the search for social and political truths.[89]

It was inconceivable for Gandhi to think of himself as unarmed when he was equipped with *ahimsa*. This was his most potent "weapon." A votary of *ahimsa*, the true *Satyagrahi*, must never bear ill-will or harbor bitterness against an evil doer, nor use offensive language against him.

> A *Satyagrahi* will always try to overcome evil by good, anger by love, untruth by truth, *himsa* by *ahimsa*. There is no other way of purging the world of evil.[90]

This means, as King noted later, that the internal and the external aspects of the self should be in unity.

> Nonviolent action without the cooperation of the heart and the head cannot produce the intended result. The violence that we had harbored in our breasts during the non-cooperation days is now recoiling upon ourselves.[91]

Gandhi is referring to the violent outbreak in 1939 in Rajkat State when people were not adequately trained in *Satyagraha* disciplines.

Gandhi was under no illusion that he was a perfect *Satyagrahi*. He often stated that he was evolving, that he was no model of *ahimsa*. Gandhi kept striving to reduce himself to zero, to place himself last, to reach the farthest limits of humility. The very last words of his *Autobiography* is a request to the reader to join him in a "prayer to the God of Truth that He may grant me the boon of *Ahimsa* in mind, and deed."[92]

e. *Noncooperation*

"Non-cooperation and civil disobedience are but different branches of the same tree called *Satyagraha*."[93] It (noncooperation) includes a broad range of responses to an evil system short of the more aggressive civil disobedience. It is practiced in the spirit of *ahimsa* with the ultimate goal being Truth.

For Gandhi, noncooperation meant the withdrawing of cooperation from the State, which in the protester's view has become immoral and unjust. It often takes the form of renouncing the benefits of the society. Gandhi and his followers renounced "the benefits of schools, courts, titles, legislatures and offices set up under the system."[94] It also could mean the operating of parallel institutions. The most universally practiced act of noncooperation was the refusal to buy foreign cloth.

Another word used to describe such a method is boycott. Gandhi was opposed, as a matter of ethical principle, to boycotting–it is retaliatory and punitive. But with regard to foreign cloth, Gandhi was prepared to talk about the utility (not the ethics) of the boycott. And he made it quite clear in the face of questioning that he was boycotting the cloth, not because it was British, but because the "dumping down of foreign cloth in India has reduced millions of my people to pauperism."[95]

King came to somewhat the same conclusion about the Montgomery boycott. He, too, sensed the possible retaliatory implications of a boycott.

> A boycott suggests an economic squeeze, leaving one bogged down in a negative. But we were concerned with the positive. Our concern would not be to put the bus company out of business, but to put justice in business.[96]

The stance of noncooperation presupposed a prior attitude toward the government which has strong Thoreauvian overtones. Gandhi claimed it is "the inherent right of a subject to refuse to assist a government that will not listen to him."[97] He observed on another occasion that a government trying to rid itself of crime would have his cooperation, but that he would never cooperate with a government continuing in corruption.[98] When asked if noncooperation was an end in itself or a means to an end, he replied, "It is a means to an end, the end being to make the present government just, whereas it has become mostly unjust. Cooperation with a just government is a duty; noncooperation with an unjust government is equally a duty."[99]

Gandhi had to answer criticism that noncooperation, like *ahimsa*, was essentially negative and passive. It is an "intensely active state" he would reply–"more active than physical resistance or violence."[100] This is so because noncooperation in the spirit of *ahimsa* involves one totally, mind and body, attitude and action.

When Rabindranath Tagore, his esteemed and helpfully critical friend, charged that noncooperation was too negative, Gandhi replied firmly,

> In my humble opinion, rejection is as much an ideal as the acceptance of a thing. It is as necessary to reject untruth as it is to accept truth.[101]

It is in this context that Gandhi made the famous statement, "Non-cooperation with evil is as much a duty as cooperation with good."

Another criticism Gandhi had to face (and King after him) was that noncooperation is a subtle form of violence or that noncooperation breeds violence. Gandhi admitted that noncooperation involved the risks of violence, but

> the risks of supineness in the face of a grave issue is infinitely greater than the danger of violence ensuing from organizing non-cooperation. To do nothing is to invite violence for a certainty.[102]

A Mr. Arthur Weatherby posed for Gandhi the dilemma of babies dying in New York if milk drivers struck and then concluded that noncooperation in India means suffering in Lancashire.

Gandhi's answer, from his point of view, was the hard logic of noncooperation; yet from another standpoint, it would seem to be an unhesitating bit of casuistry. His response was simply that noncooperation can never be an act of violence, but it may not be an act of love. That would inhere in the motivation of the act itself.

If the milk drivers were engaged in a just complaint, e.g., being underpaid by their employers and they had tried every other method to obtain higher salaries, they were justified in striking. Their act would not be violent, although it would not be an act of love.

> They were driving milk carts for the sake of their maintenance. It was no part of their duty as employees under every circumstance to supply milk to babies.[103]

By the same token, since England's trade with India had been forced on her, ruining the significant cottage industry of spinning, India was not bound to maintain Lancashire. So Indian noncooperation was not so much a deliberate attempt to injure Englishmen as much as it was an attempt to affirm the right of Indian independence. Gandhi pursues the argument by commenting that those who refuse to patronize houses of prostitution are not referred to as violent people. They may even be considered virtuous.[104]

But Gandhi's final statement in response to Weatherby points out his practical idealism (his own self-image) and his honesty in distinguishing right, duty, and love.

> Thus it is clear that noncooperation is not violence when the refusal of the restraint is a right and a duty even though by reason of its performance some people may have to suffer. It will be an act of love when noncooperation is resorted to solely for the good of the wrongdoer.[105]

Gandhi is consistent with his understanding when he sees much of Indian noncooperation as a duty, but not an act of love, because it is taken in self-defense.

Noncooperation, by its nature, is a safe option for the masses, even for children. But civil disobedience, requiring more self-discipline and more dedication to obey all laws, is practiced as a last resort.

f. *Civil Disobedience*

This is also a branch of *Satyagraha*.[106] Gandhi always entered into civil disobedience with reluctance. It was "generally rare" that he considered laws so unjust as to break them openly. But it was the only acceptable alternative to resignation or physical force.

Gandhi's own definition reflects the classical understanding of civil disobedience by most ethicists. It is a civil breach of an immoral law. While we are permitted to disobey an unjust or immoral law of a state, we are required, meekly and willingly, to submit to the penalty for disobedience.[107] This meant cheerful acceptance of jails and accompanying hardships. Unlike a criminal lawbreaker who performed his act under cover and sought to avoid punishment, the civil resister suffers the penalty without complaint.

The symbol of the jail was an important one for Gandhi. His *Satyagrahi* were to seek arrest and imprisonment, just as a soldier is willing to die in battle. The triumph of the movement was to have thousands of innocent victims behind bars. "The greater our innocence, the greater our strength and the swifter our victory."[108]

For the average thief, jail may just be a jail, but for Gandhi, it was "a palace." "I was the originator of jail-going even before I read Thoreau."[109] Civil disobedience is the "inherent right of a citizen,"[110] and Gandhi wished he could persuade everyone of this truth. Again reflecting Thoreau, Gandhi identified manhood and following one's conscience.

> It is contrary to our manhood if we obey laws repugnant to our conscience. Such teaching is opposed to religion and means slavery.[111]

This would not in Gandhi's mind lead to anarchy, a fear often expressed by critics of nonviolence. Only criminal disobedience can result in anarchy and that is why every society represses it. Since the squelching of civil disobedience is the imprisoning of conscience, only a stronger and purer society can result.[112]

Gandhi was very concerned that those involved in civil disobedience were properly trained in the techniques and spirit of *Satyagraha*. He must be a person who freely, and as a matter of duty, obeys all the laws of society. Only then, according to Gandhi, is one in a position to decide which law is just or unjust. One who does not have a thorough respect for the law may also be reluctant to face all the implications of civil disobedience. Not realizing the importance of this qualification in the Keda district resulted in his famous "Himalayan miscalculation." He vowed thereafter to prepare his followers more carefully in the strict conditions of *Satyagraha*.[113]

A note should be made about Gandhi's use of the phrase civil resistance. It sometimes is used interchangeably with civil disobedience,[114] but, in fact, it lies somewhere between noncooperation and civil disobedience. All three are subsumed under the wider frame of *Satyagraha*, but civil resistance usually falls short of the more active civil disobedience, yet is somewhat more aggressive than noncooperation.[115]

Lewis Feuer, on the other hand, makes a rather sharp distinction between civil disobedience and civil resistance. The former retains a belief in the democratic process and usually addresses itself to a specific problem. It is, on the whole, justified when a minority or other such suppressed group finds that it is being deprived of basic rights.

Civil resistance, on the other hand, according to Feuer, is overtly revolutionary, claiming that the whole society is corrupt. Its negative stance toward the society is "total and unlimited."[116] It will often be expressed in guerrilla warfare. Such groups as the Weathermen faction of the Students for a Democratic Society and the Black Panthers would be illustrations of civil resistance.

Gandhi also made a rather clear distinction between aggressive disobedience and defensive disobedience. Offensive, assertive disobedience would be the breaking of a state law that did not essentially involve a "moral issue or human dignity," but which could be understood as a "symbol of revolt against the state."

Defensive disobedience implies the more traditional conception in which there is "reluctant nonviolent disobedience of such laws as are in themselves bad and obedience to which would be inconsistent with one's self-respect or human dignity."[117]

Gandhi had to face criticisms of civil disobedience similar to those leveled against his noncooperation. Some deplored direct action. To this Gandhi replied that "never has anything been done on this earth without direct action."[118] It was direct action alone, in the form of *Satyagraha*, that brought victory in South Africa.

King justified the nonviolent direct action campaign of Selma on the basis that the Civil Rights Commission three years earlier had recommended that changes take place in certain southern communities. Nothing was done to implement these recommendations, however, until the Selma demonstrations, until such a crisis was created that the issues could not longer be ignored.[119]

To the charge that civil disobedience might lead to violence, Gandhi responded with a confession that it was likely:

> But I know that it will not be the cause of it. Violence is there already corroding the whole body politic. Civil disobedience will be but a purifying process and may bring to the surface what is burrowing under and into the whole body.[120]

Martin Luther King had to respond in much the same way throughout his career. He repeatedly said that demonstrations did not cause violence, but allowed deeply buried violence to surface.[121]

For Gandhi, civil disobedience served as a kind of "safety valve" when the only alternative was violence. Although civil disobedience may be dangerous, it is no more dangerous than the "encircling violence" from which civil disobedience provides a nonviolent escape.[122] King knew that we should eschew violence in the resolution of conflict or the world would be destroyed by violence.

D. *King's Understanding of Nonviolence*

The use of nonviolence by King, as an instrument of social change, was never meant to replace the legal activity of the NAACP, the legislation of local, state, and national governments, or the best possible education in schools.

But King knew, on the other hand, from the lessons of history and his own experiences, that law, education, and the best intentions of good men would not always or automatically bring about social change. Laws could be passed, but they must be obeyed; knowledge and education may only help us reason from our vested interest. "Privileged groups rarely give up their privileges without strong resistance."[123] In the presence of this dilemma, King held out three options which have always been open to oppressed peoples as a means of handling their oppression.[124]

One option is resignation, acquiescence. This is the easiest way, but not the moral way. "It is the way of the coward."[125] To submit, passively, to the ruling powers is to help perpetuate the myth of black inferiority and tends to increase the "oppressor's arrogance and contempt." It does not build self-respect in the victim nor create respect for the oppressed in the mind of the oppressor. This sort of "non-resistance" "merely reinforces the myth that one race is inherently inferior to another."[126]

It is within this framework that King claims, "To accept passively an unjust system is to cooperate with that system," and in this context King echoes the Gandhian principle, "Noncooperation with evil is as much a moral obligation as is cooperation with good."[127]

If there is no protest to the evil, you tacitly say to the wrongdoer, "You are right and I agree with you." His conscience will be numbed. It was this belief that formed the basis for an article by King entitled "The Social Organization of Nonviolence" in *Liberation* (October 1959) subtitled "Never let them rest." This was the advice Gandhi gave his people regarding the British during the Indian campaign for independence.

Another option available to oppressed people is that of physical violence. But violence is deceptive. It does tend to bring results, but they are often surface and almost always temporary.

. . . in spite of temporary victories, violence never brings permanent peace. It solves no social problems; it merely creates new and more complicated ones.[128]

For King, violence was a futile avenue for the Negro to travel in achieving racial justice. In his oft-used phrase, it is both "impractical and immoral–impractical because it is self-defeating–'eye for an eye' leaves everybody blind." It is immoral because instead of seeking to convert your opponent by love, you tend to humiliate him.

King refuses this option, too, because violence, thriving on hate, "destroys community," "makes brotherhood impossible," and "leaves society in monologue rather than dialogue."[129]

The third option open, says King, is the way of nonviolent resistance. King sees this as a higher synthesis, combining the truths and avoiding the error in both opposites. Negroes "today are neither exercising violence nor accepting domination."[130] He avoids the nonresistance of the latter and the violent resistance of the former.[131] The nonviolent resister agrees with the latter that violent reaction is to be avoided and with the former that some resistance must be made.

It is this method that King outlines on several occasions and which we will now examine more carefully. It comprises the essential understanding of nonviolence for King.

We will be dealing primarily with King's thoughts and ideas and not his activity, as such, although it is obviously difficult to separate them completely.

E. *King's Normative Statement on Nonviolence and an Analysis of Its Sources*

His statement is most clearly presented in *Stride Toward Freedom*, on pages 83 to 88, with an additional commentary on pages 188 and following. To complete the statement, we must examine an article, "Love, Law, and Civil Disobedience."

1. "Nonviolent resistance is not a method for cowards,"[132] not for the weak or if one lacks the ability to be violent. This would not be true nonviolence. King says, "This is why Gandhi often said that if cowardice is the only alternative to violence, it is better to fight."[133] Actually Gandhi said, "I do believe that where there is only a choice between cowardice and violence, I would advise violence."[134]

The context of the latter statement helps us to see it in a true Gandhian perspective. He immediately follows the statement about cowardice with an illustration. His son, upon finding his father almost fatally wounded in 1908, asked Gandhi what he should have done if he were present–flee and see him die or use physical force to defend him. "I told him that it was his duty to defend me even by using violence."[135]

But there is no question in Gandhi's mind that nonviolence is "infinitely superior to violence, forgiveness is more manly than punishment."[136] Strength and personal power are not construed in terms of "physical capacity" but an "indomitable will."

Gandhi affirms that nonviolence is inherent to human being while violence is the law of the animal. "The dignity of man requires obedience to a higher law–to the strength of the spirit."[137] This "higher law," nonviolence, is a "dynamic condition" which involves suffering, as one pits one's "whole soul against the will of the tyrant." There is nothing passive, submissive, or weak about this approach.[138] Richard Gregg makes the same point regarding cowardice.

> Courageous violence, to try to prevent or stop a wrong, is better than cowardly acquiescence. Cowardice is more harmful, morally, than violence.[139]

King's first point is to assure his readers that nonviolence *does resist*. He also questioned the accuracy of "passive resistance" as a description of the method. He suspects it connotes quietism, resignation, and "stagnant passivity" in the face of evil.

Gandhi referred to the "superstition" arising from "the incompleteness of the English expression, passive resistance,"[140] which allows one to conclude that it is a force to be used only by those who are not capable of meeting violence by violence.

Both King and Gandhi insist nonviolence is a method for the strong. Nonviolent resistance is "ultimately the way of the strong man."[141] "Physical-force men are strangers to the courage that is requisite in a passive resister."[142] Gregg echoes the same conviction.

> The conduct of the nonviolent resister is not one of mere passive waiting or endurance. Toward his opponent he is not aggressive physically, but his mind and emotions are active.[143]

Without a footnote credit, King says:

For while the nonviolent resister is passive in the sense that he *not physically aggressive toward his opponent, his mind and emotions are always active*, constantly seeking to persuade his opponent that he is wrong. The method is passive physically, but strongly active spiritually. It is not passive nonresistance to evil, it is active nonviolent resistance to evil.[144]

King stressed repeatedly the great difference between nonresistance to evil and nonviolent resistance. Much of the criticisms leveled against nonviolence, including those of Malcolm X and Reinhold Niebuhr, are because people fail to distinguish those two ideas. Nonresistance leaves one stagnant, passive, and complacent, whereas the other, nonviolent resistance, means strong and determined resistance, so there is no question about the nature of one's response.

Further, King had continually to make the point that the noncooperation with the Jim Crow laws, the demonstrations and picketing, although apparently a negative program, had another side, and that was the cooperation with the good and the constructive.

This constructive program is a basic part of any genuine nonviolent movement, for nonviolence is essentially a positive concept.[145]

2. "A second basic fact that characterizes nonviolence is that it does not seek to defeat or humiliate the opponent, but to win his friendship and understanding."[146] The various expressions of nonviolent protests (boycott, strike, jail, etc.) are not ends in themselves, but serve as "means to awaken a sense of moral shame in the opponent."[147]

Nonviolent resistance, effectively practiced, disarms the opponent, exposes his moral defenses, weakens his morale, and works on his conscience.[148] After a while, the opponent will have had enough. "Forced to stand before the world and his God splattered with the blood of his brother, he will call an end to his self-defeating massacre."[149]

This is what is called moral jui-jitsu by Richard Gregg. Gandhi's thought also incorporated these ideas. For him, noncooperation was not a method of forcing others to obedience by violence, but of trying "patiently to convert our opponents."[150] And the same note of moral jui-jitsu (catching or drawing your opponent off-balance is struck when Gandhi says, "if an activity is pure and that of the government impure, the latter is embarrassed by our purity."[151]

a. Gregg's Moral Jui-Jitsu

Gregg has outlined the psychological and moral mechanisms at work in nonviolent resistance. Chapter two of his book, *The Power of Nonviolence*, is titled "Moral Jui-Jitsu."

In physical jui-jitsu, the aim is to destroy the sense of balance in the opponent and to retain one's own balance. This knowledge of balance is imperative. In moral jui-jitsu the opponent loses his moral balance and therefore is converted to the position of the nonviolent resister. How this occurs is discussed by Gregg in this chapter and a brief summary follows.

First, the victim is sincerely willing to suffer and not to inflict suffering. If a blow is returned for a blow, the initial attacker is somewhat reassured and has moral support. The position of violence "on the victim's scale of moral values is the same as that of the attacker."[152] But if the victim decides to suffer and not react violently, the attacker "loses the moral support which the usual violent resistance of most victims would render him. He plunges forward, as it were, into a new world of values."[153]

Secondly, the attacker is thrown off balance, is surprised, loses his poise, may become confused in his thinking and, in short, is rendered incapable of action. In this new world of values, his "instincts no longer tell him instantly what to do."[154]

There are several reasons for this confusion and loss of efficiency.

i. Anger and hatred are very exhausting. They exact a large amount of energy from us.[155] You can become obsessed with people you hate.

ii. Another reason for inefficiency of the attacker, says Gregg, is that the nonviolent victim puts the inner self of the assailant in conflict with itself–his good, decent side with the aggressive side. This, too, is enervating.

iii. The assailant then may make the mistake of thinking his victim is a coward. He then may be even more aggressive.

iv. Then the onlookers will cause the assailant to lose poise. This is undoubtedly what happened in an incident in Birmingham. A group of Negroes wanted to have a prayer meeting near the city jail and began to march there. Bull Connor told his police to turn the hoses on the marchers. Then King relates:

> What happened in the next thirty seconds was one of the most fantastic events of the Birmingham story. Bull Connor's men, their deadly hoses poised for action, stood facing the marchers. The marchers, many of them on their knees, stared back, unafraid and unmoving. Slowly the Negroes stood up and began

to advance. Connor's men, as though hypnotized, fell back, their hoses sagging uselessly in their hands while several hundred Negroes marched past them without further interference, and held their prayer meeting as planned.[156]

v. Onlookers now will be so impressed with the courage of the victim that the assailant will feel he is "excessive, undignified, even brutal. They will see he has misjudged the character of his adversary."[157]

vi. Finally, the attacker is at a disadvantage because he is in a "suggestible and receptive state of mind and emotion." The surprising and disarming conduct of the victim presents a new idea to the attacker and so Gregg affirms, "Then the assailant has less chance of influencing the resister than the latter of influencing him."[158]

Hence, the loss of balance. The nonviolent resister has the upper hand. "He has taken the moral initiative."[159] He is not surprised or weakened by anger and not in as vulnerable a position as his attacker, who is susceptible to new ideas. The nonviolent person has been in control of himself. Eventually, the hope is that the basis of fear and anger will be eliminated from his mind and the attacker will be assured that the conflict is genuinely resolved. Or as Gregg says:

> The aim is to convert the opponent, to change his understanding and his sense of values so that he will join wholeheartedly with the resister in seeking a settlement truly amicable and truly satisfying to both sides.[160]

Gandhi sees such a statement of Jesus as "If any man will take away thy coat, let him have thy cloak also," as an example of moral jui-jitsu, although he does not use the phrase. He says,

> Your noncooperation is nonviolent when you give your opponent all in the place of just what he needs. You have disarmed him once for all by your apparent cooperation, which in effect is complete noncooperation.[161]

Gandhi also illustrated this aspect of nonviolence when he said,

> What is required is not so much the entry of Harijans to the Temple as the conversion of the orthodox to the belief that it is wrong to prevent Harijans from entering the Temples. This conversion can only be brought about by an appeal to their hearts, i.e., by evoking the best that is in them.[162]

As the appellant is pure and sincere in action and motive, so the cause will succeed. If the reformer has "consciousness of the Truth and his cause" he will be more impatient with himself than with his opponent. King echoes this same theme in his reflections on his Indian pilgrimage.

> . . . it is better to be the recipient of violence than the inflicter of it, since the latter only multiplies the existence of violence and bitterness in the universe, while the former may develop a sense of shame in the opponent, and thereby bring about a transformation and change of heart.[163]

King also indicates that he thoroughly grasps Gregg's essence of moral jui-jitsu when to a question about the meaning of "militant nonviolence," he replies:

> If you confront a man who has long been cruelly misusing you, and you say, "Punish me, if you will, I do not deserve it, but I will accept it so that the world will know I am right and you are wrong," then you wield a powerful and a just weapon. This man, your oppressor, is automatically morally defeated, and if he has any conscience, he is ashamed. Wherever this weapon is used in a manner that stirs up a community's or a nation's anguished conscience, then the pressure of public opinion becomes an ally in your just cause.[164]

In his last book, *The Trumpet of Conscience*, King describes the dilemma of the South. If southern officials would have let Negroes demonstrate and march, that would have given the lie to the myth of black contentment. If they shot them or otherwise used violent means against them, the world would witness their inhumanity. No longer would sheer threats and fear work. "Nonviolence had muzzled their guns and Negro defiance had shaken their confidence."[165] There was no mistaking who was the purveyor of evil and who was the innocent victim.

King goes on to mention a central belief of his while concluding his discussion of this second aspect of nonviolence. He mentions that the end of nonviolence, the purpose of the conversion process, is reconciliation. "The aftermath of nonviolence is the creation of the beloved community, while the aftermath of violence is tragic bitterness."[166] Just as King was concerned to win the opponent's friendship and understanding, so Gregg's aim in nonviolent resistance was not harm or humiliation, but to seek a

> solution under which both parties can have complete self-respect and mutual respect . . . a more secure, creative, and truthful relationship.[167]

3. "A third characteristic of this method is that the attack is directed against forces of evil rather than against persons who happen to be doing the evil."[168] King is quite clear that the issue is injustice, not race or color. He affirmed this in Montgomery and that perspective was not altered in his mature thought. The forces to be conquered were those of evil, injustice, and darkness, not persons who were unjust or who disagreed with him. For Gandhi, a primary qualification of a *Satyagrahi* was the ability to make and remember the distinction between evil and the evil-doer.[169] By the same token, the victory was never a personal one for the *Satyagrahi*, but a victory for Truth and justice.

This notion reflect's King's deep awareness and appreciation of the structures of society and the necessity for changing the structures so determinative of the actions and lives of individuals.

4. "A fourth point that characterizes nonviolent resistance is a willingness to accept suffering without retaliation, to accept blows from the opponent without striking back."[170] A cardinal principle in King's understanding of nonviolence is that "unearned suffering is redemptive." He was fond of quoting Gandhi's "Rivers of blood may have to flow before we gain our freedom, but it must be our blood."

King here was plumbing to the depths of the power of nonviolence. He learned from Gandhi that progress, especially in matters of prejudice, comes only by suffering. The appeal of suffering reaches beneath the rational and the conscious.

> I have found that mere appeal to reason does not answer where prejudices are age-long and based on supposed religious authority. Reason has to be strengthened by suffering and suffering opens the eyes of understanding.[171]

There is a relation here to moral jui-jitsu and the effect suffering has on the viewers of the nonviolent resister enduring his attack. A. J. Muste, whom King heard at Crozer, with whom he corresponded during the days of the movement, and whom King undoubtedly read, made suffering central to nonviolence.

> If evil rises up in its final, least rational, least excusable, most hideous form, then accept suffering at its hands and on its behalf. Let it nail you to the cross. Take suffering into your own soul; do not drive its sword into the flesh or soul of an erring child of God. Thus you will be showing the power of Divine Love, for God is Love, to outlast and outwit all opposition. . . . And

there is no power to overcome evil, to break the heart of sin, like the power of suffering love, the Cross.[172]

Nothing was more essential to *Satyagraha* than the suffering of the *Satyagrahi*. This gave the whole effort integrity and legitimacy. "A *Satyagrahi* depends only on truth and his capacity to suffer for truth."[173]

So confident was Gandhi in the power of suffering to redeem that he said, "The silent loving suffering of one single pure Hindu as such will be enough to melt the hearts of millions of Hindus,"[174] and the suffering of a *Satyagrahi* "will melt the stoniest heart of the stoniest fanatic."[175] He even measured progress by the amount of suffering that the sufferer has endured. "The purer the suffering, the greater is the progress. Hence did the sacrifice of Jesus suffice to free a sorrowing world."[176]

Gandhi's stress on suffering was consonant with his striving toward perfection, his desire to become "zero," his stress on self-abnegation at whatever cost. He was tapping one of the roots of universal religion with this emphasis–"Everybody admits that sacrifice of self is infinitely superior to sacrifice of others."[177]

Suffering in his own person, committing himself unreservedly to the service of mankind, sacrificing of self if necessary, and with no bitterness toward the other, was the goal of *Satyagraha*. This was the ideal placed before India by Gandhi; it was actually her ancient religious goal. Noncooperation, *Satyagraha*, are simply new or other names for the law of suffering.

In true sacrifice, all the suffering is on one side–one is required to master the art of getting killed without killing, of gaining life by losing it. May India live up to this *mantra*.[178]

King constantly stressed that the "way of nonviolence means a willingness to suffer and sacrifice."[179] It would mean loss of house, imprisonment, unemployment, vilification of character, harassment by law officers and neighbors. It could even mean death. But King saw all this suffering, the shedding of blood, the possibility of death as redemptive.

But if physical death is the price that a man must pay to free his children and his white brethren from a permanent death of the spirit, then nothing could be more redemptive.[180]

The direct relation between moral jui-jitsu and innocent suffering is captured by King as he presents a paraphrase of Gandhian ideals, which he hopes the American Negro could soon say to their white brothers.

> We will match your capacity to inflict suffering with our capacity to endure suffering. We will meet your physical force with soul force . . . Do to us what you will and we will still love you . . . But we will soon wear you down by our capacity to suffer. And in winning our freedom we will so appeal to your heart and conscience that we will win you in the process.[181]

King seemed certain that suffering could not only sway individuals in one-to-one relationships, but it could effect communities and civilizations as well. Suffering was an ingredient of his vision.

> . . . to see in this generation's ordeals the opportunity to transfigure both ourselves and American society. Our present suffering and our nonviolent struggle to be free may well offer to Western civilization the kind of spiritual dynamic so desperately needed for survival.[182]

5. "A fifth point concerning nonviolent resistance is that it avoids not only external physical violence but also internal violence of spirit."[183] One cannot retaliate attitudinally with hatred or bitterness any more than one can overtly react with force, if one is a true nonviolent resister. "At the center of nonviolence stands the principle of love," a love which is also able to unite the external and the internal. This for King is the Christian *agape*, which he conceives as "understanding, redeeming good will for all men."[184]

Gandhi speaks of the centrality of *ahimsa* to his conception of *Satyagraha*. For him, *ahimsa*, although literally meaning non-injury, is a "positive state of love, of doing good even to the evil-doer,"[185] and claims, as far as he is concerned, that the "true rendering of the word in English is love or charity."[186] He then proceeds to quote from I Cor. 13 and, of course, the Greek word used for love in that chapter is *agape*. Gregg asserts virtually the same in his book.

> Love is the most important of all these qualities of the nonviolent person; it may even be considered the origin of all the others.[187]

He knows the problem of the sentimentality attached to the English word and suggests that a better name might be "a sort of intelligence of knowledge." This, however, does not carry the power King or Gandhi desire to convey by the use of *agape* or *ahimsa*. Let us examine more carefully King's understanding of *agape*.

In almost every article submitted to journals, beginning with "Nonviolence and Racial Justice" in the February 6, 1957 issue of *The Christian Century* (and for about two years these articles did not differ appreciably in form and content), King makes the distinction between *eros*, *philia*, and *agape* know by all first year theology students. The distinction is again made in *Stride Toward Freedom*, reappears in the article, "Love, Law, and Civil Disobedience," and again in a sermon, "Loving Your Enemies," in *Strength to Love*.

His major statement, however, is in the first account of "Pilgrimage to Nonviolence" in *Stride Toward Freedom*. A cursory reading of his discussion here would indicate his direct reliance upon Anders Nygren and Paul Ramsey. This is not at all accidental, for one of the two texts used in his ethics course as a senior at Crozer was Ramsey's *Basic Christian Ethics*.[188] Nygren's *Agape and Eros* was also part of the assigned reading.[189]

Obviously, King's concern was an apologetic one. He was speaking of love as the center of nonviolence, relying upon Jesus's "Love your enemies," yet to his English listeners he knew love had a variety of meanings, from romance to affection to God. He wanted to make clear what he meant, for "It would be nonsense to urge men to love their oppressors in an affectionate sense."[190] King then resorts to the three main words used for love in the Greek language.[191] Here are King's definitions.[192]

> First, there is *eros*. In Platonic philosophy *eros* meant the yearning of the soul for the realm of the divine. It has come now to mean a sort of aesthetic or romantic love.

Indeed, Nygren's whole discussion of *Eros* centers around Plato's understanding of it found primarily in the *Phaedrus* and the *Symposium*. Nygren understands *Eros* as "the upward tendency of the human soul; it is a real force, which drives the soul in the direction of the Ideal world."[193] King does not use Nygren's exact wording, i.e., "acquisitive love," "egocentric love," although in the above definition he does reflect Nygren's statement, "*Eros* is man's way to the Divine."[194]

> Secondly, there is *philia* which means intimate affection between personal friends. *Philia* denotes a sort of reciprocal love; the person loves because he is loved.[195]

This is an accurate understanding of the Greek word, although it is not used to any extent by Nygren or Ramsey. It is love illustrated by mutuality, companionship, and love in response to love. But King knows if we are talking about loving our enemies, "loving those who oppose us," we cannot use either *eros* or *philia*. We must use the meaning provided by the Greek word *agape*.

> *Agape* means understanding, redeeming good will for all men. It is an overflowing love which is purely spontaneous, unmotivated, groundless, and creative. It is not set in motion by any quality or function of its object. It is the love of God operating in the human heart.[196]

Here King is actually using Nygren's phrases. In the latter's outline of *agape* in *Agape and Eros*, we find *agape* is "spontaneous and unmotivated," "indifferent to value," "creative," and "initiator of fellowship with God—*Agape* is God's way to man."[197] As can be seen, King did not include the last concept in his definition (we shall attempt to see why later). It is also to be noted that King did not refer to Nygren in this passage, nor does he ever mention Nygren by name in any of his written works.

The very next paragraph in his exposition of *agape* indicates King's direct dependence on Ramsey.

> *Agape* is disinterested love. It is a love in which the individual seeks not his own good, but the good of his neighbor (I Cor. 10:24). *Agape* does not begin by discriminating between worthy and unworthy people, or any qualities people possess. It begins by loving others *for their sakes*. It is an entirely "neighbor-regarding concern for others," which discovers the neighbor in every man it meets. There (sic) *agape* makes no distinction between friend and enemy; it is directed toward both.[198]

The above amounts to exact reproduction or paraphrasing of Ramsey and again there are no footnotes. Ramsey begins his chapter on "The Meaning of Christian Love" with a discussion of Christian love as "disinterested love for neighbor" and refers immediately to I Cor. 10:24.[199] Ramsey defines disinterested love for neighbor as "love for neighbor *for his own sake*"[200] and

> neighborly love in the Christian sense, discovers the neighbor in every man it meets and as such has never yet met a friend or an enemy. Christian love does not mean discovering the essentially human underneath differences; it

means detecting the neighbor underneath friendliness or hostility or any other qualities in which the agent takes special interest.[201]

and "Christian love means an entirely 'neighbor-regarding concern for others.'"[202] As King continues the paragraph, he again is paraphrasing Ramsey:

If one loves an individual merely on account of his friendliness, he loves him for the sake of the benefits to be gained from the friendship, rather than for the friend's own sake.[203]

Ramsey says:

In the case of a friendly neighbor it is possible in loving him to love only his friendliness toward us in return. Then he is not loved *for his own sake*. He is loved for the sake of his friendliness (in a previous sentence he used the phrase "on account of his friendliness"), for the sake of the benefits to be gained from reciprocal friendship.[204]

King concludes the paragraph with the observation:

Consequently, the best way to assure oneself that love is disinterested is to have love for the enemy-neighbor from whom you can expect no good in return, but only hostility and persecution.[205]

Ramsey's words are:

If a person has love for his enemy-neighbor from whom he can expect no good in return but only hostility and persecution, then alone does it become certain that he does not simply love himself in loving his neighbor.[206]

King goes on to say that *agape* "springs from the *need* of the other person."[207] He uses the Good Samaritan parable as evidence of this. The Samaritan was "good" because he responded to the human need that he was presented with.[208] This is, in other words, what Ramsey means by the use of the parable. It was not meant to answer the abstract question, "Who is my neighbor?" but "What is the meaning of 'neighbor-love?'"[209] And hence, Ramsey's emphasis on "neighbor-regarding love." A way of interpreting the intention of Ramsey might be to say that a neighbor is anyone to whom you can be neighborly.[210]

But King seems to miss completely two significant theological points made by Nygren and Ramsey. Nygren stresses that we are to love our neighbor because God has loved us.

> The distinctive character of the Christian ethic, as it arises out of fellowship with God, can be summed up in Jesus' words to his disciples, "Freely ye have received, freely give."[211]

And, thus, in the second place, it follows that God's love for us and our love for the neighbor is not based on the "infinite value of the human soul."[212] This judgment about man would preclude the value-creating role of *agape*, make unnecessary a decision on the part of God to love man and, as Ramsey implies, it avoids the "particularity" of the neighbor. It tends to make God's love an eternal principle and the "value of the human soul" becomes a "ground," a "condition" for God's love. As we shall see later, King opts for the "values of the human soul" as inherent, rather than the more radical Biblical idea that men have value in terms of their relationship to God.

Then, King states that *agape* is not a "weak, passive love. It is love in action. Agape is love seeking to preserve and create community."[213] Here again is a Ramsey theme. "Only an element of concern for the other person *for his own sake* creates community among men."[214] This statement is found in the section entitled, "The Work of Love in Creating Community."

But Ramsey makes a distinction between preserving and creating community. A community can be preserved by *eros* (self-love) and *philia* (mutual love) or "appeals to enlightened self-interest," but only "the work of Christian love, the work of reconciliation" can create a community where none has existed.[215]

For King, finally, *agape* means that "all life is interrelated." "All humanity is involved in a single process and all men are brothers."[216] One cannot do good or harm to another without affecting both. King's deeply held belief in the organic unity of life is symbolized by his frequent use of John Donne's "No man is an island."

Gandhi so believed in the unity of the human race that thieves were understood to be our "kith and kin." The *Satyagrahi* must "take pains to devise ways and means of winning them over," helping them to realize that kinship.[217] Also, "It is against my religion to regard any one as an enemy."[218]

At this point, Gregg is lucid. He suggests that violence presupposes separation and division and nonviolence is based on the idea of unity[219] and love may be described as a kind of "courage based upon a conscious or subconscious realization of the underlying unity of all life."[220]

It was this understanding of love that afforded King the ground for constructing his vision of the beloved community.

6. "The sixth basic fact about nonviolent resistance is that it is based on the conviction that the universe is on the side of justice."[221] Another major ethical motif in King's thought is the existence of a moral law that unfolds through history and that will not be ultimately defeated. Or as he puts it, delineating this characteristic of his nonviolent philosophy, "there is a creative force in this universe that works to bring the disconnected aspects of reality into a harmonious whole."[222]

This affirmation of King's has roots in Biblical faith (prophetism) and Personalism, but also it is a central ingredient in Gandhi's *Satyagraha*. It reflects Gandhi's observation "that life persists in the midst of destruction and, therefore, there must be a higher law than that of destruction,"[223] or more specifically:

> He (God) is love. He is the supreme Good. . . . The safest course is to believe in the moral government of the world and therefore in the supremacy of the moral law, the law of truth and love.[224]

This "cosmic companionship" (King) allows an adherent of nonviolence to have hope, to suffer without striking back and to persevere in his struggle for justice. King refers to Thomas Jefferson's misgivings about the slave issue and quotes the latter's fears from *Notes in Virginia*.

> I reflect that God is just, that his justice cannot sleep forever . . . the Almighty has no attribute which can take sides with us in such a contest.[225]

And so King concludes that the Civil Rights Movement has a faith in the future. And the movement will be vindicated because it "had something within it that says somehow even though the arc of the moral universe is long, it bends toward justice."[226] A more detailed analysis of King's understanding of the moral law will appear later in our discussion of Personalism (pages 197-199).

F. *The Statement in "Love, Law, and Civil Disobedience"*

This statement in *Stride Toward Freedom* is the distillation of King's understanding of nonviolence as of 1958. He had time enough to reflect on the Montgomery experience and time for re-reading and assimilation of Gandhi and Gregg, especially the former.

Before 1958 several religious journals printed many of his articles. These articles appeared under different titles but with virtually the same outline which included a preface indicating there was a "new Negro" in the South and stating that there are several ways to struggle against injustice–physical violence, acquiescence, and nonviolent resistance.

He then presents the 5 or 6 points of his understanding of nonviolence that we have just discussed. The article would conclude with the affirmation that the problem of race is America's greatest moral dilemma, that the churches should be taking courageous stands–the worst sin being "the appalling silence of the so-called good people." The final note in these articles is a call to be "maladjusted" to all forms of injustice.

The models for this article are "Nonviolence and Racial Justice" in *The Christian Century* (February 6, 1957) and "Out of the Long Night of Segregation" in *Presbyterian Outlook* (February 10, 1958). These were the first attempts to say what later appeared in the chapter on "Pilgrimage to Nonviolence" in *Stride Toward Freedom* and in the last chapter of the book, titled "Where Do We Go From Here?"[227] Apparently, during the preparation of *Stride Toward Freedom*, King added the characteristic of redemptive suffering. This aspect does not appear in the articles.[228]

The 1960 version of "Pilgrimage to Nonviolence" which appeared in *The Christian Century* (almost completely duplicated in the final chapter of *Strength to Love*) contains no list of nonviolent essentials. Since the *Century* series had to do with how the authors' had changed their minds, King concentrated more on theological reflection since his seminary days.

But on November 16, 1961, King delivered one of his most important addresses, entitled "Love, Law, and Civil Disobedience."[229] At the same time it reveals an enlargement of his understanding of what constitutes nonviolence and the budding of themes that find fruition in the "Letter from Birmingham Jail." This article outlines the "underlying philosophy" of the nonviolent resistance as it was being understood and practiced by the student movement in the South.

His first point or principle in this discussion is that "means must be pure as the end."[230] This is a new thought in his systematic presentation of nonviolence, although he had mentioned it as early as the Montgomery boycott. It is a major theme of King's and is found throughout his writings. For him, "ends and means must cohere." "The end represents the means in process and the ideal in the making," "the end is pre-existent in the means."[231] It was King's feeling that nonviolence made it "possible for the individual to struggle for moral ends through moral means."[232] He had several other ways of saying it.

> But as you continue your righteous protest always be sure that you struggle with Christian methods and Christian weapons. Be sure that the means you employ are as pure as the end you seek.[233]

> . . . The use of immoral means (roots) will not achieve the moral end of racial injustice.[234]

> . . . for we believe that only just means may be used in seeking a just end.[235]

> The rich man was a fool because he permitted the ends for which he lived to become confused with the means by which he lived. The economic structures of his life absorbed his destiny.[236]

> One day we must come to see that peace is not merely a distant goal that we seek, but a means by which we arrive at that goal. We must pursue peaceful ends through peaceful means.[237]

> As a race, Negroes must work passionately and unrelentingly for first-class citizenship–but they must never use second class methods to gain it. They must never succumb to the temptation of using violence in the struggle.[238]

Both King and Gandhi were fond of quoting Jesus's understanding of means-end controversy: "Those that take the sword shall perish by the sword."[239] Thomas Merton, with his usual clarity, said:

> Christian nonviolence, therefore, is convinced that the manner in which the conflict for truth is waged will itself manifest or obscure the truth.[240]

and then cites Pope Paul in his United Nations speech,

> If you wish to be brothers, let the weapons fall from your hands. You cannot love with offensive weapons in your hands.[241]

For King, the end you have in mind determines the means you will use. Or instead of "the end justifies the means" King would say "the end determines the means." A beloved community cannot be built on hostile means. A temporary victory may be obtained over an opponent by physical violence, but you probably have not created a permanent peace. This is why King insisted on the means of nonviolence because "our end is a community at peace with itself."[242]

Gregg says that peace obtained by nonviolence endures because the "outer condition reflects the inner condition."[243] There is wholeness and unity whereas peace achieved by violence tends to perpetuate division and disharmony. The outward peace does not reflect suppressed hostility.

This is also why King disagreed so vigorously with the Leninist version of Communism in which any means–lying, deceit, murder, and other forms of violence, were permitted in order to liberate the workers. And quite practically, this is why King reacted so negatively to the urban riots and the shift towards violence in the middle sixties. He had hoped black people would find their place in the American society, in the economic, housing, and educational spheres. But he knew also that these precise goals could not be achieved by violent destruction of the system.

> If one is in search of a better job, it does not help to burn down the factory.
> If one needs more adequate education, shooting the principal will not help.
> If housing is the goal, only building and construction will produce that end.

The goals needed and sought by Negroes cannot be obtained by destruction. Here again violence would be self-defeating. The end you would like established is undermined by the means you use. The vindication of truth is betrayed by the untruthful methods employed, to use Gandhi's terminology.[245]

Lacy feels that Gandhi "has left a priceless legacy to the world in the moral realm." Among other things, in that legacy, is "the inseparability of means and end," that

> means must be compatible or consistent with the end, and that nature of the means often determines the quality of the end.[246]

This is not to imply that Gandhi identified means and end, because man is still free to choose the means he desires to use. But Lacy's warning is sound, that while Gandhi and King may insist that the morality of means is essential to the morality of the act as a whole, it is a dangerous fallacy to assume further that the morality of the means *guarantees* the morality of the end.[247]

King soon found out that nonviolent means could be used for immoral ends and he wrestled with this problem. On two occasions King had to deal with this issue.

First, early in the Montgomery struggle, King realized that the boycott method could be used for unjust goals. He knew that the White Citizens Council had used the same device to discriminate unfairly against Negroes. King's aims were on a higher level.

> We would use this method to give birth to justice and freedom, and also to urge men to comply with the law of the land. The White Citizens Councils used it to perpetuate the reign of injustice and human servitude.[248]

Second, King was again faced with the immoral use of nonviolence when the Birmingham police, imitating the rather successful Chief Pritchett of Albany, decided to be restrained and nonviolent in the handling of demonstrators. This destroyed the publicity value of police brutality against innocent victims.

We have intimated that King thought it was always wrong to use immoral means to attain moral ends. "But now I must affirm that it is just as wrong, or perhaps even more so, to use moral means to preserve immoral ends." It was not appropriate, in King's view, to support racial injustice by nonviolent methods.[249] He then quotes, in support, T. S. Eliot: "The last temptation is the greatest treason; To do the right deed for the wrong reason."[250]

Gandhi was once asked if any means could be used to achieve an end. His reply was

> Your belief that there is no connection between the means and the end is a great mistake. . . . The means may be likened to a seed, the end to a tree; and there is just the same inviolable connection between the means and the end as there is between the seed and the tree.[251]

So King concludes:

> The philosophy of nonviolent resistance is the philosophy which says that the means must be as pure as the end, that in the long run of history, immoral destructive means cannot bring about moral and constructive ends.[252]

The second principle presented in this article is that of following "a consistent principle of noninjury." This is the first time this term is employed–a term used as a literal translation of the Hindu *ahimsa*, so pivotal in Gandhi's thought. But in terms of content, this answers to number five above (page 107) (it is interesting that in both accounts, this aspect receives the longest treatment).

The third point made here by King is one stressed before (number three above, page 105), namely, "That one seeks to defeat the unjust system, rather than individuals who are caught in that system."[253]

The fourth principle which "stands at the center of the movement" is that "suffering can be a most creative and powerful force." The emphasis here is essentially the same as in number four above (page 105), except that in this version King is more careful to stress the fundamental Gandhian notion that although violence and nonviolence agree that suffering can be a "very powerful social force," violence says we inflict suffering on others, while nonviolence says that suffering must be accepted by the victims, taken in to yourself, and thus it becomes redemptive.

The fifth notion in this construction of King is an addition to the *Stride Toward Freedom* list. ". . . there is within human nature an amazing potential for goodness."[254]

This affirmation is a clue to King's Christian anthropology. It is, at bottom, the liberal view that man in neither inherently sinful nor righteous, good or bad, but he has a potential for both. For King, there is "something" within every man that will respond to goodness and "that there is something within human nature that can be changed."[255]

Gandhi was probably more optimistic about man than King, who was haunted and tempered by Niebuhr's analysis of human nature. One of the conditions for a state (national) policy of nonviolence would be a vast majority of Indians willing to noncooperate with an aggressor. If a modern day Nero invaded India, we would offer ourselves as "fodder for the aggressor's cannon. The underlying belief is that even a Nero is not devoid of heart."[256]

King relied heavily on the good conscience of the oppressor and trusted he would respond to undeserved suffering.

The sixth and final principle outlined in this article is also an addition to the first list in *Stride Toward Freedom*. "It says that it is as much a moral obligation to refuse to cooperate with evil as it is to cooperate with good."[257] This statement does appear in the final chapter of *Stride Toward Freedom* in which King further expounds his nonviolent philosophy. There the statement King uses is an unacknowledged direct reference from Gandhi. "Non-cooperation with evil is as much a moral obligation as is cooperation with good."[258]

The mention of the principle of noncooperation sends King into a lengthy discussion of the nature of civil disobedience and just and unjust laws. This discussion makes the article a forerunner of the "Letter from Birmingham Jail."

G. *King's Understanding of Civil Disobedience*

1. *King and Thoreau*

While a student at Morehouse, King read for the first time Thoreau's "On the Duty of Civil Disobedience." He had already suffered many times as a result of racial discrimination and was searching for an effective method to combat the structures that made it possible. He was "fascinated by the idea of refusing to cooperate with an evil system." His first reading of the essay "deeply moved" him and he said he re-read it several times.[259]

It was during the Montgomery bus boycott that King realized the importance of the Thoreauvian insights. When it came to him that the boycott was, in fact, mass noncooperation with the evil system of segregation, he began "to think about Thoreau's *Essay on Civil Disobedience*." He was convinced that the movement in Montgomery expressed Thoreau's suggestion to "withdraw their support"[260] or "refuse allegiance"[261] or, as King put it, "We can no longer lend our cooperation to an evil system."[262]

King mentions in "Pilgrimage to Nonviolence" that Thoreau was his "first intellectual contact with the theory of nonviolent resistance."[263] This is only partly true. That is, Thoreau's refusal to pay his state taxes happened to be a nonviolent act of civil disobedience. One should not conclude from this that Thoreau was a pacifist or one who held to the principle of nonviolence. It is generally conceded that Thoreau's emphasis was on lawbreaking, not on pacifism or nonviolence[264] and, as Reddick rightly perceives, "The nonviolent principle in Gandhi and King does not come from Thoreau, only the element of *non-cooperation with evil.*"[265]

Thoreau could provide an intellectual base for King's own ideas and activity, but he was not a personal example. Although it seemed important to Thoreau to be imprisoned as a tactic, there is apparently little moral content to his going to jail. As Harry Kalven puts it, "He offers no theory about the propriety of going or not going to jail; it just happens."[266] This is a far cry from Gandhi's and King's decisions to go to jail and to accept the punishment willingly.

Also, Thoreau's own individualism, his unwillingness to be a part of or to start a movement to stop the Mexican war or to abolish slavery, betrays a kind of indifference, verging on anarchy, that was not a part of King's orientation. But Thoreau's refusal to obey unjust laws, his unyielding commitment to his conscience, his distinction between the right and the legal, surely influenced King.

2. The Basis of King's Civil Disobedience

King's resistance is in the tradition of Israel's prophets and the early Christians. It is rooted in the First Commandment and Peter's affirmation in Acts 5, "We must obey God rather than man."

King was soon forced to decide between the "cherished custom" of Montgomery or the "ethical demands of the universe." His response was "As Christians we owe our ultimate allegiance to God and His will, rather than to men and his folkways."[267] Here also is a reflection of Tillich's "Protestant Principle" in which absolute loyalty can only be given to the Absolute and not to any historical relativity.

King knew that adherence to this principle would inevitably bring one into conflict with not only social custom, but state and national law. And so "in order to be true to one's conscience and true to God, a righteous man has no alternative but to refuse to cooperate with an evil system."[268]

There is a secular, if not a Deist parallel in Thoreau, who said, "I think that it is enough if they have God on their side, without waiting for that other one. Moreover, any man more right than his neighbor, constitutes a majority of one already."[269]

3. Nature of Just and Unjust Laws

King's most articulate discussion of this distinction is in "Letter from Birmingham Jail." The following summary of his argument is from *Why We Can't Wait*.

King's explanation for obeying some laws and disobeying others rests on his belief that there are two kinds of laws–just and unjust. We are morally, as well as legally, obligated to obey the just law. On the other hand, we have a moral responsibility to disobey an unjust law. In support of his position, King quotes Augustine's dictum, "an unjust law is no law at all." King then defines a just law along the lines of classical understanding of natural law. "A just law is a man-made code that squares with the moral law or the law of God." And unjust law is the opposite. Referring to a Thomistic understanding of natural law, King says "an unjust law is a human law that is not rooted in eternal law and natural law."[270]

Further, King claims a law is just or unjust depending on how it "uplifts human personality" or "degrades human personality." Segregation codes and laws degrade people and are, hence, unjust. They lower persons to the category of things, to "its" and not "Thous" in Buber's language.

In addition, developing Tillich's idea of sin as separation, King argues that segregation, since it separates, is sinful. One could call King's logic into question here if Aristotelian syllogistic reasoning is to be used. Bosmajian points out that if the major premise is understood to mean "Separation is sin," then King's argument is valid.[271] Whether planned or unintentional (more than likely by design), King marshals arguments of Catholic, Jewish, and Protestant traditions to support his distinction between just and unjust laws.

Finally, King adds an illustration of the distinction he has made. If, for instance, a majority force a minority to obey a law it does not make binding on itself, it is unjust. He cites as an example voter registration in the South–available freely to all whites, but laden with obstacles for blacks. Says King, "this is difference made legal." "Sameness made legal" would be objective and fair adherence to the law by all parties.

As a result of this argument, King decides when a law is just, moral, and right (not just legal) and thus can be obeyed. By the same token, he decides what laws are to be disobeyed. At no time is King disrespectful of the law. He never advised "evading or defying the law" which would lead to anarchy. But when he was morally compelled to disobey what he conceived to be an unjust law, he did so reluctantly and with willingness to accept the penalty laid down by the law.

Therefore King stands in the tradition of the classical understanding of civil disobedience. Out of obedience to a higher law (God) one can follow the dictates of his conscience and break the law. And out of respect for the man-made law of the state, one accepts the consequences of his act, a punishment of some sort.

Jail, as for most civil resisters, was a significant symbol for King. He and Gandhi both agreed with Thoreau, "Under a government which imprisons any unjustly, the true place for a just man is also in prison."[272]

Early in the Montgomery struggle he sensed a certain pride in being convicted by a local court. It really meant for King a deep identification with his people who were suffering segregation. He felt he was guilty only of the "crime of desiring for my people the inalienable rights of life, liberty, and the pursuit of happiness."[273] As "filling the jails" continued in the movement King observed that going to jail became for the average Negro not a disgrace, but a "badge of honor." The racial revolution alleviated the external causes of the Negro misery and also renewed within him a sense of his own human dignity. "He was *somebody*. He had a sense of *somebodiness*. He was impatient to be free."[274] This is an echo of Thoreau's, "I think that we should be men first, and subjects afterward."[275]

The article in "Love, Law, and Civil Disobedience" concludes with the profound belief in the future made possible by the attempts at justice and the moral order of the universe. And so the participants in the movement sing, "We shall overcome."

H. *Nonviolence: Tactic and Principle*

The two main levels of nonviolence are usually termed "tactic and way of life" (Lynd), "policy and faith" (Gandhi), and "practical and moral" (King).

The method of nonviolence as a form of protest has a long tradition in America and in the world. Wherever it has been practiced on a large scale, as in the mass movement of Gandhi's campaigns or the civil rights movement in America, most participants regarded it as an effective tactical weapon to achieve their goals. In both India and in most of our southern communities the resisters were in the majority but were lacking in weapons that would make for superior physical strength.

In each movement, however, there were sufficient number of completely dedicated men and women, authentic *Satyagrahis*, for whom nonviolence was a way of life, that they leavened the masses. Gandhi and King were certainly numbered among the latter. Both held firmly to nonviolence as a principle and a tactic. Kenneth Clark, in an interview with King, asked about the relationship between nonviolent technique and love of an oppressor. King replied that the former is a "method of action," a way of alleviating or correcting a social wrong, but without the use of physical violence. The latter, on the other hand, implies the acceptance of love "as a way of life." And although many more people identify with the former than the latter, King insists he accepts both.

> I think that nonviolent resistance is the most potent weapon available to oppressed people in their struggle for freedom and human dignity.[276]

By "potent weapon," King means both morally and practically. Early in 1956, as he was beginning to think through the activity of the movement, he concluded that the use of violence would be both "impractical and immoral."[277]

King was quick to admit that there were relatively few resisters absolutely committed to nonviolence as a way of life. But because it was presented to them "as a simple expression of Christianity in action, they were willing to use it as a technique."[278] This was particularly true in the southern communities. The writer recalls that Negroes were given instructions during the Selma campaign to seek other ways of serving, i.e. driving taxis, preparing food, providing lodging, etc., if they could not accept nonviolence even as a technique. Many others during the campaign accepted it as a technique to achieve an end without making it their life ideal.

But King never refused offers for participation. He felt that even at the level of technique, people could help and if they came this far, they may even "adopt nonviolence later as a way of life."[279] So, for King, a "principled commitment to nonviolence" was not necessary before one participated in the movement.

> Far from it. It is quite possible, and even probably, that American Negroes will adopt nonviolence as a means, an instrument for the achievement of specific and limited ends. This was certainly true in the case of Gandhi himself, for many who followed him, like Nehru himself, did so on this kind of basis. Certainly, it would be wrong and even disastrous, to demand principled agreement on nonviolence as a precondition to nonviolent action. What is

required is the spiritual determination of the people to be true to the principle as it works *in this specific action*. This was the case in Montgomery, and it will continue to be the rule in further developments of our struggle.[280]

Some of the mistakes admitted by King, namely, that he should have stayed in jail in Montgomery and that the goals for Albany were too vaguely defined, could be construed as tactical errors within the framework of nonviolence.[281]

Another example of tactical maneuvering was the refusal to continue the second march from Selma to Montgomery in March of 1965. King was severely criticized for this decision. His response was, "It was not that we didn't intend to go on to Montgomery, but that in consideration of our commitment to nonviolent action, we knew we could not go under the present conditions."[282]

The above illustrations serve to show the place of compromise within the nonviolent movement. King was always prepared to compromise. He conceived it to be a necessity in a time of social ferment and transition, "but it must be the creative, honest compromise of a policy, not the negative and cowardly compromise of a principle."[283]

We may safely conclude that nonviolence as a tactic, led by a few committed to it as a way of life, was successful in southern communities where the Negro was often in the majority and could effect the economy of the community if he desired. It was successful, also, because as this group of underprivileged and deprived citizens were beaten and humiliated by police and the KKK, the conscience of America was pricked.

This "tactical theory of nonviolent direct action" was their only hope for victory. And so through various methods of demonstrations, boycotts, sit-ins, kneel-ins, stand-ins, marches, voter registration drives, all nonviolent, the movement progressed until the middle sixties. It was, as King said, the only real alternative to a blood-bath, which violence would have produced, and the black nationalism of the Muslims.[284]

King moved tactically, within the larger framework of nonviolence, from the passive resistance of boycott in Montgomery to the nonviolent direct action in Birmingham and Selma. In the latter communities, confrontation with the police and the other authorities was planned and civil disobedience was an integral part of the campaign.

In the southern communities there was a base of moral and religious tradition whose conscience could be tapped. The appeal to conscience was successful. The communities were also small enough so that a nonviolent campaign could disrupt them sufficiently to draw the attention of the state and the nation.

> In the South, a march was a social earthquake; in the North, it is a faint, brief, exclamation of protest.[285]

But a decided tactical shift took place in King's strategy for the urban northern ghettoes. He was convinced that, until justice is present, nonviolent direct action would continue to be a strategic source of power,[286] but there was a change in emphasis. This was required in order to affect the intransigence of the northern economic, ideological, and political power structures.

In *Where Do We Go From Here*, King speaks of the dual approach he hoped to use in the North. 1) There would still be the employment of mass action. He had confidence this would work in the North even though many of his friends thought that legislation, welfare, and anti-poverty programs would suffice. Some felt that after the riots in the summer of 1967, demonstrations would be rendered ineffective. 2) To supplement this direct action of masses of people would be a very serious organization of the community at the local level. In terms of jobs, housing, and education, this grassroots political organization would be indispensable in a complex urban area.[287]

The tactical shift that took place in the urban north (especially Chicago) was based on an ideological shift in emphasis. The appeal in the north, because of its "enormous, entrenched evil" could not be to conscience, but had to be to self-interest. This shift was brought about also because of the futility and despair blacks were beginning to feel as white resistance began to harden. There seemed now little ground for optimism and less basis for patience.

Now nonviolent direct action was moved up to a new level of mass civil disobedience, involving 100,000 Negroes, if necessary. The purpose would be "to make municipal operations difficult to conduct"[288] and "be a force that interrupts its (a city's) functioning at some key point."[289] This verges on what might be called nonviolent sabotage. King further reasoned,

> To dislocate the functioning of a city without destroying it can be more effective than a riot because it can be longer-lasting, costly to the larger society, but not wantonly destructive.[290]

Riots for King were counterproductive. They were self-defeating and not genuinely revolutionary, but reactionary. Riots could be more easily quelled by superior physical force than masses on the march. That is why in one of his last written articles, he claimed there was now no longer a choice between nonviolence and riots, but between "militant, massive nonviolence or riots."[291]

King was realistic enough to know that white society would ultimately resist the nonviolent tactics of Negroes. He tried to communicate that "nonviolence is a powerful demand for reason and justice," and "if it is rudely rebuked, it is not transformed into resignation and passivity."[292] The South, because of long association with black feeling and mentality, knew this. The North did not yet know that the alternative would be intolerable violence.

It was in this context and mood that the Poor People's Campaign was planned—a sustained, massive, direct action, nonviolent movement of civil disobedience on a national scale, but focused in Washington, D.C.[293]

King seemed committed to the tactic of nonviolent mass demonstrations. He was confident that just as they had dealt successfully with the social problems of segregation (public accommodations) by massive demonstrations, and just as successfully with political segregation (the right to vote), so economic segregation (jobs, housing, education) could be destroyed by nonviolent demonstrations.

However, from time to time, in Chicago and elsewhere, King was persuaded not to use those massive numbers of people in demonstrations. What they would have accomplished in Chicago one can only speculate, but they would have been unprecedented in this country. One suspects that Gandhi would have followed through on the mass marches with commitment and determination.

Once King adopted the principle of nonviolence as a way of life in Montgomery, we can trace the consistency of his loyalty to that principle through his life.

–when his home was bombed in January 1956[294]
–his resolution not to carry a gun himself[295]
–his handling of The Rev. U. J. Fields, who had mishandled M.I.A. funds[296]
–after the victory in Montgomery, he said to his fellow Negroes, "As we go back to the busses, let us be loving enough to turn an enemy into a friend. We must now move from protest to reconciliation.[297]
–the integrated bus suggestions[298]

–the practice sessions in nonviolence[299]
–King's statement upon leaving the hospital in New York September 30, 1958 after being stabbed by Mrs. Izola Curry, contained no ill will at all toward her.[300]

King was offered the Deanship of the School of Religion at Howard University by Mordecai Johnson, but declined it in a letter to Johnson dated July 5, 1957. His response contains the growing commitment to nonviolence.

> I have thought and prayed over the decision many, many times since I talked with you last. After giving this offer every consideration, I have come to the conclusion that my work in the South is not quite complete, or at least I have not been able to do several things that I would like to see done before leaving. The vast possibilities of a nonviolent, non-cooperation approach to the solution of the race problem are still challenging indeed. I would like to remain a part of the unfolding development of this approach for a few more years.[301]

However, nothing sums up King's personal convictions about nonviolence any better than a statement written in the last month of his life. It reveals his utter and radical commitment to the principle of nonviolence.

> I'm just not going to kill anybody, whether it's in Vietnam or here. I'm not going to burn down any building. If nonviolent protest fails this summer, I will continue to preach it and teach it, and we at the SCLC will still do this. I plan to stand by nonviolence because I have found it to be a philosophy of life that regulates not only my dealings in the struggle for racial justice but also my dealings with people, with my own self. I will still be faithful to nonviolence.[302]

FOUR

Christian Realism

A. *Introduction*

In the latter part of the third and the early part of the fourth decade of this century, an increasing number of American theologians became wary of some of the content and much of the fruit of Protestant liberalism.

The men most often associated with this reaction against liberalism are Walter Marshal Horton, John Coleman Bennett, H. Richard Niebuhr, Robert Lowry Calhoun, and Reinhold Niebuhr. The latter became the most influential spokesman for the movement. Indeed, the publication of his *Moral Man and Immoral Society* in 1932 usually signals the dividing line between the older liberalism and the radical re-construction of liberal theology.

It is important to emphasize the word "re-construction." All the aforementioned theologians were trained in the liberal tradition and, for one reason or another, found liberal faith inadequate to meet the needs of the times or deficient in its understanding of the nature of God and man. Most of them retained a deep appreciation for the insight of liberal theology and could more appropriately be called "post-liberals" than the somewhat incriminating label, "neo-orthodox."

In the first place, what these men were after was not simply a return to orthodoxy, much less a reversion to fundamentalism. That would have been virtually impossible for them, reared as they were in the liberal method, having been steeped in the liberal criticism of scripture, its appreciation for history and its concern for the church's relationship to the world.

Secondly, the neo-orthodox movement represented by Barth and Brunner, especially the former, was a more severe reaction to liberalism than the thought of Reinhold Niebuhr and John Bennett. The "theology of crisis," as it was also known on the continent, did, however, have some affinity with its American counterpart, especially in the areas of faith and reason, church and culture, and a renewed appreciation of the revelation of God in Christ.

On the whole, the American reaction, which has variously been called "Christian Realism" or "Realistic Theology," was a slightly more moderate reaction with a pragmatic element retained in it. This is illustrated by the concern for ethics, especially social ethics.

In any case, these men, Reinhold Niebuhr and his followers, came to the conviction that the biblical understanding of man, symbolized by the myth of the Fall, was a far more accurate, more *realistic* understanding of the human situation than either the pessimism of Christian orthodoxy or the optimism of Christian liberalism. So, as one commentator puts it, "The designation of the new movement as 'realistic theology' . . . refers primarily to its doctrine of *human nature*, and particularly to its conviction that man is a sinner."[1]

Walter M. Horton, in his classic study of realistic theology, suggests that there was a resurgence of realism about this time in many fields–political, literary, philosophical, and theological.

> Yet all these forms of realism have in common a certain temper of mind which craves objectivity and fears subjectivism; which prefers objective realities, however disagreeable, to subjective fancies, however glorious; and which means to be guided by these realities in every form of human quest, whether for truth, or for artistic beauty, or for political stability and progress.[2]

Just as there was a revolt in the name of romanticism against the rationalism and classicism of the eighteenth century, so there was now a revolt in the name of "realism" against the romanticism, the idealism, the optimism, the liberalism of the nineteenth century.[3]

The one objective and empirically verifiable base, from which more realistic theologians operated, was the doctrine of original sin or the egoistic predicament of every man. This could be documented. This was a fact of the human experience.

We shall see that Reinhold Niebuhr's Christian anthropology was determinative of his criticism of liberal and orthodox Christianity. Martin Luther King, Jr. was an heir of this movement through the influence of Reinhold Niebuhr.

B. *Reinhold Niebuhr*

Called the "most important living American theologian,"[4] Niebuhr was the moving spirit and leading mentor of the school of realistic theology. His contribution to American thought is his attempt to correlate, as well as to transcend, classical orthodoxy and American Protestant liberalism. On the one hand, orthodoxy had no satisfying social vision, and on the other hand, liberalism had inadequate theological concern.

Niebuhr's analysis resulted in a liberal social ethic with profound theological and biblical roots. This rather enigmatic combination gave rise to the observation that Niebuhr moved "politically to the left" and "theologically to the right."[5]

Like Soren Kierkegaard, Niebuhr is a dangerous author. His deeply held convictions, incisive logic, and relentless unmasking of all hidden motives in individual and social behavior have a tendency to grasp the reader. This is, undoubtedly, why King, reflecting on Niebuhr's influence, said in his "Pilgrimage to Nonviolence"

> The prophetic and realistic elements in Niebuhr's passionate style and profound thought were appealing to me, and I became so enamored of his social ethics that I almost fell into the trap of accepting uncritically everything he wrote.[6]

1. The Dialectical Stance of Niebuhr

A clue to Niebuhr's labors as critic, prophet, and apologist is found in a concluding observation to an anecdote recorded in his *Leaves From a Notebook of a Tamed Cynic*. "It is in relationships and totalities that life's meaning is revealed."[7]

He consistently refuses to be "one-sided." He knows that every finite situation has at least two sides and, hence, no historical relativity has his unqualified stamp of approval. A dialectical "yes" and "no" are pronounced upon all human achievements.

This methodology involves Niebuhr in the constant use of certain words which reflect this stance: pretension, tentative, proximate. All attempts to claim a monopoly on truth, whether it be Christian orthodoxy, Protestant liberalism, secular humanism, Marxism, or bourgeois culture, are illusory and potentially idolatrous because they have not come to grips with the totality of things.

So there is a dialectical relation between theology and politics, time and eternity, God and the world, sin and grace, spirit and nature, church and the world, reason and revelation, motive and achievement, and transcendence and immanence. This "yes and no" quality permeates his thought. This stance is seen clearly in *Beyond Tragedy*, the thesis of which, according to Niebuhr, is

> that the biblical view of life is dialectical because it affirms the meaning of history and of man's natural existence, on the one hand, and on the other insists that the center, source, and fulfillment of history lie beyond history.[8]

As the book progresses, Niebuhr indicates how central this stance is to his thinking.

> Prophetic religion is more rigorous than priestly religion. It speaks an eternal "no" to all human pretension. Priestly religion, on the other hand, appreciates what points to the eternal in all human values.[9]

> Only the word of the eternal God must be heard in the Temple, a word of judgment upon human sin and of mercy for sinners.[10]

> All of us will always have something of the false prophet in us, wherefore we ought to speak humbly. We will mistake our dreams for the word of God.[11]

> History may defeat the Christ but it nevertheless points to him as the law of life. Thus every deed of love points to an ultimate triumph in the very hour of its defeat.[12]

This dialectical approach protects man from fear by assuring him of meaning from eternity and yet it keeps him humble by exposing all the relativities of history. Or, in Niebuhr's language, this realism will save man from cynicism and defeatism on the one hand, and from sentimentality and illusion on the other. Thus it is in relationships and totalities that life's meaning is comprehended.

This rejection of absolutism is further illustrated by his criticism of the "reactionary illusions of Hegel, the bourgeois illusions of Comte and the proletarian illusions of Marx." All of them, according to Niebuhr, "imagined themselves in possession of both a philosophy and social existence which could not be challenged by the future," even though all preceding ideologies had been challenged. They thought "they had arrived at a life and thought which belonged to the 'things that are' in an absolute sense." Their downfall, their "illusion," was their assumption that "the future would no longer be a threat but only a promise."[13]

The plea for wholeness is further illustrated by his criticism of orthodox and liberal Christianity. Both have tended to dissolve the paradoxical relation of God and man in the revelation of Christ by coming down on one side or the other; orthodoxy by stripping Christ of all his radically historical qualities and liberalism by simply seeing Christ as an heroic figure who reveals the potential goodness latent in all of us. "In either case the total human situation which the myths of the Christ and the Cross illumines, is obscured."[14]

C. Themes in Niebuhr Influential on King

1. Niebuhr's View of Human Nature

Niebuhr's understanding of man is a dialectical one. Man is a composite of God-likeness on the one hand and creatureliness on the other. This creatureliness never leaves him even when he evidences spiritual depth; and in his most sinful moments, the capacity for self-transcendence is evident. He is able to see his involvement in nature's necessities, but never able to escape them. Thus man is strong and weak, free and bound, limited and limitless. He is made for eternity, yet is very much a part of the temporal.

But man is always conscious of his weakness, limitation, and dependence. This, according to Niebuhr, places man at the "juncture of nature and spirit," and involves him in both necessity and freedom. This analysis of human nature is not new. Niebuhr is dependent upon the previous observations of Paul, Augustine, Luther, Pascal, and Kierkegaard-all champions of the dialectical nature of man.

Niebuhr's unique emphasis in his doctrine of man is the prevalence of the egoistic impulse in each man and in every dimension of man's activity. It is difficult to draw a line between selflessness and selfishness. Niebuhr's examination of our motives reveals our predicament.

> The mixture of motives in any person is so complex and bewildering that none of us can be certain of any judgments which pretend to search the secrets of man's hearts. We cannot even be certain about our judgments of our own motives, perhaps least of all our own.[15]

Man cannot overcome his sinful self-contradiction, not even by well-intentioned moral action, "since every moral action, even the highest and purest, expresses it."[16]

How does something become so inwardly contradictory? What is the source of this "sickness"? Niebuhr has a simple, yet penetrating answer.

"Man is mortal–that is his fate. Man pretends not to be mortal–that is his sin."[17] This is man's absolute refusal to accept his finiteness, his creaturehood. This is rebellion against God; this is pride (*hybris*). Let us examine its inevitability.

Niebuhr feels that the Christian view of man is unique in that 1) it indicates man's capacity for self-transcendence in the doctrine of the Imago-Dei, 2) it insists on man's finiteness and dependence, since he is a part of the natural order; and 3) the evil in man is a consequence of his "inevitable though not necessary" unwillingness to accept his dependence.[18]

These three observations are indispensable clues to Niebuhr's thought. The first two are merely descriptions, while the third goes on to draw an important conclusion. The world is not evil in itself; evil is finite man attempting to be infinite. Therefore, the most concise notion of sin for Niebuhr is

> the consequences of man's inclination to usurp the prerogatives of God, to think more highly of himself than he ought to think, thus making destructive use of his freedom by not observing the limits to which a creaturely freedom is bound.[19]

Niebuhr's analysis of pride as expressed in intellectual, moral, and spiritual power is as profound as any in contemporary theology. This effort on the part of man to establish himself as his own Lord is what Christian orthodoxy has called "original sin." Man's "falling" into sin is not rationally or logically necessary, although it is inevitable. It is committed in man's freedom.

> Prophetic religion attributes moral evil to an evil will rather than to the limitations of natural evil. . . . There is, therefore, an element of perversity, a conscious choice of the lesser good, involved in practically every moral action. . . .[20]

Christianity

> does not believe that man is an egotist because he is an ego. Sin arises out of man's freedom and not out of his individuality.[21]

Because sin is the inevitable clash of man's will with God's loving will, it is a decisive act and man is responsible. "The fact of responsibility is attested by the feeling of remorse or repentance which follows the sinful action."[22] It is precisely this "depth-understanding" of man's nature that embarrassed liberal Protestantism. It could not accept Niebuhr's judgment of man's radical egoism and self-centeredness.

Some of his most biting criticism is levied against the liberal churchmen's failure to deal with the sin of man. This failure stems from a naivete which suggested that education would eventually eliminate such evils as racial prejudice, one form of original sin. According to Niebuhr.

> Race bigotry is, in short, one form of original sin. Original sin is something darker and more terrible than mere stupidity and is therefore not eradicated by enlightenment alone, though frequently enlightenment can break some of its power by robbing it of some of its instruments of stupidity. . . . Race bigotry, in other words, must be broken by repentance and not merely by enlightenment. . . . The liberal church merely preaches ethnic good will. It is too simply moralistic to come to terms with the hidden power of sin in the lives of men.[23]

And even more penetratingly

> The liberal church, which has assumed that the right kind of religious education would eliminate race prejudice, might well engage in some contrite reflection upon the fact that liberal churches have not become interracial by force of their educational program, and that there are not a half dozen churches in our whole nation that have transcended race pride in their corporate life to any considerable degree.[24]

The liberal church, its understanding of human nature largely derived from the optimism of the Renaissance and Enlightenment, assumed that men really had the resources and ability to fulfill the gospel demands.

> The faith which regards the love commandment as a simple possibility rather than an impossible possibility is rooted in a faulty analysis of human nature which fails to understand that though man always stands under infinite possibilities and is potentially related to the totality of existence, he is, nevertheless, and will remain, a creature of finiteness.[25]

The liberal church's optimism was often expressed in the idea that the problem of justice can be solved by "returning to the ideal of the good king" or by attempting to "introduce pure goodness without power into the world." Niebuhr sees the Oxford Movement as representative of the former. They thought that the Kingdom of God would come if Henry Ford or Adolf Hitler were converted. Pacifism illustrates the latter point. But absolutists or perfectionists, who think that goodness and love will be realized in human relationships if only they resolve to have it so

> do not understand the sinful contradictions in human nature and do not see that even the man who tries to live in terms of pure love will display qualities of selfishness in his life from which other men must be protected.[26]

> One of the most unfortunate facts about our contemporary moral situation is that the churches ceased to convict men of selfishness at the precise moment in history when human greed is more obvious and more dangerous than at any previous time. Nowhere has the liberal church played more false to its generation than in its optimistic and romantic interpretation of human nature, just when an industrial civilization revealed the drive of self-interest in all its antisocial power.[27]

But Marxism also is liable to the same judgment. It suffers from an "illusion" derived from a romantic conception of human nature. Marxists did not realize that men would be as evil on the other side of the revolution as they were on this side. They think

> that the inclination of men to take advantage of each other is a corruption which was introduced into history by the institution of property. It therefore assumes that the socialization of property will eliminate human egotism. Its failure to understand the perennial and persistent character of human egotism in any possible society, prompts it to make completely erroneous estimates of human behavior on the other side of a revolution.[28]

Niebuhr is convinced that controversies arising out of social, economic, and political conflict are not between the righteous and the sinful, but always between sinners. For all men are equally sinners before God.[29]

But not all men are equally guilty before God. If this were not so, there would be no preference for the victim over the oppressor and no historical distinction between the congenital liar and the moderately truthful man.

Niebuhr recalls that Biblical religion stresses inequality as much as the equality of sin. For instance, rather "severe judgments fall upon the rich and the powerful, the mighty and the noble, the wise and the righteous. . ."[30]

The prophets championed the rights of the poor and disadvantaged and strongly criticized the mighty, accusing them of pride and injustice. Indeed, Niebuhr saw a direct relation between injustice and pride. Injustice will follow pride as it follows power. If a man seeks to be the center of his own existence, he offends God, who is the authentic center of his life, but he will inevitably set himself against other lives which have a rightful place in the "harmony of the whole."

> It is interesting how clearly the prophets saw the relation to each other of power, pride, and injustice; and how unfailingly they combine their strictures against the religious sin of pride and the social sin of injustice.[31]

It is for this reason that Niebuhr says white men have sinned against Negroes in Africa and America more than Negroes have sinned against white men. The white man's ego has been allowed to expand because of the accidents of history and the possession of power. The ego has expanded

> both vertically and horizontally. Its vertical expansion, its pride, involves it in sin against God. Its horizontal expansion involves it in an unjust effort to gain security and prestige at the expense of its fellows.[32]

2. King on the Nature of Man

Although King remains fundamentally a liberal theologian, there is no question that Niebuhr qualified significantly his optimistic view of human nature received from his courses in theology from George W. Davis. When King began to read Niebuhr he was a Crozer senior and had been greatly influenced already by the liberal insights of the social gospel and personalism.

His reflections on liberal Christianity, as found in both versions of "Pilgrimage to Nonviolence," contain essentially the same material. There is an overriding appreciation of liberalism's devotion to truth and its rational method. But King questions liberalism precisely at the point of its view of human nature and does so with grateful acknowledgment to Niebuhr. Although King found Niebuhr's criticism of pacifism misguided, he was "constructively influenced" by Niebuhr's doctrine of man.

> Niebuhr's great contribution to contemporary theology is that he has refuted the false optimism characteristic of a great segment of Protestant liberalism, without falling into the anti-rationalism of the continental theologian Karl Barth, or the semi-fundamentalism of other dialectical theologians.[33]

King further acknowledged Niebuhr's insight into the behavior of man as a social being, in nations and classes, his perception of the complex character of human motivation, the relation between morality and power, and the fact that sin and evil appear at every level of man's existence.

These elements in Niebuhr's thinking helped me to recognize the illusions of a superficial optimism concerning human nature and the dangers of a false idealism. While I still believed in man's potential for good, Niebuhr made me realize his potential for evil as well. Moreover, Niebuhr helped me to recognize the complexity of man's social involvement and the glaring reality of collective evil.[34]

In the *Strength to Love* version of "Pilgrimage to Nonviolence," King places his discussion of man in the framework of Hegelian dialectic. While rejecting some aspects of liberal theology, he does not unconditionally accept the tenets of neo-orthodoxy. Liberalism tends to be too optimistic in its stress on man's essential goodness; neo-orthodoxy too pessimistic with its stress on man's essential evil.

An adequate understanding of man is found neither in the thesis of liberalism nor in the antithesis of neo-orthodoxy, but in a synthesis which reconciles the truths of both.[35]

The charge of pessimism made by King against Niebuhr must be briefly examined. He first makes it in *Stride Toward Freedom* when he is discussing the influence of Boston University. It was at the latter institution that King

came to see that Niebuhr had overemphasized the corruption of human nature. His pessimism concerning human nature was not balanced by an optimism concerning divine nature. He was so involved in diagnosing man's sickness of sin that he overlooked the cure of grace.[36]

This again is a caricature and it reveals that King did not really appreciate the dialectical nature of Niebuhr's thought. What often seems pessimistic for some liberal-minded thinkers is, in fact, Niebuhr's realistic analysis of the human situation. More careful and extensive reading in Niebuhr[37] would find that he often juxtaposes the "defeatism" of Christian orthodoxy and the "sentimentality" of liberal Protestantism and although he admits there is more "realism" in defeatism than sentimentality, he would opt for the realistic middle course in which achievement of maximum justice would be sought.

Further, Niebuhr maintains that he can appreciate the grandeur and misery of man more than the liberal[38] and criticizes the "deficiency of both bourgeois and Marxist social theory in estimating the indeterminate possibilities of historic vitalities. . . ."[39] This deficiency stems from an attempt to understand man "without considering the final dimension of his spirit; his transcendent freedom over both the natural and the historical process in which he is involved."[40]   In this way, both the creative and the destructive possibilities in man are more profoundly understood.

And in one of his essays on love and justice, he states that men "are not completely blinded by self-interest or lost in this maze of historical relativity."[41]   There always remains with them the law of love, "which they dimly recognize as the law of their being."

> It is the weakness of Protestant pessimism that it denies the reality of this potential perfection and its relevance in the affairs of politics.[42]

Gordon Harland is probably correct when he notes that it was because Niebuhr challenged the simple moralism of liberal Christianity that he acquired the reputation for being a pessimist.[43]

That King is somewhat inconsistent in his reaction to Niebuhr is found in a passage which contains the same "pessimism" with which he charges Niebuhr. It is a passage which could have been penned by Niebuhr and clearly illustrates the influence of the latter on King's understanding of man.

> You must come to see that it is possible for a man to be self-centered in his self-denial and self-righteous in his self-sacrifice. He may be generous in order to feed his ego and pious in order to feed his pride. Man has the tragic capacity to relegate a heightening virtue to a tragic vice. Without love benevolence becomes egotism, and martyrdom becomes spiritual pride.[44]

Further, in his sermon "What is Man?," King suggests that a materialistic and strictly humanistic view of man are inadequate. There are those, he said, who seek to be a "little more realistic about man," who wish to reconcile the truths of these positions while avoiding the extremes of both.

> They contend that the truth about man is found neither in the thesis of pessimistic materialism nor the antithesis of optimistic humanism, but in a higher synthesis. Man is neither villain nor hero; he is rather both villain and hero.[45]

Presumably, King agrees with those who are more "realistic," for later on in the sermon, he said:

> we err when we assume that because man is made in the image of God, man is basically good. Through his all too prevalent inclination for evil, man has terribly scarred God's image.[46]

This is precisely the dialectical nature of man which Niebuhr describes. In fact, in this sermon, King refers to Niebuhr's *Moral Man and Immoral Society*, relating the depths to which man's sinfulness can fall, e.g., white supremacy and brutal wars. He concludes by saying, "Man is a sinner in need of God's forgiving grace. This is not deadening pessimism, it is Christian realism."[47]

Perhaps the essence of King's understanding of man, however, is found in an article, "Love, Law, and Civil Disobedience" published by *New South* in December 1961. In it, he discusses six "philosophical precepts" underlying the nonviolent movement.[48]

The fifth point made by King in this exposition is that "there is within human nature an amazing potential for goodness."[49] He does not mean by this that people are basically good. He admits to a "strange dichotomy of disturbing dualism" within man and used Plato's charioteer, Ovid, Augustine, and Carlyle to document this internal conflict in the human personality.

King concludes that man is "neither innately good nor is he innately bad; he has the potentialities for both."[50] Jesus and Gandhi can appeal to the goodness in man and Hitler to their evil dimension, but, and this "but" is strategic, for what follows is determinative for King's anthropology.

> But we must never forget that there is something within human nature that can respond to goodness, that man is not totally depraved, to put it in theological terms, the image of God is never totally gone . . . the worst segregationist can become an integrationist . . . there is something within human nature that can be changed and this stands at the top of . . . the philosophy of nonviolence.[51]

If King is not moving away from a fundamental Niebuhrian dialectic, he is here more "optimistic" than Niebuhr would allow.

Another specific Niebuhrian influence on King's own anthropology is what might be called the historicity of reason. For Niebuhr there is no unprejudiced mind and no person devoid of pride. Hence our reasoning is always tainted with self-interest and tends to serve the egoistic impulse. Niebuhr thinks the distinction Whitehead made between the "speculative" reason which Plato shared with God and the "pragmatic" reason which Ulysses shared with the foxes is a valid one, but you cannot draw too sharp a line between the two.

For man's spirit is a unity; and the most perfect vantage point of impartiality and disinterestedness in human reason remains in organic relation to a particular center of life, individual and collective, seeking to maintain its precarious existence against competing forms of life and vitality.[52]

Or, more succinctly,

The will-to-power uses reason, as kings use courtiers and chaplains to add grace to their enterprise. Even the most rational men are never quite rational when their own interests are at stake.[53]

One of the prominent themes in *Moral Man and Immoral Society* is the facility of privileged groups to defend "rationally" (Niebuhr would say rationalize) their privileged position. Inequalities of privilege cannot be defended rationally, so the privileged must be extraordinarily subtle and clever in "inventing specious proofs for the theory that universal values spring from, and that general interest are served by, the special privilege which they hold."[54]

From Niebuhr's analysis of man's egocentric predicament, King learned how reason can serve vested interests, be conditioned by social status, and be under the doctrine of sin. This is obvious from the following passage.

I also came to see that the superficial optimism of liberalism concerning human nature overlooked the fact that reason is darkened by sin. The more I thought about human nature the more I saw how our tragic inclination for sin encourages us to rationalize our actions. Liberalism failed to show that reason by itself is little more than an instrument to justify men's defensive ways of thinking. Reason, devoid of the purifying power of faith, can never free itself from distortions and rationalization.[55]

Apparently King was influenced by Niebuhr's *Children of Light and Children of Darkness* and the observations concerning human nature made there. This is seen in the tone, content, and actual use of the phrase itself, as King, a black man, views "realistically" the racial problem. King knew, and Niebuhr would agree, that his most troublesome adversary was not the KKK or a Senator Eastland, who were unabashed children of darkness. Their prejudice was visible and their position known. You could deal with them in an open and honest way. The innocent, naive children of light were more difficult to deal with. They often took the form of the white liberal "who is more devoted to 'order' than to justice, who prefers tranquility to equality."[56] The white liberal is often guilty of seeing integration in terms of tokenism in society and business and is oblivious to his latent prejudice. The foolish children of light, according to Niebuhr, champion the cause of minority groups in order to prove they are not as bad as their critics say they are.

> It would be more helpful if we began with the truer assumption that there is no unprejudiced mind and no judgment which is not, at least partially, corrupted by pride.[57]

King was impressed with the eloquence of segregationist clergy and how effectively they could state their case and remarks

> It is still one of the tragedies of human history that the "children of darkness" are frequently more determined and zealous than the "children of light."[58]

King discusses how reluctantly structures of evil fall and how history teaches us that if time is not used constructively to resist, evil will remain. He then claims

> in this generation the children of darkness are still shrewder than the children of light. They are always zealous and conscientious in using time for their evil purposes. . . . But the forces of light cautiously wait, patiently pray and timidly act.[59]

Another example in King's thought of how the Niebuhrian influence grew is in King's understanding of group self-interest. In his report on his trip to India, he suggests that the United States should send large amounts of aid to that country and "whatever we do should be done in a spirit of international brotherhood, not national selfishness."[60] This, despite the fact that Niebuhr always insisted that nations and other political groups must act out of self-interest.

But King sees by the middle sixties the value of mastering the art of political alliances as the Negro attempts to develop political strength. They could expect to have allied with them the Puerto Ricans, labor groups, liberal whites, and some churches. And then with true Niebuhrian realism, he goes on:

> A true alliance is based upon self-interest of each component group and common interest into which they merge. For an alliance to have permanent and loyal commitment from its various elements, each of them must have a goal from which it benefits and none must have an outlook in basic conflict with the others.[61]

As King's experience grows, it seems that the idealist and visionary are qualified by a practical realism. At the conclusion of one of his papers on Niebuhr, written at Boston University Graduate School, King allows that the strength of Niebuhr's position lies in its

> critique of the easy conscience and complacency of some forms of perfectionism. He is right, it seems to me, in insisting that we must be realistic regarding the relativity of every moral and ethical choice. His analysis of the complexity of the social situation is profound indeed, and with it I would find very little to disagree.[62]

The one weakness he does find in Niebuhr, the one he most severely criticizes, and one which for King "runs the whole gamut of his writings" is the inability of Niebuhr to "deal adequately with the relative perfection which is the fact of the Christian life."[63] King claims that Niebuhr does not deal satisfactorily with the problem of spiritual growth, Christian values in personality, and how *agape* is concretely realized in human nature and history. He concludes his critical section of the paper with a criticism of Niebuhr made by Walter Muelder which includes the following comment

> There is a Christian perfectionism which may be called a prophetic meliorism. . . . Niebuhr's treatment of much historical perfectionism is well-founded criticism from an abstract ethical viewpoint, but it hardly does justice to the constructive historical contributions of the perfectionist sects within the Christian fellowship and even within the secular order. There is a kind of Christian assurance which releases creative energy into the world and which in actual fellowship rises above the conflicts of individual and collective egoism.[64]

3. Niebuhr's MORAL MAN AND IMMORAL SOCIETY

This book, in reality a Marxist critique of American Christian culture, had a great impact on King and the impression it made unfolds throughout his writings. It is the only book by Niebuhr he refers to by name and, indirectly, it is mentioned several times.[65]

There are three themes in *Moral Man and Immoral Society* particularly influential on King. They all relate to the central thesis of the book, namely, that a distinction should be made between the moral and social behavior of individuals and of social groups.[66] The individualistic ethic prevalent in

Protestantism is fundamentally scandalized by and ultimately irrelevant to the political and social realities indispensable for group life.[67]

Niebuhr does not mean to imply that man, individually, is essentially moral, and society is immoral. He did not intend that absolute distinction. He did mean to say that man is able to be relatively more moral than social groups. The egoistic impulse, however, is more unqualified in collectives than in personal relationships.

King, writing a sermon on the nature of man, recalls this theme. "Man's sinfulness sinks to such devastating depths in his collective life that Reinhold Niebuhr could write a book entitled *Moral Man and Immoral Society*."[68]

a. *The Appreciation of Power*

In *Moral Man and Immoral Society*, Niebuhr argues for a realistic understanding of the significance of power. Liberal moralists (secular and religious) have usually, in the face of power, defaulted to defeatism or sentimentality. This has happened because they tend to be absolutist in their ethical standards and fail to see that relations between groups are basically political, not ethical. That is

> they are determined by the proportion of power which each group possesses at least as much as by any rational and moral appraisal of the comparative needs and claims of each group.[69]

Politics is where "conscience and power," the ethical and the coercive, meet to "work out their tentative and uneasy compromises."[70] The issue at stake in most social conflict is the possession of or the lack of power. The kind of power most relevant for modern society is economic. Those classes or nations who are strong economically are able to create and maintain political and military strength. Social inequality is the result, not simply of the failure of religious and rational men to act more lovingly and reasonably, but because there is a disproportion of power. That power has the inherent ability to entrench itself infinitely, because it is the source of privilege and advantage. Hence, "dominant classes are always the slowest to yield power. . . ."[71]

b. *The Mistrust of Power*

Niebuhr says that the history of nations bears testimony to the validity of James Madison's words: "The truth is that all men having power ought to be mistrusted."[72]

This is so because power plays into the hands of proud, self-aggrandizing, sinful man. "Wherever men hold unequal power in society they will strive to maintain it,"[73] using every facility, rational and religious, legal or violent, at their disposal.

Niebuhr illustrates this demonic side of disproportionate power by his analysis of the attitudes present in the middle and proletarian classes. The latter group tends to think in terms of class solidarity, is willing to forego some of its personal freedom to attain their most cherished social goals, and probably believe that conflict, even violent, will be necessary for them to equalize the power-interests of the classes.

On the other hand, the middle class is apt to stress "liberty, respect for individual life, the rights of property and the moral values of mutual trust and unselfishness."[74]

The privileged class endorses peace and affirms that patience is virtuous because there is inevitable progress in history. The hypocrisy of the middle class is devastatingly revealed in the following statement and the truth of it must have registered in young King's mind.

> The middle classes believe in freedom, but deny freedom when its exercise imperils their position in society; they profess a morality of love and unselfishness but do not achieve an unselfish group attitude toward a less privileged group; they claim to abhor violence and yet use it both in international conflict and in the social crises in which their interests are imperiled: they want mutuality of interest between classes rather than a class struggle but the mutuality must not be so complete as to destroy all their special privileges.[75]

As an example of this hypocrisy, Niebuhr referred to southern whites in America who, while providing no adequate educational facilities for Negroes, justified their opposition to their voting rights on the basis of their illiteracy. The white minority there knew that equal education and suffrage would produce an imbalance in privilege and power.

The privileged classes resist change because they are the beneficiaries of social injustice. In their comfort they are unable to understand the problems of the victims of the injustice. Since liberal Protestantism, in the main, is

143

associated with the privileged classes, it's simple message of love is heard cynically by the dispossessed. So Niebuhr can say

> The conflict between proletarian and middle class morality is thus a contest between hypocrisy and brutality and between sentimentality and cynicism.[76]

That is also why Niebuhr contended that collective power will continue to exploit weakness and "it can never be dislodged unless power is raised against it."[77] Agreeing with Marx, Niebuhr knew, as a general rule, that the powerful, the propertied, and hence, the privileged, would relinquish neither voluntarily. It would have to be wrested from them. Religious idealism could only "qualify" the brutal and antisocial elements in the powerful, never eliminate them.

> Only the proletarian sees how the centralization of power and privilege in modern society proceeds so rapidly that it not only outrages the conscience but destroys the very foundations of society.[78]

The proletarian knows that the general welfare is not best served by a *laissez-faire* economic system. The latter sanctions a "social anarchy and political irresponsibility" that exploits the working class. And we can be sure that

> the men of power in modern industry would not, of course, capitulate simply because the social philosophy by which they justify their policies has been discredited. When power is robbed of the shining armor of political, moral and philosophical theories by which it defends itself, it will fight on without armor; but it will be more vulnerable, and the strength of its enemies is increased.[79]

So, according to Niebuhr, the oppressed, be they Indians in Asia, Negroes in America, or laborers anywhere, have a "higher moral right to challenge their oppressors than these have to maintain their rule by force."[80]

c. *Nonviolence and Social Change for the Negro*

Niebuhr concludes *Moral Man and Immoral Society* by suggesting some possibilities for the alleviation of the plight of the Negro minority in this country. He does this in a chapter called "Moral Values in Politics" in which he clearly outlines the realistic advantages the temper and method of nonviolence can yield in social conflict. Gandhi's success in India meant to

Niebuhr that "nonviolence is a particularly strategic instrument for an oppressed group which is hopelessly in the minority,"[81] and has no prospects of obtaining power enough to withstand the oppressors.

Then Niebuhr, from his realistic knowledge of intergroup tensions, his understanding of power, and his sheer prophetic insight uttered a hope in 1932 which was to prove a reality twenty-five years later in the work of Martin Luther King.

> The emancipation of the Negro race in America probably waits upon the adequate development of this kind of social and political strategy. It is hopeless for the Negro to expect complete emancipation from the menial social and economic position into which the white man has forced him, merely by trusting in the moral sense of the white race. It is equally hopeless to attempt emancipation through violent rebellion.[82]

Niebuhr realized that progress was being made in race relations. Educational advantages were being increasingly provided. Interracial study commissions helped the races better to understand one another. But all of this occurred within a system of injustice, the outer limits of which was always the tolerance level of the whites. These "progressive" measures did not fundamentally effect the black man's "political disenfranchisement or his economic disinheritance."

> However large the number of individual white men who do and who will identify themselves completely with the Negro cause, the white race in America will not admit the Negro to equal rights if it is not forced to do so. Upon that point one may speak with a dogmatism which all history justifies.[83]

But Niebuhr warned against the use of violent weapons. That would be foolish and counterproductive. Nonviolence is the relatively more effective instrument if practiced in the Gandhian manner. It could produce a greater degree of justice than either "pure moral suasion (or) violence could gain." The nonviolent campaign, says Niebuhr, could include boycotts against banks, stores, and public service corporations which discriminate against Negroes.[84] Nonpayment of taxes to states which spend a disproportionate amount of public money on white schools was also suggested.[85] Niebuhr continues his hope

> One waits for such a campaign with all the more reason and hope because the peculiar gifts of the Negro endow him with the capacity to conduct it successfully. He would need only to fuse the aggressiveness of the new and

young Negro with the patience and forbearance of the old Negro, to rob the former of its vindictiveness and the latter of its lethargy.[86]

The life and work of Martin Luther King would seem to fulfill this prophecy.

4. Influence of MORAL MAN AND IMMORAL SOCIETY on King

That King understood the meaning and necessity of power is found in Chapter 5 of Where Do We Go From Here, "Where We Are Going." He suggested in the middle sixties (when this book was written) that the Southern Christian Leadership Conference should put a priority on "studying the levers of power Negroes must grasp to influence the course of events," and let other progress assume a secondary role.

> In our society power sources are sometimes obscure and indistinct. Yet they can always finally be traced to those forces we described as ideologically economic, and political.[87]

The economic determination of morality was brought home to King in the Birmingham campaign. The Negroes there, in their struggle for equal public accommodations, sought help from United States Steel, a powerful, northern based industry, which seemingly had little to lose from involvement in the racial crisis in this Alabama City.

After some time, Roger Blough, Chairman of the Board, said that "despite United States Steel's pre-eminence in Birmingham, it would be improper for the corporation to seek to influence community policies in race relations." King responds in true Niebuhrian-Marxist language.

> If the community had enacted unreasonable taxes, or ordinances adversely affecting production, there is no doubt that the power of U.S. Steel would have been swiftly unleashed to determine a different result. Profits were not affected by racial injustice, indeed, they were benefited. Only people were hurt, and the greatest single power in Birmingham turned its back.[88]

King also sensed the easy alliance of religion and culture. "The greatest blasphemy" of the racist history of America was that the white man "ended up making God his partner in the exploitation of the Negro."

> Ethical Christianity vanished and the moral nerve of religion was atrophied. This terrible distortion sullied the essential nature of Christianity.[89]

King firmly believed that if the Church in the South would "stand up for the right of the Negroes, there would be no murder and brutality." There is some question about the truth of this unequivocal statement, given the ineffectiveness churches have in affecting social attitudes, but certainly the brutality would have been lessened. However, there is little to question about his next statement.

> The awful fact about the South is that Southerners are making the Marxist analysis of history more accurate than the Christian hope that men can be persuaded through teaching and preaching to live a new and better life. In the South, businessmen act much more quickly from economic considerations than do churchmen from moral considerations.[90]

King sees a direct relationship between privilege and power in human groups. An integrated society will be a difficult achievement because

> privileged groups, historically, have not volunteered to give up their privileges. As Reinhold Niebuhr has written, individuals may see the moral light and voluntarily abandon their unjust posture, but groups tend to be more immoral, and more intransigent than individuals.[91]

The nonrational character of a privileged group's defiance in the presence of a threat to its power is evidenced in the bitterness and hostility it expresses even when the underprivileged demand freedom in terms of love and nonviolence.[92] And even though privileged groups rarely give up their privileges without strong resistance

> when oppressed people rise up against oppression there is no stopping point short of full freedom. Realism compels us to admit that the struggle will continue until freedom is a reality for all the oppressed peoples of the world.[93]

In *Where Do We Go From Here*, the most Niebuhrian of King's books, King reaches the conclusion that "the notion that ethical appeals and persuasion alone will bring about justice" is fallacious. This contradicts his earlier optimism found in the *Nation* article "Equality Now," in which he sees the President (then Kennedy) making a "significant contribution toward the elimination of racial discrimination" by the use of "moral persuasion." And in *Strength to Love*, a confidence in rationality is expressed.

But somewhere along the way the church must remind men that, devoid of intelligence, goodness and conscientiousness will become brutal forces leading to shameful crucifixion.[94]

What King now means is that these ethical appeals "must be undergirded by some form of constructively coercive power. If the Negro does not add persistent pressure to his patient plea, he will end up empty handed."[95]

Then, in the same context, Booker T. Washington, who heretofore has been uncritically mentioned, comes in for his first real criticism from King. And it was precisely the point where King benefited most from Niebuhr.

> Washington's error was that he underestimated the structures of evil; as a consequence his philosophy of pressureless persuasion only serves as a springboard for racist Southerners to dive into deeper and more ruthless oppression of the Negro.[96]

It is interesting to note how King becomes more critical of Booker T. Washington and more appreciative of the more "radical" W. E. B. Du Bois.[97] One of the difficult lessons King learned in the civil rights struggle was that "you cannot depend upon American institutions to function without pressure."[98] King, as a young man, was apparently not sociologically sensitive enough to know that institutions are, inherently, conservative. As he matured he discovered that one has to deal directly with the evil structures of society, the systems of injustice and modify, if not remove them. Thereby a moral balance is established in which all citizens can develop their highest potential. "The thing to do is to get rid of the system and thereby create a moral balance within society."[99]

5. Niebuhr's Understanding of Love and Justice

D. B. Robertson has suggested that the relationship between love and justice is the "primary area of emphasis" in Niebuhr's thought and the "major problem" for Niebuhr in the elaboration of a social ethic.[100] For Niebuhr, the relationship between love and justice is a dialectical one and it is best expressed by him in a passage from the second volume of The Nature and Destiny of Man.

> The positive relation of principles of justice to the ideal of brotherhood makes an indeterminate approximation of love in the realm of justice possible. The

negative relation means that all historic conceptions of justice will embody some elements which contradict the law of love.[101]

That is to say, love and justice for Niebuhr can be distinguished but they are not to be separated nor to be seen as different in kind.[102] Or as Niebuhr puts it briefly, "love is both the fulfillment and the negation of all the achievements of justice in history,"[103]–fulfillment in that it serves to expand the agapeic potential of justice and negation in that it always transcends justice, to bring under judgment every realization of justice.

The ethical demands for the Christian as laid down by Jesus in the Sermon on the Mount and elsewhere, are absolute and unconditional. We are to love our neighbor in the way God has loved us, i.e., in the sense of *agape*, disinterestedly, unqualifiedly, with no thought of worth or deserving in the object of love. This ethical demand is unavoidable in Jesus's teaching.

Here we have an ethic, says Niebuhr, that we cannot disavow on the one hand, because it judges our prudential decisions nor perfectly achieve on the other, because of our self-interest.

This is what Niebuhr means by an "impossible ethical ideal."[104] But there is a profound relevance of this unattainable ideal for both the personal and the social dimensions of life, even though Jesus made no such distinction. It is a relevant ideal because, although never attained in history, it gives us an "absolute standard by which to judge both personal and social righteousness. It is one standard by comparison with which all human attainments fall short . . ."[105] or

The love ideal which Jesus incarnates may be too pure to be realized in life, but it offers us nevertheless an ideal toward which the religious spirit may strive.[106]

We more nearly approximate the love ideal in personal relations, in I-Thou encounters. Here we can be indiscriminate and more completely self-giving. We can meet the needs of the neighbor without weighing and measuring his needs against those of the self. Love is therefore "ethically purer" than justice, which is prompted by calculation, reason, prudence, and discrimination. It must be remembered, however, that Niebuhr finds the love ideal unavoidable and maintains a deep appreciation for the love which he calls a "fruit of the religious sense of the absolute."[107]

But as one enters multipersonal relationships and must decide between competing neighbor-claims, the love ideal is necessarily refracted. In the area of social behavior and conflict, where the egoistic impulse is almost unmanageable, our goal would have to be something less than the agape ideal.

In complex human relations of society, the ethical goal is not love, but the achievement of justice. Love is expressed in social relationships in terms of justice. This is not to denigrate love. Indeed, love demands justice, which is the highest approximation of love that finite man can realize in his social existence. Niebuhr described basic justice as dependent upon the

> right organization of men's common labor, the equality of their social power, regulation of their common interests, and adequate restraint upon the inevitable conflict of competing interests.[108]

Justice is the goal in "immoral society" because sacrificial love is not a simple historical possibility there. But love is always related to justice because it is a factor in all approximations of justice and as the source of the norms of justice. The organic interrelationship of love and justice is further revealed in the following observation by Niebuhr.

> In so far as justice admits the claims of the self, it is something less than love. Yet it cannot exist without love and remain justice. For without the 'grace' of love, justice always degenerates into something less than justice.[109]

Liberal Protestantism did not understand the necessary tension between love and justice because, as mentioned earlier, it did not fully grasp the depth of self-interest in man. It therefore often succumbed to the alternative of sentimentality and proposed love as a cure for every social problem.[110]

And much American Christianity did not sense the inordinate power of vested interests in social groups and classes. Because of this, it was impossible to ask nations and races to love one another. They could, however, do justice to one another, having a high sense of mutual obligation, and attempt to give each other its due.

Because of this point of view, churchmen often substituted "the law of love for the spirit of justice instead of recognizing love as the fulfillment and highest form of the spirit of justice."[111] This simple Christian moralism which admonished men to be unselfish can degenerate into "pure philanthropy without regard for the difficult task of achieving social justice (and) becomes a cloak behind which social injustice hides itself."[112]

This is brought home in a vivid fashion to Niebuhr as he reviews the conflict in the small mining community of Pineville, Kentucky. The struggle resulted from the desire to unionize the mines. He found that, ironically, liberal and fundamentalist clergy often shared the same naivete when it came to the application of Christian love to social structures.

> It is the tendency to make philanthropy the proof of the Christian spirit of love and of the honest interest of the church in the plight of the underdog, while every effort of the disinherited mass of miners to achieve social justice through concerted pressure is regarded with abhorrence, partly because it is believed to be 'unchristian' and partly because it is felt that a union scale in the mines would wipe out the whole coal industry in the state.[113]

The churchmen's fear of exerting pressure reveals their sentimentality in dealing with the real world. The church's failure to deal with power of self-love and the power of interest groups is in direct proportion to its failure to be socially effective. Power, for Niebuhr, is not necessarily evil. It may be used for good or evil ends. He criticizes the Quaker attitude of placing love and power in contradiction to each other. The children of light often forget that all forms of justice have been realized by some equilibrium of power. This contradiction leaves out the whole problem of the attainment of justice. Justice may be the servant of love, and power may be the servant of justice.[114]

He then makes a distinction between force and power, indicating that force in a narrow sense "may be an element in the arsenal of power." However, power is wider than force. "It includes all the vitalities of life by which men seek to accomplish their ends."[115] The "balance of power" is extremely important in Niebuhr's social ethics. He appreciates realistically what he calls "second-rate goodness" and the "tolerable harmonies of life." He readily concedes that a balance of power is different from and inferior to love. But it is one expression of love under sin or a basic ingredient in justice, given the sinfulness of man. Niebuhr stresses the fact that "a balance of power does not exclude love."

> In fact, without love the frictions and tensions of a balance of power would become intolerable. But without the balance of power even the most loving relations may degenerate into unjust relations, and love may become the screen which hides the injustice.[116]

151

Although he would hasten to say that all justice established by pressure should be qualified by love, he would also say that the church could do more for the cause of reconciliation if

> instead of producing moral idealists who think that they can establish justice, it would create religious and Christian realists who know that justice will require that some men shall contend against them.[117]

So, for Niebuhr, love and justice are the essentially Christian virtues while patience, longsuffering, and acceptance of the *status quo* are lesser virtues. He pleads for a profound Christian faith that would not be illusory enough to think that it could achieve unqualified justice in a sinful world and yet realistic enough not to ignore the matter of justice by an appeal to the good will of individuals and their ability to love. Rather, Niebuhr would "encourage men to create systems of justice which will save society and themselves from their own selfishness."[118]

This understanding enables Niebuhr to appreciate the place of law in society. The only realistic way to love a neighborhood or a disadvantaged segment of society is to see that humane legislation is passed which would bring as much justice to bear as possible. The amelioration of social evil will not be rapid relying on the power of the law, but it will be much more effective in a shorter time than relying upon a changed individual.

> The whip of the law cannot change the heart. But thank God it can restrain the heartless until they change their mind and heart.[119]

6. King on Love and Justice

Although King did not systematically delineate his understanding of the relationship of love to justice, it is one of the main themes in his writings. And the influence of Niebuhr is obvious and implied.

King's devastating criticism of the white liberal's sentimentality reflects Niebuhr's own analytical skill. King insists that it is insufficient for a white man to say, "We love Negroes, we have many Negro friends." He knows, as only a member of a disadvantaged group can, that the Negro needs justice, not merely love. In fact, says King, we must demand justice for Negroes, and in Niebuhrian language states

Love that does not satisfy justice is no love at all. It is merely sentimental affection, little more than what one would have for a pet. Love at its best is justice concretized.[120]

While King is here speaking of love in social relationships, "a love that demands justice," he also in the same context talks of the ideal love, *agape*; love as unconditional and oblivious to value, love that can be best experienced in personal relations.

It (love) is not conditioned upon one's staying in his place or watering down his demands in order to be considered respectable. He who contends that he "used to love the Negro, but . . ." did not truly love him in the beginning, because his love was conditioned upon the Negroes' limited demands for justice.[121]

When King speaks of justice, he means that a man must have "his due" in the Aristotelian sense and for him there is nothing abstract about this justice. "It is as concrete as having a good job, a good education, a decent house, and a share of power."[122]

For the white man, who is in a position of power, truly to love the black man, would mean the relinquishing of his power and the working toward these basic goals of social justice. This will probably be accomplished most effectively by legislation and, to a lesser degree, court orders. For, as King knew, the power would not be voluntarily surrendered.

Concerning the relationship of love and law, King is most realistic. Upon several occasions[123] King responds to the critics who claim laws are not the answer. To those who affirmed, "morality cannot be legislated," he agreed and countered with "but behavior can be regulated." As he often said, "It may be true that law can't make a man love me, but it can keep him from lynching me."[124]

He would not take sides with those who said education was the solution to the racial dilemma nor with those who advocated legislation. He chose to be dialectical again–both education and legislation were needed. The former, along with religion, would help change the attitudes and the hearts of men, while the latter would effectively control behavior.

Judicial decrees may not change the heart, but they can restrain the heartless. The law cannot make an employer love an employee, but it can prevent him from refusing to hire me because of the color of my skin. The habits, if not the hearts of people, have been and are being altered every day by legislative acts, judicial decisions, and executive orders. Let us not be misled by those who argue that segregation cannot be ended by "the force of law."[125]

King felt that it was an "immoral act" to compel a person to endure injustice waiting for another man's heart to be changed. He knew that it was impossible to change one's internal feelings through legislation. The law was never meant to do that. But that is no reason for quietism and political inaction. Laws can be passed which do not seek to control our internal feelings, but which seek to control the external effects of those feelings.

King's understanding of the place and importance of power vis-a-vis justice reveals Niebuhr's influence. The white liberal would have to reconcile himself to the fact that there would be no painless transition from the old order of injustice to the new order of justice. The exchange of entrenched power is always fraught with tension and conflict. The Negro had not achieved any of his rights without confrontation with or exerting constant pressure upon the white power structure. And King sadly concludes, "the Negro is now convinced that white America will never admit him to equal rights unless it is coerced into doing it."[126]

In one of his last published statements, King confesses in a tone more bitter than the somewhat irenic phrases of the late fifties, that the main road of escape from the ghetto will be a more equitable sharing of political power between Negroes and whites. He now sees how integrally related are power and justice.

> "Integration" is meaningless without the sharing of power. When I speak of integration I don't mean a romantic mixing of colors. I mean a real sharing of power and responsibility.[127]

King's most articulate presentation of the interrelationship of love, power, and justice is found in the chapter in *Where Do We Go From Here* entitled "Black Power." Here King, the moderate, the rational liberal, is agonizing over the shift in emphasis in the civil rights movement. He sees that the slogan of Stokely Carmichael and the increasingly militant youth of the movement has justification. Not enough progress has been made. As King said, "black power" was a cry of disappointment.

But King, being forced to confront squarely the matter of power, produces a statement that is a distillation of much of his mature ethical thought. I will quote it in full. Note especially the call for a "balance of power" and the foolishness of setting love over against power, both Niebuhrian themes.

Power, properly understood, is the ability to achieve purpose. It is the strength required to bring about social, political, or economic changes. In this sense power is not only desirable but necessary in order to implement the demands of love and justice. One of the greatest problems of history is that the concepts of love and power are usually contrasted as polar opposites. Love is identified with a resignation of power and power with a denial of love. It was this misinterpretation that caused Nietzsche, the philosopher of the "will to power," to reject the Christian concept of love. It was this same misinterpretation which induced Christian theologians to reject Nietzsche's philosophy of the "will to power," in the name of the Christian idea of love. What is needed is a realization that power without love is reckless and abusive and that love without power is sentimental and anemic. Power at its best is love implementing the demands of justice. Justice at its best is love correcting everything which stands against love.

There is nothing essentially wrong with power. The problem is that in America power is unequally distributed. This has led Negro Americans in the past to seek their goals through love and moral suasion devoid of power and white Americans to seek their goals through power devoid of love and conscience. It is leading a few extremists today to advocate for Negroes the same destructive and conscienceless power that they have justly abhorred in whites. It is precisely this collision of immoral power with powerless morality which constitutes the major crisis of our times.[128]

It is to be noted how dependent King is, in this passage, upon Tillich's discussion in *Love, Power, and Justice*. Tillich's words are

Love and power are often contrasted in such a way that love is identified with a resignation of power and power with a denial of love. Powerless love and loveless power are contrasted. This, of course, is unavoidable if love is understood from its emotional side and power from its compulsory side. But such an understanding is error and confusion. It was this misinterpretation which induced the philosopher of the "will-to-power" (i.e., Nietzsche) to reject radically the Christian idea of love. And it is the same misinterpretation which induces Christian theologians to reject Nietzsche's philosophy of the "will-to-power" in the name of the Christian idea of love.[129]

King came to realize how important political power was for the Negro. And in the political arena, one must face power struggles and the pitting of interest against interest. King, finally, had to face that reality.

Before we leave the discussion of love and justice, we must deal with criticisms James Sellers has made of King, with special reference to his understanding of Niebuhr. They are contained in an article entitled, "Love,

Justice, and the Nonviolent Movement" which appeared in *Theology Today*.[130] His comments betray lack of maturity, misunderstanding, and error.

Sellers claims that sometime in the movement, King "explicitly rejected Niebuhr's views" and substituted "personalistic idealism" for "Niebuhrian realism."[131] This assumes that King was at one time a Niebuhrian, which is patently untrue. King was early influenced by the liberal tradition of the social gospel and personalism at Crozer and concluded his graduate work in a theological faculty at Boston University dedicated to the same tradition.

Niebuhr was never a major determining influence on King, although he was a significant one (as we have just shown). King himself admits that much of Niebuhr was unacceptable to him. King disagreed with Niebuhr's views of pacifism, his suspicion of reason, his pessimism concerning human nature, and his criticism of utopian communities. Although King benefited from reacting to Niebuhr, he almost always saw him from the framework of his liberal thought, which was his self-admitted philosophical position.

The other criticism by Sellers of the sit-in demonstrations, including King, is that in "the nonviolent movement, justice seems to stand as the highest goal of a Christian society, with love, accordingly, subordinated as the method or device by which that goal is to be attained."[132] Sellers continues

> Despite the realism that breaks through now and then, the sit-in theology maintains that love has its place as a means to the end of justice. And now we see why the sit-in theorists do not hold with Reinhold Niebuhr; their theology is Niebuhrianism turned upside down.[133]

Sellers sees justice as the reality which stands at the end of the civil rights struggle; "it is the goal rather than the weapon." And in place of justice, love is the weapon which advances men toward their goal. This is a serious criticism and deserves serious attention. First of all, Sellers, writing in 1961, did not have the benefit of the whole corpus of King's writings, as we have today. One would be more sympathetic with his critique, however, if he were not so confident in his assertions and conclusions. There is a sense in which Sellers is technically right. King did say, in his first speeches and articles in 1956, that

> ... this is a movement of passive resistance and the great instrument is the instrument of love.[134]

This love might well be the salvation of our civilization. This is why I am so impressed with our motto for the week, "Freedom and Justice Through Love."[135]

This would seem to contradict Niebuhr's very clear and representative statement in the preface to his 1956 edition of *An Interpretation of Christian Ethics*, first published in 1935.

I still believe, as I believed then, that love may be the motive of social action but that justice must be the instrument of love in a world in which self-interest is bound to defy the canons of love on every level.[136]

But Sellers fails to see King's instrumentality of love in the perspective of the ends-means framework so important for King.[137] There is an organic relationship between ends and means, i.e., a loving end can only be achieved by loving means. "The end is pre-existent in the means." King *did* speak of love as a "way." However, it was not the ideal love of which he spoke, not *agape*, but a refracted love, appropriate content for a technique in the struggle for social change. In fact, King uses "love" and "nonviolent resistance" interchangeably. In another article written about the same time as the ones referred to above, he said, "We have discovered a new and powerful weapon–nonviolent resistance."[138]

As we have seen, nonviolence involved a variety of factors for King–calculation, strategy, weighing and measuring alternatives, etc.–and nonviolence as a pragmatic principle and tactic certainly answers to Niebuhr's "justice being an instrument of love."

It is conceded that King was, at this point, not nearly as dialectical as Niebuhr. And he was certainly not dualistic. There is a sense in which he is monistic–love and justice seem to merge into one. But it is not a "justice monism" as Sellers indicates. It is more like a "love monism."[139]

Another perspective which neutralizes, if not corrects, Sellers's comments, is the one found in "The Ethical Demands of Integration,"[140] an article that is indispensable for understanding King. Here King sets forth a philosophy of race relations which sees our society moving from segregation to desegregation to integration. Desegregation removes the legal and social prohibitions but is essentially negative. Integration is the "positive acceptance of Negroes into the total range of human activities. Integration is genuine intergroup, interpersonal doing."[141]

Since integration is the ultimate goal of King's striving, desegregation is a short range goal, a step on the way to a higher level of experience. The important thing to notice here is that King associates justice with this middle ground of desegregation. "Man-made laws assure justice" and "court orders and federal enforcement agencies are of inestimable value in achieving desegregation."[142] The final goal, integration, the realization of "genuine inter-group and interpersonal relationships," is a virtual synonym for the "community of love" which is produced by a "higher law," one that is written of the heart.

Finally, Sellers fails to grasp King's obvious concern to outline the power and normative character of love. He quotes John Wesley as a corrective to King. "The law of God . . . will always be 'the spirit of love' taking a necessarily painful form. 'And yet love is the spring of all.'"[143] Even though Sellers did not have access to some later King material, it does seem strange that he does not see love as the "spring" of all King's activity.[144] His two sermons in *Strength to Love*, "Loving Your Enemies"[145] and "Love in Action," are ones in which love as "potent instrument" and impelling force and normative behavior are all combined.[146]

Sellers again states that in the Movement's ideology (and hence in King), "love does not always occupy the pinnacle, the position of the *summum bonum*."[147] But in a sermon, "Paul's Letter to American Christians," preached in 1955, King asks,

> What is the *summum bonum* of life? I think I have found the answer, Americans. I have discovered that the highest goal is love. This principle is at the center of the cosmos. It is the great unifying force of life. God is love. He who loves has discovered the clue to the meaning of ultimate reality. . . ."[148]

Sellers has put his finger on an important issue. It is not that he is altogether wrong, but that he seems to lack a comprehensive grasp of King's thought.

7. Niebuhr and Pacifism

Niebuhr's attack on pacifism, which has become a classical rationale for nonpacifists, must be seen in historical perspective. He was a pacifist, himself, along with many liberal clergymen, in the post-World War I era. But the growing international crisis in the late twenties and early thirties, especially in Germany (which he had visited), caused him to disavow his pacifist convictions. The pacifism he denounces, however, is the kind suggesting that war should never be an instrument of national policy. He thought this to be utterly unrealistic in the actualities of the then current international power struggles. Nonviolence, on the other hand, could be an effective pragmatic technique for some oppressed minorities.[149]

But regarding international conflict, there was an insistence that pacifism was futile and self-defeating. Niebuhr based his argument on the preference of war over tyranny. If it would come to a decision between the two, Niebuhr would choose war, which he also calls anarchy. The latter, at least, is open-ended and allows for possibilities of creating alternatives.

> Pacifism either tempts us to make no judgments at all, or to give an undue preference to tyranny in comparison with the momentary anarchy which is necessary to overcome tyranny.[150]

Tyranny will not destroy itself; in fact, it will continue to grow if it is not resisted in some way. In order to resist it, "the risk of overt conflict must be taken."

Niebuhr's conviction strengthened through the years. In a more recent book, *Man's Nature and His Communities*, he speaks in even stronger language.

> It may be significant that the brutalities of open conflict are spiritually less debasing than the enslavement of one tribal group by another. The brutalities of tyranny, whether in Nazi Germany or in South Africa or in Mississippi, are more wounding to human self-esteem than any conflict.[151]

This is why Niebuhr often sees the violent conflict of war as a "lesser evil" or a "negative good." He is fearful that an absolute disavowal of war would mean the disavowal of the effort to establish justice. And for Niebuhr justice was always dependent on a "decent equilibrium of power." So conflict is not ruled out completely. Let us continue, briefly, to examine the basis for Niebuhr's argument against pacifism.

a.   *The Nature of Man*

The force of Niebuhr's contention is grounded in his understanding of man. Pacifists do not know human nature sufficiently to be concerned about the contradiction between the law of love and the sin of man.

Man, whose egoistic impulse ultimately frustrates the realization of love in personal and group relationships, cannot always be relied on to practice or

159

receive pacifism. The pacifist is the embodiment of what Niebuhr calls the absolutist-perfectionist ethic, who believes that love is a "simple historical possibility."

> The validity of the pacifist position rests in a general way upon the assumption that men are intelligent and moral and that a generous attitude toward them will ultimately, if not always immediately, discover, develop, and challenge what is best in them. This is a large assumption which every specific instance will not justify.[152]

Liberal, optimistic man believes that with a little more education, piety, time, and longsuffering, the demonic persons and structures of society will eventually crumble. Controversies will be resolved by clearing up misunderstandings and by exercising one's imagination to a greater degree. The "simple moralism of the modern church" is mistaken in its belief that love will prevail if only good men are more resolute and more forgiving of their antagonists. Niebuhr comments that a forgiving spirit can be exploited. "Has not the white man taken advantage of the forgiving spirit of the Negro."

> . . . it seems that the world in which we live is not so spiritual that it is always possible to prompt the wrongdoer to contrition merely by appealing to his conscience and to that of the society in which he lives.[153]

Niebuhr believes that the pacifists are fundamentally unappreciative of the Pauline-Reformation doctrine of Justification by Faith, and believe that man is able to transcend the brokenness and ambiguity, "claims and counterclaims," of history. They conceive of the gospel as the law of love and not as a message for men who break that law.

Niebuhr's radical understanding of justification is the source of his dialectical understanding of man. It is this doctrine which enables him to fathom the depth of sin. If the fate of pure love (Christ) in history is always crucifixion and if the Kingdom of God must always enter the world by way of a crucifixion, then appeals to good will and conscience will ultimately be of no avail. He states this theological position clearly.

> The question is whether the grace of Christ is primarily a power of righteousness which so heals the sinful heart that henceforth it is able to fulfill the law of love; or whether it is primarily the assurance of divine mercy for a persistent sinfulness which man never overcomes completely.[154]

Forgiveness of the foe has meaning for Niebuhr, only if it comes from one who senses he also is a sinner in need of forgiveness.

b. *Nonresistance and Nonviolent Resistance*

Here Niebuhr argues on the same ground as the pacifists–the New Testament and the example of the Cross. He claims that pacifists are guilty of doing what their less legalistic friends do, namely, "diluting the ethic of Jesus for the purpose of justifying their position."

Upon discovering that nonresistance is not relevant to the relativities of life, they propose that what Jesus really meant was not nonresistance but nonviolent resistance. For Niebuhr this is a blending of the perfectionist and pragmatic which has no warrant in the New Testament. Living by "way of the Cross" means precisely that one will practice nonresistance.

> There is not the slightest support in Scripture for this doctrine of nonviolence. Nothing could be plainer than that the ethic uncompromisingly enjoins non-resistance.[155]

> They will find nothing in the gospels which justifies nonviolent resistance as an instrument of love perfectionism.[156]

And Niebuhr goes on to insist that there is no absolute distinction between violent and nonviolent resistance. If it is made absolute, we arrive at the morally absurd position of giving moral preference to the nonviolent power which Doctor Goebbels wields over the type of power wielded by a general."[157]

He cites Richard Gregg's *The Power of Nonviolence* as the *reductio ad absurdum* of this position. In this book, according to Niebuhr, Gregg suggests that one's foe may be overcome more effectively by the use of nonresistance, which will eventually break his morale.[158] But, for Niebuhr, the ethic of the Christian gospels is a perfectionist one which logically issues in complete nonresistance.

c. *Elements of Coercion in Nonviolence*

It is this judgment by Niebuhr that most threatened King. Niebuhr assumed that no society can exist without some coercive power, that the "achievement of harmony and justice between groups requires a measure of coercion."[159]

Once this is accepted as a given in group relations, pure pacifism has disappeared and there cannot be drawn an "absolute line of demarcation between violent and nonviolent coercion."[160]

If it comes to the matter of the least coercive approach to make, we must admit that even the coercion in nonviolence can also result in the destruction of life and property–the inevitable results of violent coercion. Here, however, the result is not intentional, but indirect. For example, a community can be destroyed by a sufficiently intense boycott. Pressure, sometimes destructive, can be brought to bear by nonviolence. The innocent and the guilty suffer together in this conflict as in more obvious kinds of warfare.

We are to realize the sinful element in all resistance and coercion. The liberal church, says Niebuhr, was usually blind to the fact that nonviolence may be covert violence. In a statement, "Why I Leave the F.O.R.," Niebuhr expresses his apprehension over the relationship between blindness to coercion in nonviolence and the exploitation of the disinherited.

> If . . . we will use nonviolent coercion in behalf of the disinherited but will discourage any coercion that may issue in nonviolence, we feel that we would give an undue moral advantage to that portion of the community which is always using nonviolent coercion against the disinherited.[161]

There was a certain hypocrisy in the kind of pacifism practiced by the liberal church. Its constituency was primarily among the middle class, who had the economic power to forego violent forms of coercion and condemn them when practiced by the disinherited who suffered from the hidden violence (coercion) of the privileged.

d. *Pacifism as "Heresy"*

Niebuhr actually considered most modern forms of Christian pacifism heretical. His judgment is made on the basis that the normative Christian experience and the essence of the Gospel is found in the Pauline-Augustinian-Lutheran tradition of Christianity. It is also made on empirical grounds. The facts of history and human existence do not conform to the world-view espoused by the liberal Christian pacifist. Most modern forms of Christian pacifism

> have really absorbed the Renaissance faith in the goodness of man, have rejected the Christian doctrine of original sin as an outmoded bit of pessimism,

have reinterpreted the Cross so that it is made to stand for the absurd idea that perfect love is guaranteed a simple victory over the world, and have rejected all other profound elements of the Christian gospel as "Pauline" accretions which must be stripped from the "simple gospel of Jesus."[162]

e. *Value of Pacifism*

Notwithstanding his stringent attacks on pacifism, Niebuhr does see two significant contributions it can make. In the first place, provided a pacifist and especially a thoroughgoing one, is able to understand and avoid the sin of Pharisaism, i.e., be sufficiently aware to what degree he is a "parasite on the sins of his fellowman"

> he may become a valuable reminder to the Christian community of the fact that the Kingdom of God has come and that his law is the law of life, even though men cannot maintain themselves in the world of sin by obedience to it.[163]

The church is wise to protect its pacifists. They bear a relevant witness to the love that is unattainable and yet a love which must be the object of our striving–a love which judges and ultimately heals us.

Secondly, Niebuhr justifies a pragmatic pacifism. Not accepting "the law of the Cross" as its model, it accepts the world as it is, in which there are plays for power and the need to restrain the violent competition of selfish interests. Pragmatic pacifism's

> interests lie in mitigating the struggle between contending forces, by insinuating the greatest possible degree of social imagination and intelligence into it and by providing the best possible means of arbitration so that violent conflict may be avoided. Such a pacifism is a necessary influence in every society because social violence is a great evil and ought to be avoided if at all possible.[164]

Here Niebuhr is true to his presupposition that life must be understood in terms of "relationships and totalities."

8. *King's Response to Niebuhr*

King had apparently carefully read Niebuhr's analysis of the contradiction in absolute pacifism. His summary paragraph of Niebuhr's position in *Stride Toward Freedom* is an accurate presentation of Niebuhr's main argument.[165]

But his personal response was one of bewilderment. "Niebuhr's critique of pacifism left me in a state of confusion."[166]

The confusion is understandable in a seminary senior who had spent two years drinking in the liberal doctrine of man and the possibilities of history. Pacifism was probably not questioned in Davis's courses. He, himself, was a pacifist. Gandhi was also accepted without undue criticism. Reinhold Niebuhr must have burst like a bombshell in King's theological-ethical world. King had basically two reactions to Niebuhr, both of which, in their own way, amount to abiding influences.

a. *King's Understanding of Nonviolent Resistance*

The first reaction dealt with Niebuhr's understanding of nonresistance. King felt that Niebuhr was misguided in his views of pacifism at this point, especially when he identified nonresistance to evil as strictly passive and as an expression of naive trust in the power of love. King said this is a "serious distortion."

His correction of Niebuhr is based on his study of Gandhi, who convinced King that "true pacifism is not nonresistance to evil, but nonviolent resistance to evil."[167] King said there is a "world of difference" between these two positions. King implies that in nonviolent resistance to evil one actively resists, but with love and not hate. Niebuhr would reply that there is a relative difference between the two positions, relative in the amount of love and aggressiveness used and in the violence that results.

Then King uses an argument Niebuhr accused most Christian pacifists of utilizing. "True pacifism is not unrealistic submission to evil power, as Niebuhr contends. It is rather a courageous confrontation of evil by the power of love. . . ."[168] King is informed here primarily by Gandhian philosophy, although the redemptive power of love as witnessed in the Cross is implied.

The fact is that King did not take pains to answer Niebuhr's charge that Christian pacifists, if they take the Cross seriously, should be practicing nonresistance. Perhaps he did not have the time or interest to do the New Testament exegesis done by G. H. C. Macgregor in his reply to Niebuhr.

Macgregor suggests that the stress in the New Testament is much more on "non-retaliation" than on "non-resistance." He notes that some scholars say that the logic of the "non-resistance" sayings of Matthew 5 demand "retaliate not upon evil," rather than "resist not evil." He further mentions that the Greek rendering suggests a "possible mistranslation of the original Aramaic" which would then read, "Do not render evil in return for evil." Then, concludes Macgregor, the most accurate translation of Jesus would coincide with Paul's version in Romans 12:14, "Render to no man evil for evil."[169]

There is no evidence that King read Macgregor's competent criticism of Niebuhr from a pacifist point of view. He would have, however, endorsed the argument and incorporated it into his own defense of nonviolence. In terms of this first reaction, King learned from Niebuhr by reacting against him, thereby indirectly strengthening his own position.

b. *Realistic Pacifism*

The second main reaction King had to Niebuhr, which was more direct, resulted in a positive influence. It is included in both versions of "Pilgrimage to Nonviolence."[170]

Niebuhr's probing analysis of the "complexity of man's social involvement,"[171] and his exposure of self-righteousness in the most saintly, apparently forever qualified King's pacifist orientation. King felt that many pacifists failed to see the duplicity and ambiguity in all human acts. Their "unwarranted optimism concerning man" placed them perilously close to self-righteousness.

> It was my revolt against these attitudes under the influence of Niebuhr that accounts for the fact that in spite of my strong leaning toward pacifism, I never joined a pacifist organization. After reading Niebuhr, I tried to arrive at a realistic pacifism. In other words, I came to see the pacifist position not as sinless but as the lesser evil in the circumstances. I felt then, and I feel now, that the pacifist would have a greater appeal if he did not claim to be free from the moral dilemmas that the Christian non-pacifist confronts.[172]

The lesson of Niebuhr that perfectionist-absolutist pacifists suffer from moralistic illusions had not been lost on King. He now appreciates the relativities of life, that to be involved in this world is to be "in sin." This can be illustrated by two references to King's writing.

His attitude toward war, as such, was not determined by strictly pacifist ideology. He admits being suspicious of nonviolence as a strategy in international relations for a long time. Until 1960, when the second version of "Pilgrimage to Nonviolence" was written, he felt that war, although never a positive good, could be a negative good by thwarting the growth of evil. The Niebuhrian influence here is obvious. "War, horrible as it is, might be preferable to surrender to a totalitarian system."[173]

But he then came to the conviction that the destructive power of nuclear weapons was so unlimited that war had ceased being a negative good. So, in order to survive, man must find an alternative to war. It is, as he often said, a matter of "nonviolence or nonexistence." Interestingly enough, the reason for opposition to war is not an absolute pacifist one, but a pragmatic one, i.e., human survival.

King became, in the last three years of his life, a sharp critic of the Vietnam War. But his opposition was primarily based on the political miscalculation of this country, its overt imperialism, and that we are "on the other side of revolution." He spoke of the "casualties" of the Vietnam War.[174] The casualties he mentions, beyond the appalling physical loss of life, are the United Nations Charter, the spirit of self-determination, the Great Society, the humility of our nation, the principle of dissent, and prospects for mankind's survival.[175]

In other addresses and articles[176] his opposition is essentially pragmatic and centers around the unity he felt there existed between the civil rights issue and the issue of the Southeast Asian war. He did not intend to "segregate moral concerns."[177] There is never in his discussion of the war a strong pacifist tone in the tradition of A. J. Muste and other orthodox pacifists. In fact, as early as the Crozer days, he was "far from convinced of the practicability of his (Muste's) position."[178]

The other illustration is King's attitude toward necessary coercion in a society in serious conflict. He regretted, for instance, that it took the National Guard, Army troops, and Federal Marshals to secure James Meredith's admission to the University of Mississippi. As a "devotee of the nonviolent discipline," he regretted the use of force, but concluded "it was necessary and justifiable."

> Whereas I abhor the use of arms and the thought of war, I do believe in the intelligent use of police power. Though a pacifist, I am not an anarchist. Mississippi's breakdown of law and order demanded the utilization of a police action to quell the disorder and enforce the law of the land.[179]

So King was not, as he admits, a "doctrinaire pacifist." Niebuhr would rejoice in the practicality of the following expression of King's self-understanding.

. . . I tried to embrace a realistic pacifism which finds the pacifist position as the lesser evil in the circumstances. I do not claim to be free from the moral dilemma that the Christian nonpacifist confronts.[180]

c. Niebuhr's Evaluation of King

It is for these reasons that Niebuhr commended King's efforts. D. B. Robertson quotes Niebuhr as saying that "Martin Luther King's position is right." King's 'sentimentality' Niebuhr discusses critically, but he still believes that Martin Luther King is "the most creative Protestant, white or black."[181]

Again, in the Foreword to a pamphlet on the Vietnam War issued by Clergy and Laymen Concerned About the War in Vietnam,[182] Niebuhr calls King "one of the great religious leaders of our time." In defending King's position on nonviolent resistance to evil, Niebuhr says

Many of the journals and the public have confused his position with absolute pacifism, which they reject. I think, as a rather dedicated anti-pacifist, that Dr. King's conception of the nonviolent resistance to evil is a real contribution to our civil, moral, and political life.[183]

Finally, in a letter to the writer, Niebuhr said that although he and King never met personally, he did write King a letter once "declaring my admiration for his endeavors despite my anti-pacifism." Niebuhr went on in the letter to say that in a review of his book (presumably *Stride Toward Freedom*),

I said that my enthusiasm for Dr. King's nonviolence despite my anti-pacifism was due to my distinction between a pacifism designed to prove our purity and a pacifism designed to establish justice.[184] I thought that Dr. King leading a ten per cent Negro minority was a good combination of idealism and of pragmatic realism.[185]

Niebuhr's letter continues

Again in a television debate with the Negro novelist, James Baldwin, I was horrified to know that many Negro leaders had seriously misjudged his pacifism as an inert loving forgiveness of the white man, despite his injustice. I sought to convince Baldwin, partially successfully, that King's policy as regard to race was akin to Lincoln's who was intent that the rebels fire the first shot, as they indeed did at Fort Sumter.[186]

Niebuhr's insight is essentially correct and properly emphasizes the pragmatic, realistic dimensions in King's pacifism. It seems that Niebuhr has modified the rather hard line he held in the thirties. Then he seemed to have no sympathy with what he felt was an irresponsible fusion of the perfectionist and the pragmatic.[187]

9. Niebuhr and the Possibility of Community

Before we conclude our discussion of Niebuhr's influence on King, we will examine briefly the Niebuhr's understanding of the prospects for human community and his views on the symbol of the Kingdom of God. Niebuhr appreciated the social dimension of life and saw it as indispensable for the fulfillment of individual life. "The individual cannot be a true self in isolation."[188] There is a necessary organic interrelatedness of the individual and the community. The individual's decision, achievements, and aspirations find their greatest fulfillment and final meaning in the community.

> The highest reaches of individual consciousness and awareness are rooted in social experience and find their ultimate meaning in relation to the community.[189]

It is conceivable that King's *Where Do We Go From Here*, already mentioned as the most Niebuhrian of his books, was inspired, to some degree, by Niebuhr's *Children of Light and Children of Darkness*. The final chapter in Niebuhr's book is entitled "The World Community" and the final chapter in *Where Do We Go From Here* is called "The World House."

> The problem of overcoming the chaos and of extending the principle of community to world-wide terms has become the most urgent of all the issues which face our epoch.[190]

a. Value of the Millennial Hope

Authentic religious standards exaggerate the distance between the ideal and real as well as contain impatience with the resulting "compromises, relativities, and imperfections of historic society." When this happens there usually arises a millennial hope which looks beyond the antimonies of history toward the resolution of all conflict and the equalization of all inequities. It is the "classical religious dream."

Niebuhr says that the Christian Kingdom of God is a "highly spiritualized version" of this Jewish concept of the millennium, which was construed in this-worldly terms. The vision of Second Isaiah represents this hope. The presence of the millennial hope is important because "courage is maintained to continue in the effort to redeem society of injustices." One is disillusioned in the striving for an egalitarian society if his vision is limited to temporal experience.[191] On another occasion, Niebuhr calls this dream "the transcendent perspective of religion," which

> makes all men our brothers and nullifies the divisions, by which nature, climate, geography and the accidents of history divide the human family. By this insight many religiously inspired idealists have transcended nation, racial and class distinctions.[192]

Some interpreters of American religious history have noted how this "classical religious dream" has been fused with the "American dream," thinking that democracy is the most appropriate political and social experience of Christianity, and that the god of the American dream is really an American god. Even here, however, the transcendent element in the dream overcomes domestication of the Divine.

> . . . yet he is god and not just American, because the freedom of opportunity which America offered the class-ridden peoples of Europe, when America was at her best, was a human and not just an American value.[193]

But the dream is never fully realized in history. One of the tragedies of history is that any future peace and justice of society will depend upon the admixture of coercive and moral power.

> So difficult is it to avoid the Scylla of despotism and the Charybdis of anarchy that it is sage to hazard the prophecy that the dream of perpetual peace and brotherhood for human society is one which will never be fully realized.[194]

b. *The Impossible Possibility of the Kingdom of God*

The realization of the Kingdom of God is bound to the same fate as the practice of Christian love–it is not a "simple historical possibility." This position of Niebuhr's is a clue to his view of history. For him, there is only one New Testament interpretation of history, one that "pictures history as moving toward a climax in which both Christ and anti-Christ are revealed.

The New Testament does not, in other words, envisage a simple triumph of good over evil in history. It sees human history involved in the contradictions of sin to the end."[195] Because the "liberal children of light" linked the goodness of man with the idea of progress, "modern culture imagined history itself to be redemptive."[196]

But Niebuhr is never more firm than in his insistence that the Kingdom of God is not an "ideal society" toward which modern culture believes itself to be evolving.[197] The Kingdom is a "divine reality,"[198] coming only "through the intervention of God"[199] because the rational, moral, and religious resources available to man are simply not "sufficient to guarantee it."

> A sentimental generation has destroyed this apocalyptic note in the vision of the Christ. It thinks the Kingdom of God is around the corner, while he regards it as impossible of realization except by God's grace.[200]

The same generation

> failed to understand the persistence and power of the pride of nations or to comprehend the inertial force of traditional loyalties.[201]

The Kingdom of God will eventually resolve the contradictions of history. But when it does, that will be the end of history. For history is not self-fulfilling, self-containing, or self-explanatory. This is the significance for Niebuhr of the symbol of the Second Coming of Christ.[202]

Just as love is related to justice dialectically, in that it negates and fulfills justice, judges and yet is capable of infinitely expanding the possibilities of justice, so the Kingdom of God "is relevant to every moment of history as an ideal possibility and as a principle of judgment upon present realities."[203]

Sometimes allegiance to the Kingdom of God will so defy the world that martyrdom will result; at other times obedience will neutralize the force of evil sufficiently to make possible a new and higher justice; still, on other occasions, the powers of the Kingdom will be forced to cooperate with the powers of this world to achieve an approximation of justice.

"Martyrs, prophets, and statesmen may each in his own way be servants of the Kingdom"–martyrs in that they remind us of the "illusion that the Kingdom of Caesar is the Kingdom of Christ in embryo"; prophets in that they remind us that "each moment of human history faces actual and realizable higher possibilities"; statesmen in that they remind us of the uses of "power to correct the injustices of power." Without the latter

> we might allow the vision of the Kingdom of Christ to become a luxury of those who can afford to acquiesce in present injustice because they do not suffer from it.[204]

So the task of building a world community is man's "final necessity and possibility, but also his final impossibility."[205] It is possible because of man's freedom; it is impossible because of man's finitude. As such, the world community is the "perpetual problem as well as the constant fulfillment of human hopes." This discussion will be continued when we discuss, at greater length, King's notion of the "Beloved Community" in the last chapter.

FIVE

Personalism

A. *Introduction*

Although King was introduced to the basic elements of personalism at Crozer in courses with George W. Davis, he became thoroughly acquainted with this philosophy during his doctoral studies at Boston University.

For almost a century now, Boston University has been identified with the personalist school of philosophy. Borden Parker Bowne, the most prominent American personalist, was appointed professor of philosophy there in 1876 and Peter Bertocci, a student of Edgar Sheffield Brightman, is currently professor of philosophy at Boston. In between were such outstanding personalist scholars as Brightman in philosophy, Albert Knudson (probably the most significant theologian of the movement), Walter Muelder in social ethics, and L. Harold DeWolf in theology.

King owed a great deal to these men. Brightman, Muelder, and DeWolf, the latter his major professor and advisor through his dissertation research, had a strong influence on him, personally and intellectually. We have mentioned King's debt to Muelder in the chapter on nonviolence.

King's own indebtedness to the Boston school of personalism is put in brief, summary form in the first version of "Pilgrimage to Nonviolence."

> I studied philosophy and theology at Boston University under Edgar S. Brightman and L. Harold DeWolf. Both men greatly stimulated my thinking. It was mainly under these teachers that I studied personalistic philosophy–the theory that the clue to the meaning of ultimate reality is found in personality. This personal idealism remains today my basic philosophical position. Personalism's insistence that only personality–finite and infinite–is ultimately real strengthened me in two convictions; it gave me metaphysical and philosophical grounding for the idea of a personal God, and it gave me a metaphysical basis for the dignity and worth of all human personality.[1]

On another occasion, King is quoted as saying in response to a question about the teacher who had contributed most to the formation of his character and philosophy, that it was "Dr. Edgar Sheffield Brightman who had contributed most to the shaping of his character."[2]

Because King was, in intellectual terms, a social ethicist and not a philosopher, one does not find fully developed philosophical positions and concepts in his writings. One sees the metaphysical base and philosophical presuppositions of his world view behind his writings, not so much articulated in them.

But that personalism was a pronounced influence on his thought cannot be denied. One has only to look at the innumerable references to the "sacredness of human life," "the legacy of dignity and worth" to which every man is heir, and to his constant reference to the "moral law" which irrefutably unfolds itself through history.

Before we deal with King's own version of personalism and specific instances of personalism's influence on his thought, we will outline in some detail the elements of personalist philosophy which had a formative bearing on King's ethical thought.

B. *Rudolf H. Lotze*

Lotze was a nineteenth century German idealist philosopher who, through his influence on Borden Parker Bowne, his most famous student, was the father of personalism as we know it in America. He was an heir of the western idealist tradition stemming from Plato, but he considerably modified the Absolute Idealism of Hegel.

Lotze's system is set forth in his major work, *Microcosmos* Volumes I and II. A pervading theme of this work is the unity of all things. His world-view, generally, is monistic. Book Nine of Volume II is entitled "The Unity of Things" and two chapters in that book, "The Real and The Ideal" and "The Personality of God,"[3] illustrate his understanding of the unity of life. This unity reflects his commitment to the idealistic tradition. "Idealism opposes to the realistic acknowledgment of the unknowable nature of things the bold assertion that Thought and Being are identical."[4]

Lotze sensed that divisions had occurred in contemporary thought between science and philosophy, mind and material, logic and value judgments. He attempted to reconcile, if not synthesize, these disparate elements.

One of the important aspects of Lotze's thought which constituted a reaction against Hegel was his reliance on experience as a way of knowing. This gave rise to the rational empiricism in later personalism.

The idealism of Hegel was so absolute that logical reflection could plumb the depths of reality without any recourse to or dependence upon experience. "It was Lotze's aim to grant perception, or empirical knowledge of nature, its place in thought."[5] Lotze stressed the central place of experience and suggested that we can understand it only "as we grasp its inner continuity." Succeeding personalist interpreters have echoed this note.

> We have again and again pointed out that experience is first and basal in all living and thinking, and that all theorizing must go out from experience as its basis and must return to it for verification.[6]

> The theory of reality must, therefore, begin with experience; and its task must be not to construct or reconstruct it, but to interpret it.[7]

One of the principal realities we experience is the "subjection of the actual world to the rule of that truly spiritual ideal world from whose content shines forth in clearest light the absolute worth of moral Ideas."[8]

For Lotze, the whole of reality depends upon a "principle of Good." This Supreme Good "is the ultimate Reality in whose existence all other realities find their ground."[9] Lotze maintains truth is comprehensible in a world in which nature depends upon this principle of Good. We learn to know this "in Living Love itself."[10] It is the primary work of this Love

> to establish an universal order and regularity, within which various individuals, comparable in kind, could be brought into a connection of reciprocal action. If this eternal sacredness and supreme worth of Love were not at the foundation of the world, and if in such a case there could be a world of which we could think and speak, this world, it seems to me, would, whatever it were, be left without truth and order.[11]

It is the purpose of the "Supreme Good" which Lotze conceives to be the World-Ground, which leads him to a Person, who is the content of ultimate reality. As the soul longs to apprehend this highest good, it is unsatisfied with "any form of the existence of that Good except personality."[12] The "notion of a Personal God" is the goal toward which we strive.

It is the conception of the World-Ground as personal that suggests the predominant feature in Lotze's thought and the one that is indispensable for later personalism. Since man relates to the personal God at a level deeper than reason, namely one of feeling and emotions, values emerge and, hence, ethics must be taken seriously.

For Lotze, it was inconceivable to separate metaphysics and ethics. Metaphysics, as the science of being, does not have a right to exist independent of ethics. As one commentator on Lotze said, "Indeed we cannot properly speak of ultimate reality except in terms of ultimate value."[13]

There are two impulses which give rise to the notion of God and belief in Him, according to Lotze.

> Metaphysical attributes of Unity, Eternity, Omnipresence, and Omnipotence determine Him as the ground of all finite reality; ethical attributes of Wisdom, Justice, and Holiness satisfy our longing to find in that which has supreme reality, supreme worth also.[14]

Even though Lotze strongly intimated that "true reality and complete personality are to be found only in the Absolute" and believed that "personality was the key to reality," Knudson feels that he did not attempt a thorough and systematic exposition of this principle.[15] But Lotze's attempt "to give ultimacy to personal values in an age of science has its repercussions in this country in the form of the 'personal idealist' movement at the turn of the century."[16]

The primary spokesman of this movement was Borden Parker Bowne, a friend and student of Lotze. According to Knudson, the task of radically making personality the organizing principle of a philosophical system fell to Bowne. Perhaps this was easier for Bowne, who regarded religion as the focal point of thought and who maintained "that metaphysics and logic are enlightened by the fundamental question of religion, and are to be understood only in connection with it."[17] In any case, it was Bowne who developed a

> systematic methodological personalism. It was he who first took the personalistic conception of reality, grounded it in the Kantian epistemology, developed its implications in a comprehensive way, and made it the center and constitutive principle of a complete metaphysical system.[18]

C. *Personalism as an Idealism*

Idealistic content is seen throughout the literature of personalist philosophers. Indeed, personalism is best understood within the framework of the western idealist tradition. Knudson said that "thoroughgoing personalism is idealistic."[19] Bowne, in his classical work, *Personalism*, said that we "ourselves are invisible." Further, reflecting Platonic thought, he said that the physical organism which is known by the senses is "only the instrument for expressing and manifesting the inner life, but the living self is never seen."[20] Hence, our human significance, the meaningful order of life, comes out of the invisible, from beyond the sensible. This idealistic assumption about the nature of reality allowed personalism to posit unity and continuity of reality. Flewelling reminds us that

> Lotze pointed out the fact that we must discover some continuity behind the ebb and flow of matter and even of human experience if we are to find out the meaning of the world.[21]

Bowne actually found the continuity in personality which alone could unite all the varied experiences of time and space. Unity is possible in this world only through personality. A final or ultimate unity is in the thought of a "Supreme Personality."

> . . . upon reflection it appears that this world is a function of intelligence in such a way that apart from intelligence it has neither existence nor even meaning.[22]

Brightman also reflects this concern in his discussion of the interrelationship of mind and body. He admits this has been a difficult problem for philosophy, especially if mind and body are thought of as belonging to completely different orders of being. His own solution, typical of personalism in general, reveals an Hegelian influence.

> But if one adopts the personalistic hypothesis that physical things are the energizing of a Supreme Mind, and thus regard the body itself as an expression of this Mind, the difficulty decreases. For the problem of interaction between mind and body becomes the problem of the interaction between human mind and the Supreme Mind.[23]

On another occasion, Brightman stresses the unity of reality. He attacks the "realistic" creed of "every man for himself" by stating that, although there is conflict and selfishness in life, there is also self-sacrifice and love of peace and truth. King would certainly endorse Brightman's affirmation that conflict is meaningful and that beyond all war there is peace, beyond all chaos there is order, beyond all seeming contradictions there is coherent truth. Everything noble in human history grows out of some dim apprehension of this truth. If there is no unity, every person and every event is entirely unrelated to any other. There is no law, no order, no cosmos.[24]

The invisibility of the personal world is strongly defended by Brightman. He is a dedicated apologist for the reality of the nonsensible. We may see the body, but not personality. Sensations do not give us a direct perception of the experience in another's mind. In fact, he even questions whether sense alone can give us knowledge of the body.

The visible (and all the sensible) consists of experience patterns within consciousness. In this sense, the visible itself is invisible to any external observer; only I can see and feel exactly what I do see and feel.[25]

It is on this basis that Brightman attacks behaviorists, semanticists, and logical positivists, all of whom attempt to restrict meaning and knowledge to the sensible, i.e., if it cannot be verified in sense experience it is not true. Brightman's rather forceful argument is the following.

Imagine what human culture would be if this restriction were taken seriously, and all references to ideals, purposes, truth, and consciousness were actually supposed to be meaningless.[26]

Brightman also compares idealism favorably to materialism and naturalism. He claims that personalism is more empirical than naturalism because the latter tends to ignore or reject the "most essential characteristic of all experience, namely, that it is personal consciousness. Persons are the only experienced reality."[27]

Further, personalism is more inclusive than naturalism, in that naturalists "deliberately omit personality and value from consideration" in their concentration on physical objects and biological organisms. Since personalists view personality and value as indispensable clues to understanding reality and as essential to the interpretation of all sense observations, it is more inclusive and, indeed, more factual than naturalism.

Finally, personalism is as scientific as naturalism. The former depends upon and respects the findings of science, but disagrees with the naturalist who asserts that scientific knowledge is all that can be known or hoped for. It is personalism's task to ask questions of meaning ("pre or post scientific questions") (Brightman).

How can we determine what is truly good, just, beautiful, holy, or true? How can we rightly define the total reality that is disclosed by our whole experience–scientific and extrascientific?[28]

So, concludes Brightman,

Personalism is a philosophy whose interpreters seek for a unity that includes all the facts–the facts of value and personality as well as the facts of the sense order.[29]

There is a practical, existential aspect to personalism, although the two philosophies, personalism and existentialism, differ markedly. It reacts against the impersonal absolute Mind of Hegel, much as Soren Kierkegaard did, in the name of the personal. Of course, as we shall see later, personalism was much more socially oriented than the individualism of existentialism.

Bowne claims that philosophy can bring "the infinitely far God . . . infinitely near," but belief in such a deity must be practical and concrete. For the "practical realization of this divine presence, logic and speculation can do little for us. This belief must be lived to acquire real substance or controlling character."[30]

We are not abstract intellects nor abstract wills, but we are living persons, knowing, feeling and having various interests, and in the light of knowledge and under the impulse of our interests trying to find our way, having an idea of experience also and seeking to understand it and to guide ourselves so as to extend to enrich that experience, and thus to build ourselves into large and fuller and more abundant personal life.[31]

Knudson, in his excellent book, *The Philosophy of Personalism*[32] stressed the voluntaristic and activistic over the rationalistic and deterministic, when discussing theories of the self. Personalism "lays more stress on the will than the intellect and inclines to the view that life is deeper than logic."[33] Brightman wants to make it clear, however, that he is on the side of those who

defend reason and idealism on the ground that a rational idealistic personalism is truer to the facts of experience and to man's ideal aspiration than in naturalism or neosupernaturalism. . . . Neosupernaturalism is confused truth; naturalism is confused error.[34]

He is so convinced of the validity of his position that he contends one could legitimately say "down with personalism" only if he really believed "there is no personal God, or that value is not personal, or that matter is not the personal energizing of God."[35]

D. *Personalism as a Theism*

The idealist presuppositions of personalism became also a basis for its theism. The God of theism is best understood by comparing him to the god of deism (radically transcendent) and to the god of pantheism (radically immanent). The theistic god is both transcendent and immanent, both free and personal, both creative and moral, or as Bowne puts it, we have

> a cause that was and that also is–a cause that does not lie temporarily behind the process, but is immanent in the process as the abiding power on which it forever depends.[36]

Knudson suggests that the typical theistic personalism which was espoused by Bowne and Brightman had its chief sources in the spiritual individualism and activism of Leibniz, in the immaterialism of Berkeley, in the epistemology and ethical conceptions of personality of Kant and finally in Lotze, "who took the personalistic elements contributed by his predecessors and wove them into a new type of theism."[37] This understanding of theistic personalism would obviously be the most rationally accessible way to Christianity. There is a great deal of affinity between personalism and traditional theism.

Since personalism stresses the "true genius of the Christian religion" in the emphasis on the personality of God and the sacredness of human personality, it is *"par excellence* the Christian philosophy of our day."[38]

Christian theism was particularly appealing to Bowne. When one refers to the World-Ground as intelligent, personal, and ethical, one may use "God" and "World-Ground" interchangeably. The latter is a philosophical version of the Biblical God who is righteous Lord and Father. On several occasions he states the adequacy of Christian theism. It affirms a free Creator and free creatures and makes "the moral nature of man the manifestation of an omnipotent and eternal righteousness which underlies the cosmos."[39] Theism was greatly enhanced by Christianity's "new conception of God and man and their mutual relations."

By making every man the heir of eternal life it (Christianity) gave to him a sacredness which he could never lose and which might never be ignored. By making the moral law the expression of a Holy Will, it brought that law out of its impersonal abstraction and assured its ultimate triumph.[40]

It was for this reason that Bowne was unhappy with Comte's conclusion to dismiss the theological stage of life and thought. Bowne agrees that the abstract metaphysical "should disappear," but he was desirous of retaining the other two.

We are positivistic in respect to science, and theologians as respects causation. This view conserves and satisfies all our essential human interests in this field, and vacates a mass of impersonal philosophizing which criticism shows to be baseless.[41]

For Knudson, personalism approximates most accurately a theistic representation of the Christian faith. This is so because of the stress placed on the personality of God and the notion that the highest revelation of divine truth is found in the person of Christ.

The magic word "personality," by virtue of the new insight it gives us into the nature of reality and into the conditions of knowledge, binds together historical Christianity and the personalistic philosophy.[42]

Brightman held somewhat the same position. Although personalism is not a science, it is a "sane philosophy of science;" although personalism is not a religion, it is an "introduction to the understanding of religious experience and religious revelation." "The personalist cannot assert that his is the only thinkable philosophy, but he can view it as offering light on many of the dark places of the world's thought and life."[43]

E. Personalism: A Definition

In one form or another personalistic philosophers hold firmly to the ontological reality of personality. The Supreme Being is personal in nature and all reality participates to some extent in that person-ness, with man having a special dignity and worth among created things.

Lotze set the tone for all future attempts at definition. He claimed that all judgment and reflection depend upon the conception we have of "the significance of our own being, of the dignity proper to man, and of the ends which he should attain."[44] What impressed him about the cruelty of savage

181

tribes was not their apparent absence of justice, "but only a failure to understand the worth of life."[45]

For Lotze, personality was the only conceivable form of God, the Supreme Cause of the universe. "Perfect personality is in God only" and all finite minds are "but a pale copy thereof."[46] Probably the most succinct definition was given by Knudson. "The metaphysics of personalism may be summed up in the statement that personality is the key to reality."[47] A similarly brief, but illuminating definition comes from Brightman. "In the broadest sense, personalism is the belief that conscious personality is both the supreme value and the supreme reality in the universe."[48]

What Brightman means by this definition is clarified in the chapter "What is Personal Idealism?" in his *An Introduction to Philosophy*. Personality, as the supreme philosophical principle, implies that the ultimate cause and reason of all reality are found in some process of personal experience. Personal idealism or idealistic personalism (these terms are synonymous for Brightman)

> makes the further assertion that persons and selves are the only reality, that is, that the whole universe is a system or society of interacting selves and persons–one infinite person who is the creator, and many dependent created persons.[49]

For personalism, therefore, the universe is a society of persons and the central, most creative person is God. As a result of his critical reflections, Bowne affirmed a world of persons with a Supreme Person at the head.[50] It is for this reason that Brightman saw personality as fundamental to all knowledge as well as fundamental to all reality.

> If all experience is personal, perhaps the energies which produce and sustain it are also personal; perhaps nature itself is the experience and the energizing of a person who is more than nature.[51]

1. *Self and Personality*

Brightman was concerned to distinguish "self" and "person." "A self is any conscious process; a person is a self that can experience values and judge itself by rational norms."[52] A person or a personality is a more inclusive entity than a self, for the former includes many experiences; among them are memory, purpose, value, will, activity, and interactions with its environment. Bowne understood by personality or personal being, "only self-knowledge and self-control." If these elements were present, personal being was present. If these elements are absent, the being is impersonal.[53]

This distinction on the part of personalists was apparently an attempt to indicate the relative priority of the human and the personal over the unvaluing and nonrational dimensions of creation. Knudson held that a person is a self who has "attained a certain degree of intellectual and moral development; a slave is not a person, nor is a child. Personality implies freedom and more responsibility."[54] This is why for personalists the category of "person" transcends the psychological and the metaphysical and assumes a "distinctly ethical character." This is also why King, steeped in this philosophy, could indict discrimination and segregation as depersonalizing.

This distinction may be further appreciated in Brightman's list of the first principles of a personalistic philosophy of life near the end of his *Nature and Values*. The first principle is "respect for personality." This respect finds expression in three levels of personhood. It involves a healthy self-respect, i.e., "never knowingly to violate either my reason or my love." It involves respect for others–the neighbor whose dignity and worth must always be regarded. In a language reminiscent of Kant, Brightman stated the Law of the Ideal Personality: "All persons ought to judge and guide all of their acts by their ideal conception . . . of what the whole personality ought to become both individually and socially."[55] Finally, it involves respect for God, the Divine Personality. Unlike ourselves and others, who may be respected for what we can become, God can be respected for what he is. In fact, "Faith in God" simply means that he can be respected because his being, his unchanging nature, he himself, will respect personality."[56]

A second principle of the personalist philosophy is that nature is "a revelation of Divine Personality." This notion reflects the inclusiveness and unitary thrust of personalism. Nature is not separated from super-nature in any radical way as some theologians, notably Karl Barth, have attempted to separate natural theology from revealed theology.

For Brightman, nature is not simply man's instrument, much less his enemy. God is revealed through nature. Nature has a sacramental character–it is a "sensible sign . . . of grace and God's good will toward us." Personalism believes that nature is God in action and literally God's handiwork. It is "God's will directing, shaping, controlling the phenomenal area of God's conscious experience." In short, says Brightman, the "only substance of nature is the Divine Personality."

This deep appreciation for nature bespeaks the openness and inclusiveness of personalism. It serves to unify science and religion, harmonize nature and revelation in theology as well as the rational and romantic in philosophy, and to reconcile differences among the world's major religions.[57]

A third major principle of personalistic philosophy is "spiritual liberty." Brightman is impressed with the fact that "the whole of history is man's struggle for freedom." This freedom of which he speaks is not just the classical understanding of freedom of choice. That is assumed in personalism. It is even more than the political freedom of democracy, although that is necessary. The essence of spiritual liberty "comes through a life in touch with the sources of truth and power . . . 'the truth shall make you free.'"[58]

This liberty is a personal freedom that allows a person to become what he was meant to be as a person, to develop his potential to the fullest as a human being, to be permitted to experience worth, dignity, and value or in religious terms to know himself loved as a child of God. (The first and third principles had considerable impact on King's ethical philosophy.)

2. The Personal God

We mentioned in the previous section the belief of personalism that God is the Supreme Person, that the ultimate nature of Being is personal. Reality can be understood most appropriately in the categories of the personal. At the center of a society of persons is a "supremely rational and supremely loving Person . . . God, the only Eternal Person."[59]

What is meant by saying "God is personal" or "God is a person?" Any definition would have to be related to the affirmation that man is a personal being. Bowne insisted that any being, finite or infinite, is personal if it has self-knowledge, self-consciousness, and self-control. The term personal has no other meaning.[60]

For Bowne's student, Brightman, belief in God as a person is belief that the "unbegun and unending energy of the universe is conscious rational will."[61] That is, the "fundamental and eternal energy of the universe is conscious rational will, a conscious purpose that is coherent, selective, and creative."[62]

So, in Brightman's understanding of the personal God, for instance, these themes constantly reappear and may be understood as content for the category of "Person": spirit, eternal consciousness, thinking, willing, controlling, loving, rational purpose. God as personal means God as self-conscious, loving will. To believe in a personal God is to believe that:

> God is a spirit, a being whose *esse* is to be conscious, to experience, to think, to will, to love, and to control the ongoing of the universe by rational purpose.[63]

Both Bowne and Brightman, on the other hand, go to some length to assure the reader that belief in "God as a person" is not to be identified with "man as a person." They sense that much of the objection to the personalist conception of God is based on what is an alleged anthropomorphism. They insist that there is a difference between a personal God and an anthropomorphic deity.

Bowne argues that man's essential personality is as "unpicturable and formless as God." Personality is not to be defined in terms of space, time, and measurement. It is not a "psycho-physical organism" (Brightman) and "personality and corporeality are incommensurable ideas" (Bowne). One cannot visibly see nor literally picture the essence of personality—"selfhood, self-consciousness, self-control, and the power to know."

> Laying aside, then, all thought of corporeal form and limitation as being no factor of personality, we must really say that complete and perfect personality can be found only in the Infinite and Absolute Being, as only in Him can we find that complete and perfect selfhood and self-possession which are necessary to the fullness of personality. In thinking then, of the Supreme Person we must beware of transferring to him the limitations and accidents of our human personality, which are no necessary part of the notion of personality, and think only of the fullness of power, knowledge, and selfhood which alone are the essential factors of the conception.[64]

Brightman suggests three arguments for the evidence of a personal God.[65] First, there is the presence of law and order, purpose and adjustment, in the universe. This suggests a personal mind at work. He concedes that order does not automatically imply mind, "but mind necessitates order and order is coherent with mind."

The second source of evidence is often used by theists. History and sociology seem to point toward a monotheism and the ideals of cooperation and benevolence. ". . . One supreme personal God is at work in all religious experience."

Thirdly, the theist believes that the "referent" of all our conscious experiences is most coherently related to the data of our experience when it is viewed as personal. "Value is inherently a personal experience, and if the cosmic source of value is itself a value, it must be a person realizing ideals."[66]

So, the theistic argument for belief in a personal God rests "on its greater coherence with all the facts of experience than any alternative belief."[67] We can see now how avowedly theistic personalism is. Rather than asking if a philosophical thinker can believe in God, the personalist, says Brightman, would ask "can he reasonably avoid belief in God?" The existence of a supreme person and his energizing will helps us "most coherently and completely" to understand all of life and matter.[68]

3. *Logos* and *Agape*

Two norms or ideals which portray the New Testament God are *logos* and *agape*, reason and love, or, better still, says Brightman, "reasonable love." This enables him to ask sincerely and answer with affirmation the question about absolute standards and "fixed ends." Even though human knowledge is subject to error and is often incomplete, we do make a distinction in thought between the relatively less certain and the relatively more certain.

Some of our beliefs when shown to be inadequate or in error may or may not make an appreciable difference to the meaning of our existence. But, claims Brightman, there are some convictions so basic, so all-determining, so full of certainty, that if they are proved false, no amount of readjustment will suffice for harmony in life; "all meaning is gone." There are at least

> two fundamentally unchangeable goals of all human action. They may be called intelligence and cooperation, or respect for truth and respect for personality, or reason and love (the *logos* and *agape* of the New Testament).[69]

Logos and *agape* are "the noblest powers" of the world of persons and the goal of life is the maximum development of these powers. To put it in other words and more simply, the purpose of life is that persons live together adequately and cooperatively.

> Still more simply, the purpose of life is reasonable love or loving reason–they mean the same thing. Love without reason as well as reason without love is a maimed and self-defeating thing.[70]

These are true norms and "fixed ends" and if universally applied would make for peace and unity. If reason is a false norm, science would be impossible.

If love, i.e., respect for personality, is not a true norm, all value is eliminated, since all value is personal experience that is respected.[71]

Brightman suggests that these two ideals have universal appeal to all races and creeds. Under different names they appear in most philosophies and religions. He saw the "Four Freedoms" delineated by Franklin Roosevelt (freedom of speech and religion, freedom from want and fear) as an "effort to make the norm of reasonable love . . . concrete; each of the freedoms is an expression of rational respect for personality."[72] Brightman is confident that these principles of reason and love are true norms. And although no one is completely reasonable or loving, they (love and reason) "define fixed directions in which humanity must forever move if it is not to destroy itself."[73]

With this emphasis, Brightman is representative of the best in liberal thought. It reveals his optimistic assumptions about the nature of man and history. Both were deeply imbedded in the thought of King.

4. *Value*

The category of value is of central importance to personalism. We have seen how Lotze united the metaphysical and the ethical by way of his emphasis on value. He was undoubtedly influenced at this point by Kant's primacy of the practical reason, which was the unique contribution of Kant to philosophical thought.

Kant's emphasis upon freedom and duty implies a precedence over theoretical reason. For Brightman, this means that value is "more fundamental than nature; what ought to be (as Lotze later hints) is the explanation of what is."[74] This symbolizes the pivotal place value holds in the personalist world-view.

Brightman makes a distinction between values and ideals. An ideal simply serves as a definition of a value. However, a value is more than just a definition; "it is the experience of a realized ideal."

> The value is an ideal plan carried out in personal life. That men ought to cooperate is an ideal norm; actual cooperation of Negroes and whites, Gentiles and Jews, Japanese and Chinese, is a value.[75]

What, then, is the meaning of value? For Brightman, value "means whatever is actually liked, prized, esteemed, approved, or enjoyed by anyone at any time."[76] It is important to note that he uses the word "actual." In the light of the above-mentioned distinction between ideal and value, we can appreciate Brightman's contention that a value "is the actual experience of enjoying a desired object or activity."[77] A desired object is a potential value, while actual value is present realization of desire.

In ethical thought, good is often synonymous with value. One should remember, however, that good is most often used in connection with morality, while value can apply to a wide variety of areas–the esthetic, the logical, the religious, as well as the moral.

Brightman further distinguishes intrinsic and instrumental values. The former refers to "immediate, consummatory ends" and the latter to "contributory, mediate, causal means."[78] An instrumental value is anything which has the intention of producing an experience of intrinsic value. On the other hand, an intrinsic value is anything desired or enjoyed for its own sake "as an end in itself." Obviously, for Brightman, the only true intrinsic value we know is personality. This suggests the relation of value to religion. God is the only source of value as well as the conserver of values.[79] A religious man asserts the "predominance of good in the universe" and has always thought of God "as something assuring or symbolizing the permanence of those values."[80]

Although, according to Brightman, "religion is man's concern about his own value and destiny," we learn from religious experience that the "idea of God in some form is the highest religious affirmation of man's value and destiny."[81]

> In general, the whole domain of value experience . . . is even more explicitly coherent with the hypothesis of a personal God than are other facts of law and order. . . . Value is inherently a personal experience; and if the cosmic source of value is itself a value it must be a person realizing ideals.[82]

5. The Moral Law

Theistic personalism is convinced that there is an objective moral law in the universe to which men must adjust themselves. The presence of this moral law is one of King's strongest convictions and most prominent themes. It is affirmed with clarity by Brightman.

> Idealists hold that moral experience points to an objective moral order in reality, as truly as sense experience points to an objective physical order, and most idealists believe that the objective existence of both orders can be understood rationally only if both are the activity or thought or experience

of a supreme mind that generates the whole cosmic process and controls its ongoing.[83]

Brightman defined a moral law as "a universal principle to which the will ought to conform in its choices. If it is not a universal principle, it is not a law; and if it does not apply to the obligation of the will in choosing, it is not moral."[84] Walter Muelder summed up the belief for personalists. "Morality is a part of reality. We seek it but we do not make it."[85]

There is obviously here a dependence upon Kant's categorical imperative and the *a priori*, i.e., the universal and necessary character of the practical reason. Lotze, following Kant, suggested a direct relationship between the World-Order and the moral world and agrees with Fichte that "the ground of all other certainty" is "this moral order of the world."[86]

For Bowne, there is an empirical basis for the postulate that the world-ground has a moral character. It is based on the moral nature of man, the structure of society, and the course of history. "The first two are held to point to a moral author, and the last reveals a power not ourselves, making for righteousness, and hence moral."[87] The centrality of the moral is obvious in Bowne's philosophy and typical of personalism in general. Men cannot live together without constructing a society which rests on moral ideals. When these ideals are absent or when oppression and injustice are sanctioned by law, "social earthquakes and volcanoes begin to rock society to its foundations."

Neither man nor society can escape the need of righteousness, truthfulness, honesty, purity, etc. No cunning, no power, can forever avail against the truth. No strength can long support a lie. The wicked may have great power and spread himself like a green bay-tree, but he passes away . . . no lesson is more clearly taught by history than that righteousness exalteth a nation while sin is a reproach to any people. The one truth, it is said, which can be verified, concerning the world-ground is that it makes for righteousness.[88]

By now, we can see that the objectivity of value, the objectivity of the moral law is directly related to the personalist concept of God. Without a belief in God, the moral order would collapse and our ideals be shattered. The moral law depends upon the will and nature of God.

Knudson said that of the three main arguments for the existence of God–conceptual (ontological), causal (cosmological), and valuational (moral), personalism opts for the latter, for "worth is the key to reality,"[89] and "all religion is based on faith in the goodness of the world-ground."[90] A God

189

without righteousness, goodwill, and moral concern, i.e., void of value, might be all-powerful and all-knowing, but he could never be an adequate object of religious faith. For religious faith is primarily concerned with the moral character of God, "his personality in the full ethical sense of the term."[91] Thus, for personalism, the moral nature of the universe presupposes a moral author. Bowne, in quasi-scriptural language, concluded, "He that formed the eye, shall not he see? . . . He that implanted in man an unalterable reverence for righteousness, shall not he himself be righteous?"[92]

Brightman, in a chapter significantly titled, "The Autonomy of Moral Law," and in more philosophical language, claimed:

> If religion be defined as cooperation between man and his God, expressed both in worship and in the conduct of life, then two important implications follow at once: First that God is regarded as the embodiment of the moral ideal, and, secondly, that he is viewed as the very source or creator of a moral order in the universe.[93]

The interrelationship of ethics and metaphysics in personalism should be noted here. Theistic metaphysics provides a base and support for ethics while ethics, the "interpretation of the phenomena of moral experience" can furnish metaphysics with subject matter. But since there is an "autonomy" in the moral law, it remains true within its realm, "the realm of human living, irrespective of what may lie beyond human experience or beyond the grave."[94] The deepest truths about life, about reality as a whole, are not derived from speculation or purely intellectual processes, but from the ethical and spiritual nature of man and history, from experience that is prior to and deeper than logic.

As we shall see, one of King's central themes is the presence in the universe of a moral order man could not defy and which inexorably is working its way through history. It was the philosophy of personalism that provided King with a sound intellectual base for his religiously motivated ethical concern.

6. Community: The Social Nature of Personality

For personalism there is a logical relationship between the personal and the social. "The world of persons is a social world."[95] "For personalism, social categories are ultimate."[96] "The structure of experience is social."[97] "Men are born to live together, and apart from this togetherness would not be truly human."[98] "The maxim 'Think for yourself' is basic; but the further maxim 'Think socially' must be added if philosophy is to do its whole duty."[99]

Hence, man naturally expresses himself in terms of community and naturally needs fellowship with other persons. Persons are constantly interacting with other persons in the world of persons. This interaction affects each of us, determining to a great extent our experience, consciousness, and history. This is in no way an attempt to deny the importance of individual personality, or self-identity, but it is to say that each of us is a person in relationship and never completely personal apart from the social. We develop and grow as persons interacting with others in our social relationships. There is also a mutual interdependence of persons. We come to need and to rely upon each other. This, for Knudson, is the meaning of a "Christian world."

> The real Christian world is a world of mutually dependent beings. It is a social world, a world of interacting moral beings; and in such a world love is necessarily the basic moral law.[100]

So we see also that the social nature of personality is ultimately grounded in the nature of the Divine Personality. Although strictly speaking, God does not require persons for his existence

> his moral nature is love, and love needs comradeship. God, then, is not a solitary, self-enjoying mind, He is love; he is the "Great Socius," the Great Companion.[101]

It is for this reason that experiments in human community, such as democracy, are seen as attempts to "live politically in tune with the Infinite."[102] It is out of this love that the Christian community eventually arises, a community "created by and devoted to that love."[103] Therefore, personalism, with all types of idealism, "recognizes the community as at once the support, the fulfillment, and the ideal goal of the individual."[104]

7. The Ideal of the Human Community

Personalism's hope for a "world of values" must be seen in the light of the sacred treatment of human personality and from within the liberal, optimistic view of human nature prevalent in the first third of this century.

For instance, Brightman's "ideal of inexhaustible perfectibility" (as opposed to perfection), is evidence of the possibilities open to man. The perfectionist strain is found in Knudson, who said that the true church is composed of people who are not only saved *in* their sins (as classical orthodoxy suggests), but who are also earnestly seeking to be saved *from* their sins.[105] The church is a regenerated body of believers which points to a "redeemed and perfected human society." We are not trapped in the "pessimistic" paradox of Luther's *simul justus, simul peccator*, but we can become less selfish and more loving, less sinful and more obedient persons.

In discussing the universal human longing for perfection, Brightman desires to eschew the label "optimism" and uses instead "meliorism," which signifies the possibility of human betterment and improvement. That is, evil is a real force in the universe, but good is dominant and the "universe is always susceptible of improvement."[106] Value will ultimately hold sway over disvalue.

Another concept, important for Brightman, is "cooperation." In fact, it is the essence of religion. It is, first of all, cooperation with God, involving receptivity and response to him, without which there is no religion at all. And further it would involve "cooperation with the unshakable purpose of the Eternal Person," primary among them being respect for personality. Thus, in the second place, religion means cooperation with man, "a devotion to personal values."

> . . . not to cooperate with men for the social realization of those values is at the same time not to cooperate with God's purpose. Religion, when conscious of its own destiny, is best defined as *cooperation with God and man for the realization of individual and of shared values.*[107]

The level of cooperation is the most significant level of the third principle of personalistic philosophy, the level of spiritual liberty. Here man is liberated from selfishness and is able to open himself to the needs of his neighbor, willingly sharing with and working for him. On the level of cooperation, also, reason and love "find the best soil for their growth." "Here is the Kingdom of God in which all races and creeds can meet, learn, and respect each other in religious liberty."[108]

Another basis in personalism making for the possibility of universal human community is the concept of unity. It is directly related to the principle of respect for personality. As long as there is regard for the value of human personality, there can be human unity–a unity that does not preclude nor repress differences of opinion or of cultures.

Brightman cites Jesus as the very incarnation of that principle. "His heart was warm toward Jews and Greeks, Samaritans and Gentiles."[109] And although Brightman sees Jesus's teaching of love "slowly and painfully" being applied by men in democracy and worldwide cooperation, "men have much to learn about the principle of spiritual liberty."

> . . . yet the profoundest fact about religion is not its separation and divisions; the profoundest fact is that religion, like science and philosophy, is a search for unity and that it is a faith, which science and philosophy too often ignore or lack, that the source of all being is in the unity of divine personality, divine ideals, and divine liberty.[110]

Brightman's method for achieving the "world of values" is one of appeal to the best in man, his sense of fairness, his spiritual depth, his rationality. It is what Plato called "persuasion" or what Christianity means by "conversion." Brightman calls it "rational love in education." Given the reluctance of man fully to respond to reason and love, however, the world of values lies somewhere in the future. But his faith in man's perfectibility and his firmly held belief in the worth of personality gives Brightman hope.

> Any philosophy or religion or political theory that treats personality seriously and sacredly has in it the seeds of hope–hope that humanity may see that nature and values are one world, a world which can be realized effectively only by the labors of reason and love, human and divine.[111]

The themes here of meliorism, inclusiveness, cooperation, unity, and the value of personality provide the philosophical basis for King's dream of the beloved community.

F. *Personalism in King*

With the exception of the above-mentioned quotation from *Stride Toward Freedom*, King makes no specific reference to personalism as such. However, in many places throughout his writing, in short phrases as well as in sustained but relatively brief discussions, the influence of the theistic idealism of personalism is unmistakably evident. This influence is most obvious in King's discussion of the injustices of segregation, a discussion which allows him to reveal his personalist understanding of man and God.

1. *The Inherent Worth of Man*

The operative word here is inherent. King felt there was deeply rooted in our political and religious heritage the conviction that "every man is an heir to a legacy of dignity and worth," and that "every human being has etched in his personality the indelible stamp of the Creator."[112]

> Our Judeo-Christian tradition refers to this inherent dignity of man in the Biblical term "the image of God." "The image of God" is universally shared in equal portions by all men.[113]

What King meant by this was apparent in what immediately followed the reference to the "image of God."[114] He goes on to say that "human worth lies in relatedness to God. An individual has value because he has value to God."[115] Later on in the same work, King seems to equate "image of God" with "infinite metaphysical value."[116] This means for King that every person, by virtue of birth, is a child of God and related to him as a son to a father.

The worth of a man does not inhere in the measure of his intellect, his racial background, or his social status or, as King said on another occasion, not in his "specificity, but his fundamentum."[117] The worth of man lies in the relationship of value every man has to God. Man is to be respected because he is a "reflection of divinity"[118] and because God loves him, not because of an exigency of history or an accident of birth. "In the final analysis, says the Christian ethic, every man must be respected because God loves him."[119]

Here King distinguishes himself from traditional orthodox theology which has affirmed that as a result of the Fall, man's primal disobedience, the "image of God" in man was broken. The qualitative relationship with God was no longer inherent in him. The atoning work of Christ was needed to restore God's image and to heal the broken relationship between God and man.

King does not concentrate his attention, in either sermons or other writings, on the atonement as an event which significantly altered the God-man relationship. He does appreciate the sinful nature of man. The influence of Niebuhr was indelible at this point. But King's understanding of sinful man was ultimately within the framework of the perfectibility of man and the inherent worth and sacredness of human personality. It was always against the background of the intrinsic value of the person that King discussed the nature of man.

But, the image of God *can* be broken. This occurs when men treat each other unjustly or destroy that in man which constitutes his true essence. Because of the divinity reflected in man, "every act of injustice mars and defaces the image of God in man."[120] So long as the Negro, or any other man, is treated as something less "than a person of sacred worth, the image of God is abused in him and consequently and proportionately lost by those who inflict the abuse."[121]

This was the theological and philosophical rationale for King's attack on segregation. King persistently claimed that segregation was "morally wrong and sinful" precisely because it is based on pride and hatred. Segregation is "unbrotherly and impersonal." "Two segregated souls never meet in God. Segregation denies the sacredness of human personality."[122]

> The undergirding philosophy of segregation is diametrically opposed to the undergirding philosophy of our Judeo-Christian heritage, and all the dialectics of the logicians cannot make them lie down together.[123]

Further, segregation is immoral because it treats men as "means" rather than "ends," and thereby "reduces them to things rather than persons." King conceived of man as an end in theological terms, i.e., he is a child of God. But he reminds the reader of Immanuel Kant's concern that "all men must be treated as *ends* and never as *means*."[124] So man is not a means, a thing, an "animated tool" and, accordingly, must not be related to as such. He must be dealt with "as a person sacred in himself." "To do otherwise is to depersonalize the potential person and desecrate what he is."[125]

One of King's strongest criticisms of totalitarian communism is based on this Kantian personalist understanding of man. This political system denies man his freedom and relegates him to the status of a thing, rather than elevating him to the status of a person. Hence man can never be made for the state, never a means to the end of the state. Man is an end, for which the state is created.[126]

King assumes that democracy at its best is "person" oriented and not "thing" oriented and that a truly integrated society would mean that the quality of "thou-ness" would be restored to the Negro as his due "because of the nature of his being."[127] Within this framework, Negroes could have a feeling of "somebodiness," "self-respect," and "human dignity."[128] The alleviation of human need is motivated by and grounded in this

195

understanding of man. If man would accept as a "profound moral fact" the "infinite metaphysical value" of the human person, we would not "be content to see men hungry, to see men victimized with ill-health, when we have the means to help them."[129]

King's nonviolence, both in principle and tactics, is directly related to the affirmation of ultimate value of all human life. "Thou shalt not kill," really means that life is "too sacred to be taken on the battlefields of the world." And

> when we truly believe in the sacredness of human personality, we won't exploit people, we won't trample over people with the iron feet of oppression, we won't kill anybody.[130]

2. The Personal God of Love

King revealed personalistic thought in his sermon, "The Death of Evil on the Seashore." He said that God could not deal with evil in any "overbearing way," a way we might desire. If he did that, he might defeat his ultimate purpose. For he said, "we are responsible human beings, not blind automatons; persons, not puppets."[131] Man has been given freedom by God and, in doing so, God placed upon himself a good deal of restriction. He is not free to impose his will upon man. He now runs the risk of receiving from us a willing and free response–this is his purpose for men. If God were to act through "sheer omnipotence" he would, thereby, defeat that purpose.[132]

More specifically, King speaks of God as "the ground and essence of all reality, a Being of infinite love and boundless power." He relates God to value as creator and sustainer and, echoing personalist categories, he says that God is a "Conserver of values."[133] Within the context of theistic idealism, he criticizes naturalism and materialism of all kinds.

> Reality cannot be explained by matter in motion or the push and pull of economic forces. Christianity affirms that at the heart of reality is a Heart, a loving Father who works through history for the salvation of his children.[134]

And in the second version of "Pilgrimage to Nonviolence," King has his most complete presentation of the personalist God. The passage is prefaced by a personal confession, couched in meditational and deeply moving tones, that he had long believed in the personality of God–his theological and philosophical training had guaranteed that. But the "personal God" had remained on the academic level. During the civil rights struggle, with the many harried days and nights, threats on his life, family, and property, God as a living reality became real to him. Here is the passage which summarizes the understanding of God King learned from Edgar S. Brightman.

> I am convinced that the universe is under the control of a loving purpose, and that in the struggle for righteousness man has cosmic companionship. Behind the harsh appearances of the world there is a benign power. To say that this God is personal is not to make him a finite object besides other objects or attribute to him the limitations of human personality; it is to take what is finest and noblest in our consciousness and affirm its perfect existence in him. It is certainly true that human personality is limited, but personality as such involves no necessary limitations. It means simple self-consciousness and self-direction. So, in the truest sense of the word, God is a living God. In him there is feeling and will, responsive to the deepest yearnings of the human heart; *this* God both evokes and answers prayer.[135]

3. King and the Moral Law

As a result of his biblical training and his roots in personalist philosophy, King affirms as strongly as he possibly can the moral foundations of reality. This is perhaps his most central and determinative theological and metaphysical principle. His immediate debt is owed, of course, to the formulations of personalism, i.e., the uniting of the metaphysical and the valuable in a profound appreciation of the ethical. Kantian and Hegelian influences are found in King's discussion of the moral law, with the Kantian elements the most predominant. The former is illustrated by such phrases as "cosmic companionship" in the struggle for justice,[136] and "all reality hinges on moral foundations."[137] The latter, Hegelian, influence is illustrated by the following: "some creative force that works for universal wholeness;"[138] and the constant reference to "something in history" operating for good.[139] In fact, for King, history is often the subject of verbs as it if had a personal character.

Obviously, King's theological training should not be overlooked. His deep roots in the Hebrew prophetic tradition enabled him to transpose the moral law of Kantian idealism and the dialectical process in history of Hegelian idealism to God, the Lord who operates in and through history in the name of love and justice.[140] It is instructive to note that this theme appeared in his earliest writings and speeches. In an address in San Francisco on June 27,

197

1956, describing the Montgomery boycott, he used language that would reappear in almost every article and book he wrote:

> We have the strong feeling that in our struggle we have cosmic companionship. . . . We feel that the universe is on the side of right. . . . We must press on because freedom and justice are ethical demands of the universe.[141]

In "Facing the Challenge of a New Age," references to William Cullen Bryant and James R. Lowell appear–references to which he returns repeatedly when he sought to justify his optimism in resistance to opposition. It is in this article that he mentions the historical tension between Good Friday and Easter with "evil being ultimately doomed by the powerful, inexorable forces of good." In addition, he states that the cross, symbol of weakness and suffering, divided all of history into A.D. and B.C.[142]

4. The Moral as Ultimate

Whatever else King firmly believed, he affirmed the moral structure of the universe. As he understood history, good has always been vindicated and, relying upon the Crucifixion-Resurrection symbol of Christianity, good always will be vindicated, truth will ultimately conquer evil, love will eventually emerge victorious over injustice. It is the "structure of the universe." Or, in other words, "God is able to conquer the evils of history. . . . He has placed within the very structure of the universe certain absolute moral laws."[143]

Evidence that this structure is operative in history, proof that reality hinges on moral foundations, "is the fact that when men and governments work devotedly for the good of others, they achieve their own enrichment in the process."[144] The Cross of Christ is a "telescope" through which we view love, the "most durable power in the world," and King concludes that "at bottom (it is) the heartbeat of the moral cosmos."[145] This love, which is the moral law of the universe, or the law of God, radically affirms the value of human personality. A man-made law is just or unjust depending on how it identifies with the moral law. The uplifting of human personality is the purpose of law and "any law that degrades the human personality is an unjust law."[146]

For this reason, King insisted that the civil rights issue was not an "ephemeral, evanescent domestic issue" to be manipulated by self-seeking and reactionary politicians, but it was "an eternal moral issue."[147] In opposing integration, we are not only opposing the noble principles of democracy, "but also the eternal edicts of God himself."[148] So, the Negro should be given his freedom–not just because it is "diplomatically expedient, but because it is morally compelling."[149]

5. *God in History ("There is something in the universe . . .")*

King comes very close to identifying the historical process with God. The personal and moral character of God is virtually synonymous with positive forces of history working for good. Were it not for his biblical moorings, he would at times be an Hegelian in terms of history being a process of divine self-manifestation–the Absolute Spirit (*Geist*) realizing itself in history. This Hegelian note is struck in the following passage.

> . . . there is something unfolding in the universe whether one speaks of it as some unmoved mover, or whether someone speaks of it as a personal God. There is something in the universe that unfolds for justice and so in Montgomery we felt somehow that as we struggled we had cosmic companionship.[150]

Somewhat the same thought is found in a passage from *Stride Toward Freedom*. King assumes that most people

> believe in the existence of some creative force that works for universal wholeness. Whether we call it an unconscious process, an impersonal Brahman, or a Personal Being of matchless power and infinite love, there is a creative force in this universe that works to bring the disconnected aspects of reality into a harmonious whole.[151]

He is saved from Absolute Idealism by his appreciation of the Exodus as a reliable model of God's activity in history.[152] One of King's better sermons, "The Death of Evil on the Seashore,"[153] suggests that although evil may be recalcitrant and apparently in power, "there is a checkpoint in the universe."[154] That "checkpoint" was seen in the confrontation Moses had with Pharaoh and in the ensuing conflict between the Israelites and the Egyptians. The Red Sea spelled the destruction of Egyptian bondage, an evil which carried the seeds of its own doom. And so every

> Red Sea passage in history ultimately brings the forces of goodness to victory, and the closing of the same water marks the doom and destruction of the

199

forces of evil . . . evil has a self-defeating quality. It can go a long way, but then it reaches its limit. There is something in this universe that Greek mythology referred to as the goddess of Nemesis.[155]

King sensed behind and within the civil rights struggle a supra-rational force, a divine dimension. As we have seen, it made little difference to King by what label it was called. It could have been Whitehead's "principle of concretion," Wieman's "process of integration," Tillich's "Being-Itself," or the Christian's "personal God."

> Whatever the name, some extra-human force labors to create a harmony out of the discords of the universe. There is a creative power that works to pull down mountains of evil and level hilltops of injustice. God still works through history his wonders to perform.[156]

In order that the reader be convinced that King believes in a personal God who is willing love, he said the Hebrew-Christian God we worship

> is not some Aristotelian "unmoved mover" who merely contemplates upon himself, he is not merely a self-knowing God, but another loving God who forever works through history for the establishment of His kingdom.[157]

Because the universe is on the side of justice, because love beats in the heart of the moral cosmos, because God is good and just, "history does not pose problems without eventually producing solutions."[158] The solution produced in the latter half of the sixth decade of this country was the "peaceful weapon of nonviolent direct action."

For many of the disadvantaged and disinherited, belief in the personal God who holds the reins of history enabled them also to adhere to the principles of nonviolence. It gave them hope beyond despair and a "deep faith in the future." It inspired them to sing "We shall overcome." It was the reason the nonviolent resister could accept suffering without retaliation.[159] Again, there was faith and hope in the movement because there is "something within it that says somehow even though the arc of the moral universe is long, it bends toward justice."[160]

Thus, King's Christian faith that good will eventually triumph, that the Resurrection is the ultimate symbol of the nature of reality, gave him confidence in the presence of evil forces in history. Their seemingly irresistible power will be "crushed by the battling (sic!) rams of the forces of justice."[161] His faith, a religious reflection of a "silent, invisible imperative, akin to the laws in the physical world" assures him that life will work only in a certain way. He was impressed with Hugo's observation in *Les Miserables*. Napoleon lost at Waterloo not because of the superior military strength and ingenuity of Wellington or Blucher. He lost because "he had been impeached before the Infinite. . . . He vexed God." So, King concludes that Waterloo is symbolic of an eternally true fact.

> . . . in the long run of history might does not make right and the power of the sword cannot conquer the power of the spirit.[162]

The providence of loving God has both a theological and metaphysical base for King. It is grounded in the Biblical God who provided a Red Sea in history for Israel and victory over evil in the Cross for Christianity. It is grounded as well in the personal nature of ultimate reality as defined by the idealistic theism of personalism. In both cases, there is the belief that "the contradictions of life are neither final nor ultimate"[163] and "that beyond time is a divine Spirit and beyond life is Life," a God who will ultimately "join virtue and fulfillment."[164]

G. *Hegel's Influence on King*

As we have suggested, while Kant had a determining influence on personalism, Hegel also was of considerable significance to this philosophical position. This is particularly true in the monism of Bowne and Brightman. The Hegelian dictum, "The Real is Rational and the Rational is Real" is found in Bowne's contention that:

> The world of experience exists for us only through a rational spiritual principle by which we reproduce it for our thought, and it has its existence apart from us only through a rational spiritual principle on which it depends, and the rational nature of which it expresses.[165]

It was an assumption of Bowne and Brightman that Being was orderly and rational. The implication that God is a Being of rational order was most forcefully articulated by Hegel. The primacy of reason obtained everywhere–in nature, history, and religious experience. Bowne felt that one creative purpose embraced all systems of reality in one plan. They are really stages in God's unfolding plan and purpose and work.[166] In another place, Bowne refers to the world as "not merely a thought, but a thought expressed in act. It is God idea; it is also God's deed."[167] These two elements must be held together for a proper understanding of the world.

Hegel's influence on Brightman can be seen in his discussion of "the dialectic of desire" in his *A Philosophy of Religion*. Brightman understood by dialectic the "mind's search for completeness and coherence."[168] Wholeness is a goal toward which we work; we do not start with it. The presence of Good in the universe "leads to a dialectic of desire that finds coherent culmination only in a personal God."[169] The personal God is the complete, coherent, whole structure of reality. This reflects Hegel's attempt to transcend analysis and to synthesize opposites, unite differences and ultimately to resolve tension. The universe, for Hegel, was a coherent whole.

King met Hegel in his courses in theology under Davis and in survey courses in philosophy.[170] However, he was most clearly subjected to Hegelian thought in a year long (1952-53) seminar on Hegel taught by Brightman.[171] Although King could never become an Hegelian in substance, Hegelian methodology pervades his thinking and writing. The net result of his study of Hegel was that King thought dialectically (in terms of wholes) and he appreciated the broad sweeps of history.

1. *The Dialectic in King*

It is not insignificant that in his address delivered at the First Annual Institute on Nonviolence and Social Change in Montgomery, Alabama, December 1956, in which King begins to reflect upon the meaning of the boycott, he places the struggle in the framework of historical change. "We stand today between two worlds–the dying old and the emerging new."[172] Soon after the address begins (in the second paragraph), as he seeks meaningfully to interpret what is happening in Montgomery, he draws upon his philosophical training.

> Long ago the Greek philosopher Heraclitus argued that justice emerges from the strife of opposites, and Hegel, in modern philosophy, preached a doctrine of growth through struggle. It is both historically and biologically true that there can be no birth and growth without birth and growing pains.[173]

King refused to see the Montgomery boycott and the subsequent civil rights movement as isolated events. They had to be viewed against the background of history–a history in which the moral laws of justice and truth are gradually unfolding. On the one hand, that is why King always included the white man with his prejudice, as well as his understanding, in his interpretation of the racial crisis in America. On the other hand, it is why King repeatedly refused to see the racial conflict simply in terms of white and black, but in a much larger perspective of justice and injustice.

So King said to the Montgomery Improvement Association, on its Fourth Anniversary, December 3, 1959, that when he became its president in 1955, he did not have to create unity; "You had already been brought together by the forces of history."[174] Rosa Parks, whose arrest December 1, 1955, precipitated the boycott in Montgomery, was part of a much larger process at work in history.

> She was anchored to that seat by the accumulated indignities of days gone by and the boundless aspirations of generations yet unborn. She was a victim of both the forces of history–the force of destiny. She had been tracked down by the *Zeitgeist*–the spirit of the time.[175]

So, for an oppressed people, the yearning for freedom eventually manifests itself. Something within the American Negro reminded him of his birthright of freedom and that this can be realized. "Consciously or unconsciously, he has been caught up by the *Zeitgeist*"[176] that is sweeping the world, prompting all oppressed peoples to move toward freedom. History has forced upon this generation and this time "an indescribably important destiny–to complete a process of democratization which our nation has too long developed too slowly."[177]

We can see that King allowed for polarities within a position and hoped for reconciliation, if not a synthesis of the two. He tended to view conflict from a larger, more cosmic perspective, one that transcended lesser divisions. In interpreting the history of race relations in American history, King employs the dialectic. He disagrees with the optimists who feel the problem will soon be solved and we have made great strides in civil rights. He also disagrees with the pessimists who claim that virtually nothing has been accomplished and that integration is impossible.

King adopts a third position which he denotes "the realistic attitude." "Like the synthesis of Hegelian philosophy, the realistic attitude seeks to reconcile the truths of two opposites and avoid the extremes of both."[178] We have come a long way, but we have a long way to go, was his conclusion.

In fact, King saw evolutionary growth in race relations as he viewed the total spectrum of racial history in America. On many occasions in the late fifties, when he was the primary spokesman of the Negro and the most articulate interpreter of his experience, King employed the following argument. He suggested there have been three distinct periods in the history of race relations in the United States, "each representing growth over the preceding period." The thought patterns of each period were legitimized by a Supreme Court decision. The period of slavery, 1619-1863, was climaxed by the Dred Scott decision in 1857. The period of segregation, 1863-1954, was symbolized by the Court decision, Plessy vs. Ferguson, in 1896. Since 1954, we have been in the era of "constructive integration."[179] Thus, the process of history continues to unfold, moving to a purer and more refined sense of truth and goodness.

However, for King, it was not inevitable that history would produce justice. Time was often the ally of the power structure and the *status quo* or, at best, time was neutral. Historical change comes about by human responsiveness to the *Zeitgeist*. This involves one in a style of reasoning that is somewhat foreign to the classical educational tradition of the West. The latter has been determined by syllogistic, rational thought of Aristotle.

But there is another way to reason–the dialectical. Here a thesis is confronted by an antithesis (e.g., the powerful social, political, economic systems of a southern community by a united, committed, oppressed people). Out of this tension and conflict emerges a synthesis, a new reality combining the best in each position, but a qualitative leap forward is made in history. So growth and development are achieved through conflict. The impression this method left on King was deep. It finds expression not only in his activity, but in his presentation of ideas.

The fascination for the dialectic began in the Hegel Seminar in Boston. Peter Bertocci recounts that King, usually quiet in class, became quite attentive when his fellow students began discussing Hegel's dialectical relationship of master to slave. That the master could come to depend so much on the slave that the latter would emerge in a dominant position in the relationship was a determining insight for King and colored much of his method of thinking thereafter.[180]

One practical outcome of the lesson learned from Hegel was that King always tried to avoid adopting extreme positions. He tended toward mediation and conciliation. He desired to avoid the extremes of the "militant and the moderate,"[181] the courses of "gradualism or directionless spontaneity,"[182] "acquiescence or violence" in face of oppression,[183] "hotheadedness or Uncle Tomism"[184] and endorsed "both education and legislation" as viable methods to achieve racial progress.[185] "Negroes are neither African nor American, but both African and American."[186] His concern was to unite the apparently irreconcilable into a working harmony. On the first page of *Strength to Love*, his orientation is clearly stated.

> But life at its best is a creative synthesis of opposites in fruitful harmony. The philosopher Hegel said that truth is found neither in the thesis nor the antithesis, but in an emergent synthesis which reconciles the two.[187]

One can understand why King was self-conscious in the presence of black power. He could appreciate it and his chapter on the subject in *Where Do We Go From Here* is one of the most balanced and sensitive to be found anywhere. But black power was an extreme just as white supremacy was an extreme. Both positions had built into them an antithesis that would eventually modify each. There are striking substantial dissimilarities between Hegelian philosophy and personalism and King sided with personalism in each case.

First of all, in terms of man's nature, personalism was more voluntaristic than Hegel's rather deterministic rationality. Personalism held that "life is deeper than logic." Here, it seems that personalism is more Kantian in holding to a formal freedom–the freedom of an individual within the system. Hegel, on the other hand, thought that freedom was bound to the system. Even though the latter may be changed, it does not mean that the individual person will be more free.

Secondly, Hegel's Absolute Mind or Spirit is essentially impersonal, whereas personalism holds irrevocably to the personal nature of ultimate reality. For Hegel, God was a logical "Universal" inherent in all things, an Identity in which differences disappear. For personalism, God is the personal will of love who initiates relation with his children and to whom they pray with confidence.

In the next place, Hegel's epistemology rests on the power of rational reflection, while personalism relies on the experience of human consciousness as a *bona fide* way of knowing. One is reflective, the other experiential. There is a practical, existential quality about personalism which distinguishes it from the abstract, impersonal rationality of the Absolute Idealism of Hegel.

Finally, the state is the highest historical value for Hegel, while the person and the person-in-community are the supreme value for personalism. Community for Hegel (and to a great extent for his American disciple, Josiah Royce) did not allow for the individuality of the person. His uniqueness was denied and he was absorbed into the All. Personalism, however, always made an indispensable place for the unique, individual person in community.

Our conclusion is that while King was greatly influenced by Hegel's method of dialectic and his desire to envision history in terms of general trends and counter-trends which transcend more parochial interests, King could never adopt the content of Hegel's philosophy.[188] Hegel's Absolute Idea was not the personal Biblical God of Exodus and the Cross, who operates in history to bring his people from bondage to freedom.

SIX

King's Vision
of the
Beloved Community

A. *Introduction*

King's devotion to the realization of the beloved community was his primary goal. It was the organizing principle of his life and around which all of his thought and activity centered. His writings and his involvement in the civil rights struggle were illustrations of and footnotes to this fundamental preoccupation.

All of his other intellectual concerns find themselves in an instrumental position with regard to the priority given the beloved community. The social gospel provides a theological framework in which to articulate it. Nonviolence provides the means by which to establish it. Personalism provides the philosophical base for supporting the personal nature of the community. And Niebuhr's realism serves to qualify King's optimism about its possible realization in history.

The concept of the beloved community can be traced from those early formative addresses delivered by King in 1955-56. In one of his first published articles, "We Are Still Walking," he said, reflecting Rauschenbusch, "We are striving for the removal of all barriers that divide and alienate mankind, whether racial, economic, or psychological."[1] In "Facing the Challenge of a New Age,"[2] King stated that the bus boycott was not an end in itself. The real purpose of the Montgomery campaign was healing; its "end is reconciliation; the end is redemption; the end is the creation of the beloved community."

Toward the end of *Stride Toward Freedom*, published in 1958, King discusses the relationship of nonviolence to the goal of "genuine . . . interpersonal living." Then he concludes, "Only through nonviolence can this goal be attained, for the aftermath of nonviolence is reconciliation and the creation of the beloved community."[3] In a sermon, "Loving Your Enemies," King calls upon his hearers to follow the "impractical" method of love. Communities have been wrecked when they followed the "practical" methods of violence, hatred, and vengeance. The "obligation to love" remains with us. "While abhorring segregation, we shall love the segregationist. This is the only way to create the beloved community."[4] Again in 1962 in an address, "The Ethical Demands of Integration," King emphasized the importance of community. For him, the "most creative turn of events" in man's long history was when he gave up his stone axe to cooperate with his neighbor.

> That seemingly elementary decision set in motion what we know now as civilization. At the heart of all that civilization has meant and developed is "community"–the mutually cooperative and voluntary venture of man to assume a semblance of responsibility for his brother.[5]

In the *Playboy* interview of 1964 (published in January 1965), King persists in his claim that all Americans have "got to live together. We've got to find a way to reconcile ourselves to living in community, one group with the other."[6] He continues, "It is the keystone of my faith in the future that we will someday achieve a thoroughly integrated society."[7]

King posits two alternatives for American society in the title of his next-to-last book, *Where Do We Go From Here: Chaos or Community?* In this book King speaks of the necessity of an international community. He sees the world as a "large house" and since we all now live in one house, we must "transform this world-wide neighborhood into a world-wide brotherhood. Together we must learn to live as brothers or together we will be forced to perish as fools."[8] The latter note of world perspective is repeated in *The Trumpet of Conscience* and there is here also a renewed stress, found in the early addresses, on the eradication of barriers of all kinds. "Our loyalties must transcend our race, our tribe, our class, and our nation. . . ."[9] This is reminiscent of Rauschenbusch, who asserted that the Christian God is:

> a barrier of barriers from the first. All who have a distinctively Christian experience of God are committed to the expansion of human fellowship and to the overthrow of barriers.[10]

The Kingdom of God for Rauschenbusch ultimately transcends all divisions of nationality, religion, and race.

1. Beloved Community and Josiah Royce

The concept of beloved community has been widely known in philosophical circles at least since the appearance of Josiah Royce's *The Problem of Christianity*. In this book Royce outlined his understanding of the beloved community.[11] The latter is a community of love and loyalty, the highest expression of corporate Christian faith. Due to his own idealistic, Hegelian orientation, Royce's beloved community is more of a rational construct than King's more historical and biblical conception. King was desperately concerned that it be realized and that it reflect certain specific ideals of justice and love.

King never once mentions Royce and it is not known from surveying his graduate courses and term papers that he read extensively in Royce. He undoubtedly was acquainted with him, at least indirectly, by way of his graduate philosophy courses at University of Pennsylvania, Boston University, and at Harvard. He certainly read about the community in Rauschenbusch's *Theology of the Social Gospel*, in which there is a positive interpretation of Royce's understanding of the ideal human community.[12]

The phrase is used by King as if the reader would recognize and understand its meaning. It is obviously not a creation of King's.

2. The Interrelatedness of Life

Integral to King's understanding of community was his conception of the "solidarity of the human family."[13] A phrase he used innumerable times, as late as March 31, 1968, was "We are tied together in the single garment of destiny, caught in an inescapable network of mutuality."[14]

To support his belief that "whatever affects one directly affects all indirectly," he repeatedly uses in his writings the oft-quoted observation of John Donne, "no man is an island, entire of itself."[15] There is an "interrelated structure of reality."[16] This structure means that we are dependent on each other. What we have and are we owe to many people who have preceded us. "Whether we realize it or not, each of us is eternally 'in the red.' We are everlasting debtors to known and unknown men and women."[17] This element of debt and implied gratitude destroys an unhealthy

209

self-sufficiency in men which isolates them as individuals and then destroys community.

Secondly, this "structure" means that we need each other for personal fulfillment. Our individual maturity and personal growth cannot take place apart from meaningful relationships with other persons. The interrelated, interdependent character of life means that "I" cannot reach fulfillment without "Thou." "The self cannot be self without other selves."[18] These fulfilled selves constitute the real human community.

The third implication of this "structure" and its most serious one is the corporate effect of injustice and immorality summed up in one of King's favorite lines, "Injustice anywhere is a threat to justice everywhere."[19] This observation is ultimately King's argument against the "outside agitator" ploy used by many southerners against people (even Atlanta-born King himself) who came into their state to intervene in local affairs.[20]

King understood that the denial of constitutional rights to anyone potentially violated the rights of all citizens. The victims of electric cattle prods and biting police dogs were the entire national community. Discrimination against ten per cent of our population weakens the whole society. South Africa and the southern United States were mutually affected by discrimination in each area. The poverty and racial issues are not merely sectional problems; they are American problems. By the same token, the liberation of black men means the full freedom for the white man. King took seriously the indivisibility of our country and the indivisibility of life. So he contends:

> In a real sense, all life is interrelated. The agony of the poor impoverishes the rich; the betterment of the poor enriches the rich. We are inevitably our brother's keeper because we are our brother's brother. Whatever affects one directly affects all indirectly.[21]

This is what King means by being "tied together in a garment of mutuality" and this reinforces his Donne reference: "and therefore never send to know for whom the bell tolls; it tolls for thee."[22] Because of this solidaristic understanding of life, King saw the civil rights movement contributing "infinitely more to the nation than the eradication of racial injustice. It will have enlarged the concept of brotherhood to a vision of total interrelatedness."[23] That is to say, our society will be approaching the ideal of the beloved community. That human life is initially and ultimately social was bequeathed to King by Rauschenbusch's strong emphasis on the solidarity of life and Brightman's contention that all life was social.

B. *Definition of the Beloved Community*

In a SCLC Newsletter in 1957, shortly after the new civil rights organization was formed, King described its purpose and goal.

> The ultimate aim of SCLC is to foster and create the "beloved community" in America where brotherhood is a reality. . . . SCLC works for integration. Our ultimate goal is genuine intergroup and interpersonal living–*integration*.[24]

An integrated society where "brotherhood is a reality" succinctly summarizes King's understanding of the beloved community. To appreciate the positive meaning King attaches to integration, one must review how he distinguishes segregation, desegregation, and integration.

Segregation is "prohibitive," denying the Negro equal access to schools, parks, restaurants, and libraries. Desegregation is "eliminative and negative"–it merely removes the legal prohibitions. Integration, on the other hand, is more far-reaching than desegregation; it is more "creative" in that "integration is the positive acceptance of desegregation and the welcomed participation of Negroes into the total range of human activities. . . ."[25]

It is clear to King that a desegregated society is not an integrated society. In that desegregation makes available public facilities and services to all people, it usually precedes integration. But there is no necessary nor automatic shift from desegregation to integration. The latter is "much more subtle and internal, for it involves attitudes: the mutual acceptance of individuals and groups."[26]

Integration, as King understood it, is a matter of personal relationships created by love; thus an integrated society cannot be legislated. Once segregationist laws have been stricken from the books, Negroes and whites will have to relate to each other across these nonrational, invisible psychological barriers which have traditionally separated them in our society. King hoped our society would eventually be "stricken gloriously and incurably color-blind."[27] King's high expectation for integration is seen in the following statement.

> It (desegregation) gives us a society where men are physically desegregated and spiritually segregated, where elbows are together and hearts are apart. It gives

211

us special togetherness and spiritual apartness. It leaves us with a stagnant equality of sameness rather than a constructive equality of oneness.[28]

Integration meant primarily for King "black and white together." Chapter six in *Why We Can't Wait* is entitled "Black and White Together" and a significant verse of the civil rights hymn "We Shall Overcome" contains the same words. But integration for King was broader than simply racial equality.

King never sought black supremacy to transplant white supremacy. His search was for brotherhood. King was not interested in black justice as opposed to white justice. He was interested in justice for all. He hoped for a day when Negro newspapers and Negro churches would become American newspapers and Christian churches. As a result of a commitment to solving the problem of racial hatred and oppression

> the sense of brotherhood springs as a practical necessity, and once this happens, there is revealed the vision of a society of brotherhood. We seek new ways of human beings living together, free from the spiritual deformation of race hatred–and free also from the deformation of war and economic injustice. And this vision does not belong to Negroes alone. It is the yearning of mankind.[29]

In his address at the Prayer Pilgrimage in Washington, D.C. in May of 1957, King unequivocally states:

> We must not become victimized with a philosophy of black supremacy. God is not interested in merely freeing black men, brown men and yellow men; God is interested in freeing the whole human race. We must work with determination to create a society in which all men will love together as brothers and respect the dignity and worth of human personality.[30]

And the elimination of the unjust system will permit each person to develop his unique potential. The presence of freedom for all will "create a moral balance in society which will allow all men, Negro and white, to rise to higher levels of self-completion."[31] Some specific indications of what the beloved community will be like are found in the "Dream Speech" of August 1963. These indications point to King's overriding concern for integration.

> . . . sons of former slaves and the sons of former slave owners will be able to sit down together at the table, of brotherhood.

> The injustice and oppression of the state of Mississippi "will be transformed into an oasis of freedom and justice."

. . . my four little children will one day live in a nation where they will not be judged by the color of their skin but by the content of their character.

Even the state of Alabama will be transformed so that

little black boys and black girls will be able to join hands with little white boys and white girls and walk together as sisters and brothers.

But it is not simply black and white joining hands–

. . . all of God's children, black men and white men, Jews and Gentiles, Protestants and Catholics, will be able to join hands. . . .[32]

The beloved community, however, is not completely constitutive of the subtle, internal, spiritual relationships between people embodied in the rhetoric of the "Dream Speech." King evidenced impatience with the meaninglessness of "human dignity" and "brotherhood" if these words and phrases were not concretely expressed in the transformation of society. Every man must now have food and the material necessities of life for his body as well as education and dignity.

Let us be dissatisfied until rat-infested, vermin-filled slums will be a thing of a dark past and every family will have a decent sanitary house in which to live. Let us be dissatisfied until the empty stomachs of Mississippi are filled and idle industries of Appalachia are revitalized. . . . Let us be dissatisfied until our brother of the Third World–Asia, Africa and Latin America–will no longer be the victim of imperialist exploitation, but will be lifted from the long night of poverty, illiteracy, and disease.[33]

This comment made in 1968 is an enlargement upon, yet an echo of an early and consistent concern of King's, namely, an egalitarian, socialist approach to wealth. In 1956, he chastised America for "taking necessities from the masses to give luxuries to the classes." To bridge the gap between poverty and wealth was to be a goal of America. King continues his admonition.

You can use your powerful economic resources to wipe poverty from the face of the earth. God never intended for one group of people to live in superfluous inordinate wealth, while others lived in abject deadening poverty.[34]

The beloved community would be an expression of God's intention that no one was meant to be without the necessities of life. It is for this reason that King, in the last two years of his life, began to advocate the creation of jobs and a guaranteed annual minimum income. He sensed that the civil rights struggle had not seriously dealt with the economic problems of the Negro.[35] In early 1968, when he was interpreting the meaning of the Poor People's Campaign, he said, while referring to the Negro

> I am speaking of all the poor, I am not only concerned about the black poor; I am concerned about poverty among my Mexican-American brothers; I am concerned about poverty among my Puerto Rican brothers; I am concerned about poverty among my Indian brothers; I am concerned about poverty among my Appalachian white brothers, and I wish they would realize that we are struggling against poverty for everybody and would join in a movement to get rid of poverty.[36]

King could not envision a human community apart from the alleviation of economic inequity. Harvey Cox says that King has here combined two traditionally biblical concerns–the "holiness of the poor" and the "blessed community." In King's movement, the Negro became the embodiment of "the poor" and "integration" now points to the vision of the holy community.

> It is also essential to notice that the two elements, the holy outcast *and* the blessed community, must go together. Without the vision of restored community, the holiness ascribed to the poor would fall far short of politics and result in a mere perpetuation of charity and service activities.[37]

King's vision of the beloved community included all races, all classes, all religions, all ethic groups, and, ultimately, all nations. The community transcended economic, social, political, and cultural lines.

C. *The Evidence of Community in the Movement*

The people who made up the movement–who participated in demonstrations, who attended mass meetings, who worked in other necessary ways–were from every facet of the community's life. They were a foretaste of King's beloved community. Although there was a majority of lower- and lower/middle-class working people, professional leaders (teachers, lawyers, clergy, doctors) willingly walked and worked with domestics and these day laborers. The educated and the illiterate,[38] the affluent Negro and the welfare recipient, white and black-people who had long been separated by rigid social mores and laws, found themselves working together.

After the March to Montgomery in the Spring of 1966, several thousand people were delayed at the airport, waiting for their planes to arrive. King was impressed by the heterogeneity of the crowd and yet its obvious unity.

> As I stood with them and saw white and Negro, nuns and priests, ministers and rabbis, labor organizers, doctors, housemaids and shopworkers brimming with vitality and enjoying a rare comradeship, I knew I was seeing a microcosm of the mankind of the future in this moment of luminous and genuine brotherhood.[39]

In fact, that there was such a representative cross-section in the movement was a design of King's. He called upon whites to help in the campaigns. His base of involvement was as widely divergent as conceivably possible. A special feature of the struggle was its universal character. "Every social stratum is involved-lower, middle and upper classes-and every age-children, teenagers, adults and senior citizens."[40]

In every major phase of the movement, from Montgomery to the Poor People's Campaign, King desired to have a representative group of citizens marching with him as a symbol of the unity to which human community can aspire and which it can eventually realize. The inclusiveness and transcending of barriers typical of his dream were found already in the movement itself.

D. *The Dream Theme in King's Thought*

King is probably best known in the popular mind for his "I Have a Dream" speech, delivered at the March on Washington on August 28, 1963. However, the major motifs in this speech, as with so many of King's central themes, were first formulated during the Montgomery pastorate. The subsequent years saw an elaboration of the theme, but it seemed to have had its inception while King was preaching at Dexter Avenue Baptist Church in 1955-57 and while he was interpreting the bus boycott through the nation at the same time.

As early as December 1956, in an address delivered at the First Annual Institute on Nonviolence and Social Change in Montgomery, King speaks of a "challenge of a new age"–"an age in which a new social order is being born."[41] The "new world" of which King spoke then was a world

> in which men will live together as brothers; a world in which men will beat their swords into ploughshares and their spears into pruning hooks; a world in which men will no longer take necessities from the masses to give luxuries to the classes; a world in which all men will respect the dignity and worth of all human personality.[42]

Then King concludes the address by quoting the first verse of "America" and asserting, "This must become literally true." In a final paragraph, we find some of the same phraseology he was to use seven years later in Detroit and Washington.

> Freedom must ring from every mountain side; Yes, let it ring from the snow-capped Rockies of Colorado, from the prodigious hilltops of New Hampshire, from the mighty Alleghenies of Pennsylvania, from the curvaceous slopes of California. But not only that. Let freedom ring from every mountainside–from every mole hill in Mississippi, from Stone Mountain of Georgia, from Lookout Mountain of Tennessee, yes, and from every hill and mountain of Alabama. From every mountain side let freedom ring. When this day finally comes, "The morning stars will sing together and the sons of God will shout for joy!"[43]

In a speech he delivered at the Golden Anniversary Conference of the National Urban League, which appeared in the December 1960 issue of YMCA Magazine,[44] King associates the democratic and Christian aspects of the dream. When discrimination is removed from our society, the "dream of American democracy" will be realized. At the end of this address, King continues to elaboration of his understanding of the dream. It will be:

> A dream of equality of opportunity, of privilege and property widely distributed; a dream of a land where men will not take necessities from the many to give luxuries to the few; a dream of a land where men do not argue that the color of a man's skin determines the content of his character; a dream of a place where all our gifts and resources are held not for ourselves alone but as instruments of service for the rest of humanity; the dream of a country where every man will respect the dignity and worth of all human personality, and men will dare to live together as brothers–that is the dream. Whenever it is fulfilled we will emerge from the bleak and desolate midnight of man's inhumanity to man into the bright and glowing daybreak of freedom and justice for all of God's children.[45]

Again, in a commencement address at Lincoln University on June 6, 1961, King definitely outlines his meaning of the American dream.[46] In this address King repeats his concern for the creation of a society where all men can live together as brothers, where every man "will respect the dignity and worth of human personality."[47] Then, in the final paragraph of this speech, he restates his belief that through a certain "maladjustment" (to the evils of segregation, discrimination, and injustice)

> We will be able to emerge from the bleak and desolate midnight of man's inhumanity to man into the bright and glittering daybreak of freedom and justice.

And here appears, apparently for the first time, the refrain with which he concludes many of his speeches on the "Dream."

> That will be the day when all of God's children, black men and white men, Jews and Gentiles, Catholics and Protestants, will be able to join hands and sing in the words of the old Negro spiritual, "Free at last! Free at last! Thank God Almighty, we are free at last."[48]

After the Birmingham campaign, King spoke in Detroit on June 23, 1963 to the largest crowd yet to hear him. The address, which was about thirty-five minutes in length, included themes King had been emphasizing throughout the country on lecture tours–the failure of the last one hundred years, the immorality of segregation, the urgency of the moment, and the centrality of nonviolence in the struggle. But for this Detroit speech, King prepared as his concluding remarks a passage centered around "I Have a Dream," which was repeated and added to in the August 28, 1963 "I Have a Dream" speech. Some specific material prepared for the Detroit speech which reappeared in the Washington speech is the following.

> I have a dream that one day on the red hills of Georgia the sons of former slaves and the sons of former slave-owners will be able to sit down together at the table of brotherhood.

> I have a dream that my four little children will one day live in a nation where they will not be judged by the color of their skin but by the content of their character.

> I have a dream that one day every valley shall be exalted, every hill and mountain shall be made low, the rough places will be made plain.

217

King concluded the Detroit speech with the familiar hope of "all of God's children" joining hands in a community of love, singing "Free at last! Free at last! Thank God Almighty, we are free at last!"[49]

One is struck by the similarity between the last four minutes of the Detroit speech and the second half of the Washington speech. William Robert Miller claims that the Detroit speech was a preliminary version of the one delivered at the March on Washington.[50] This is partly true because many of the themes do appear again. David Lewis simply states that at Washington King kept the refrain from the Detroit speech having to do with the "Dream."[51] There is less truth to this assertion.

The truth is more likely the following. Each speaker at the Washington March was allowed eight minutes. King decided to speak about the "bad check" the black man had been given one hundred years before–one which had come back marked "insufficient funds."

> We refuse to believe that the bank of justice is bankrupt. We refuse to believe that there are insufficient funds in the great vaults of opportunity of this nation. So we have come to cash this check–a check that will give us upon demand the riches of freedom and the security of justice.[52]

This was to have been the main thrust of his remarks on that August afternoon. According to Coretta King, he was tempted to repeat his "dream of a free united land, but in view of the shortness of the time given him, he decided against using that theme."[53] But the crowd's response was so enthusiastic and so overwhelmingly affirmative that near the end of the prepared text, he moved into the "dream theme" which he had used at Detroit, expanded it, and concluded with the inclusiveness now typical of King's hope.

> When we let freedom ring . . . we will be able to speed up that day when all of God's children, black men and white men, Jews and Gentiles, Protestant and Catholics, will be able to join hands and sing in the words of the old Negro spiritual, "Free at last! Free at last! Thank God Almighty, we are free at last!"[54]

An analysis of the Washington speech will reveal that, in fact, it is comprised of two literary units. The prepared text ends quite naturally with the paragraph, beginning "Go back to Mississippi, go back to Alabama, go back to South Carolina, go back to Georgia, go back to Louisiana, go back to the slums and ghettos of our northern cities."[55] The second unit of the speech begins with the words, "I say to you today, my friends, that in spite of the difficulties and frustrations of the moment, I still have a dream."[56] We should note the word "still." It was a dream King had had for some time, as the foregoing survey indicates, not something he planned to say for the first time in August of 1963. However, the Washington speech is King's normative statement and has come to be called the "Dream Speech," although only half of the speech dealt with his dream.

Dr. Harold DeWolf related to the writer that King thought God had the dream and that King was, in essence, God's prophet or spokesman. The dream was originally in the mind of God and came through King to the American audience.[57] This, of course, would be consistent with the biblical God who inspired the prophetic teachings on justice and mercy so often quoted by King. Although there is no mention of a dream in the acceptance speech in Oslo on December 10, 1964, King does evidence his disavowal of cynicism and reaffirms his hope for the future of human society.

> I have the audacity to believe that peoples everywhere can have three meals a day for their bodies, education and culture for their minds, and dignity, equality and freedom for their spirits. I believe that what self-centered men have torn down men other-centered can build up. I still believe that one day mankind will bow down before the altars of God and be crowned triumphant over war and bloodshed, and nonviolent redemptive goodwill will proclaim the rule of the land. "And the lion and the lamb shall lie down together and every man shall sit under his own vine and fig tree and none shall be afraid." I still believe that we shall overcome.[58]

The dream theme is seen again with real force on the last three pages of *The Trumpet of Conscience*. Here King admits that though he has been a "victim of deferred dreams," he still has a dream.[59] It is a dream of brotherhood, the unity and dignity of all men, and a reflection of that ideal society laid down by Amos, Micah, and Isaiah. The last sentences of the sermon are:

> With this faith we will be able to speed up the day when there will be peace on earth and goodwill toward men. It will be a glorious day, the morning stars will sing together, and the sons of God will shout for joy.[60]

Finally, in an address delivered six weeks before his death, King reiterates his hope and faith that the forces of justice would triumph, that "we shall overcome."

219

With this faith we will be able to transform the jangling discords of our nation into a beautiful symphony of brotherhood. With this faith we will be able to transform international energy into a creative psalm of peace and we will build rightly–and in this land–a nation where all of God's children, black and white men, Jews and Gentiles, Catholics and Protestants, and all ethnic groups in the land can join hands and sing in the words of the old Negro spiritual: "Free at last! Free at last! Thank God Almighty, we are free at last!"[61]

One cannot illustrate the centrality of the dream to King's thought without mentioning the two book dedications. *Why We Can't Wait* is dedicated to his four children "for whom I dream that one day soon they will no longer be judged by the color of their skin but by the content of their character." And *Where Do We Go From Here: Chaos or Community?* is dedicated to

the committed supporters of the civil rights movement, Negro and white, whose steadfastness amid confusions and setbacks give assurance that brotherhood will be the condition of man, not the dream of man.

The figure of the dream is used by King as an instrument to communicate the content of the beloved community. The "Dream" and the beloved community are directly related but are not to be identified.

The meaning of the beloved community for King comes to us by way of his participation in and reflection of the classical religious dream. Reinhold Niebuhr observed in *Moral Man and Immoral Society* that when "religion concerns itself with the problems of society, it always gives birth to some kind of millennial hope."[62] Every vital religion contains such a hope, according to Niebuhr, because "the religious imagination is as impatient with the compromises, relativities and imperfections of historic society as with the imperfections of individual life."[63] Israel's prophets dreamed of the messianic era, a time when all life would be lived in harmony; Jesus proclaimed the Kingdom of God in which there would be authentically embodied love and peace; Paul envisioned a life "in Christ" in which there would be neither racial, sexual, nor political boundaries.

King's dissatisfaction with the status quo brought about by a reluctant society to fulfill its promises to its citizens and the certainty that King had that God meant it another way forced him into the tradition of those prophets who call attention in society to the distance between what ought to be and what is.

1. King's Dream and the American Dream

King's vision is not only a prophetic and religious one. As he said in his Washington speech, it is "deeply rooted in the American dream." These roots are made very clear by King in his Lincoln University Commencement Address in which he said that "America is essentially a dream." And even though it is a dream not yet fulfilled

> It is a dream of a land where men of all races, of all nationalities, and of all creeds can live together as brothers. The substance of the dream is expressed in these sublime words, words lifted to cosmic proportions: "We hold these truths to be self-evident–that all men are created with certain inalienable rights; that among these are life, liberty, and the pursuit of happiness." This is the dream.[64]

Two elements of this passage strike King as particularly significant. One is the "amazing universalism" of the dream. It includes all men, not just white Protestants, for instance. Another aspect of the dream for King was that "each individual has certain basic rights that are neither conferred by nor derived from the state . . . they are God-given."[65] King construed the involvement of the students in the civil rights movement of the early sixties as recalling America to its original intention and as an attempt to heal the "schizophrenic personality" Americans had developed.

> They are seeking to save the soul of America. They are taking our whole nation back to those great wells of democracy which were dug deep by the Founding Fathers in the formulations of the Constitution and the Declaration of Independence. In sitting down at the lunch counters, they are standing up for the best in the American dream.[66]

King understood the American dream as belief in the "dignity and worth of human personality,"[67] and believed that the black man could provide a

> new expression of the American dream that need not be realized at the expense of other men around the world, but a dream of opportunity and life that can be shared with the rest of the world.[68]

The American dream has been understood usually as a combination of the religious hope for the Kingdom of God on earth advocated by the Puritans, and secular dream of democracy derived from the eighteenth-century enlightenment. The latter was espoused by such men as Jefferson and

221

Franklin.[69] The goal of the democratic ideal and the kingdom hope was a perfected society in which there would be opportunity and equality for all, a place where people of all backgrounds and races could live harmoniously together–an earnest and microcosm of what mankind could be. Even Paul Tillich sensed this about America as he autobiographically relates his impressions upon coming to this country. In contrasting America to the "tragic self-dismemberment" of Europe, he said America

> is the image of one nation in whom representatives of all nations and races can live as citizens. Although here too the distance between ideal and reality is infinite and the image is often deeply shadowed, nonetheless it is a kind of symbol of that highest possibility of history which is called "mankind."[70]

Reinhold Niebuhr contends that many people identify Christianity with the religion of the "American dream" and many churchmen have imagined democracy as the social and political expression of Christianity.[71] From the point of view of both Tillich and Niebuhr, this would be idolatrous, a violation of the Protestant principle. There should always remain a healthy tension between the ideal of Christianity's kingdom hope and the social, political, and religious approximations of it.

King's own liberal orientation, which permitted him to see history as somewhat inherently redemptive and to stress the possibilities of man, came near to seeing the beloved community as synonymous with the American dream. The *spirit* of American law, he once said, was "commitment to the democratic dream of integration."[72] The "Dream Speech" of August 1963 combines ideals from both secular democratic philosophy (freedom and equal opportunity for all) and the biblical prophetic tradition (dignity and human worth of each individual). They are not only combined in that speech, but interwoven in a way which suggests that they are virtually indistinguishable.

But King was primarily a religious thinker. There probably was a necessary apologetic reason for referring to the American dream on that late summer afternoon in 1963. It was a kind of *ad hominem* argument, designed to broaden the appeal of his message. However, King's own convictions about such ultimate matters were theologically conditioned, and for him the dream was radically rooted in the biblical prophetic vision. James Cone is undoubtedly right when he claims that King's dream was one "grounded not in the hopes of white America but in God."[73] King is finally indebted, not to the secular enlightenment tradition, but to his religious faith, primarily Israel's prophets, for the understanding of the inclusive human community.

E. *Theological Base for the Beloved Community*

The vision of the beloved community is solidly grounded in the biblical tradition. It rests upon Judaism's hope for the Messianic era and Christianity's expectation of the coming Kingdom of God. The Judeo-Christian heritage of concern for communal life and corporate faith, its call for universal justice, its hope for a transformed society; all found expression in Rauschenbusch's social gospel and through that to King's concept of the beloved community. Although King never systematized his theology, his fundamental theological base is a liberal version of the biblical doctrine of creation, the prophetic appeal for justice and the Christian ideal of *agape*. It comes down to what is familiarly known as the fatherhood of God and the brotherhood of man.

1. *Creation*

In February 1957, King wrote the statement issued by the National Council of Churches for Race Relations Sunday.[74] King notes here that all men are created in the image of God and, therefore, are inseparably bound together. On another occasion he said that all human beings are "made from the same basic stuff . . . molded in the same divine image."[75] The radical humanness we possess as men is a deeper identity than Jew or Gentile, Negro or white, Russian or American, and this humanness is for King the essence of the image of God.

He was deeply disturbed when segregationist Christians would attempt to justify their ideology on biblical grounds. To the popular mythology which claimed that the Negro is inferior by nature because of Noah's curse on Ham's children, King reminds his hearers how blasphemous and antithetical this was to the Christian religion.[76]

In the National Council of Churches statement King uses two biblical texts. The first is a combination of Acts 17:24 and 26. "God that made the world and all things therein . . . hath made of one blood all nations of men for to dwell on all the face of the earth." The second text is the conclusion of the third chapter of Galatians (Gal 3:28): "There is neither Jew nor Greek, there is neither slave nor free, there is neither male nor female; for you are one in Christ Jesus." King discerns here a "broad universalism" which stands at the center of the Christian gospel, making "segregation morally unjustifiable" and "brotherhood morally inescapable."

We have one Creator-Father and hence all his children are brothers. Each man derives his dignity and human status from his relation of sonship to the Father. It is this which makes for unity and community among men. Racial segregation, on the other hand, "is a blatant denial of the unity which we have in Christ . . . (and) is utterly opposed to the noble teachings of our Judeo-Christian tradition."[77] This was *sine qua non* for King. To him it was impeccable logic and a position from which he never moved. It is not unlike an observation, made from another theological perspective, by Reinhold Niebuhr.

> The transcendent perspective of religion makes all men our brothers and nullifies the divisions, by which nature, climate, geography and the accidents of history divide the human family. By this insight many religiously inspired idealists have transcended nations, racial and class distinctions.[78]

2. *Prophets*

As we have intimated, King's conception of the beloved community reflects the prophetic vision of justice, mercy, peace, righteousness, freedom, equality and harmony which was to be realized in the messianic era. As we have also seen, King repeatedly drew upon the prophets in his cry for justice. In a "Christmas Sermon for Peace,"[79] King combines six prophetic references in a closing paragraph in which he reiterates his dream. As with Rauschenbusch, the prophet is the model of social religion.

> I still have a dream today that one day justice will roll down like water, and righteousness like a mighty stream.[80] I still have a dream today that in all of our state houses and city halls men will be elected to go there who will do justly and love mercy and walk humbly with their God.[81] I still have a dream today that one day war will come to an end, that men will beat their swords into plowshares and their spears into pruning hooks, that nations will no longer rise against nations, neither will they study war any more.[82] I still have a dream today that one day the lamb and lion will lie down together,[83] and every man will sit under his own vine and fig tree and none shall be afraid.[84] I still have a dream today that one day every valley shall be exalted and every mountain and hill be made low, the rough places will be made smooth and the crooked places straight, and the glory of the Lord shall be revealed, and all flesh shall see it together.[85]

King seems to grasp the uniqueness of the Hebrew religion–its concern for history and ethics. Yahweh was the Lord of history and a just and righteous

God who required righteousness and justice in his children. There was no attempt on the part of King to spiritualize this demand or postpone it indefinitely to the world-to-come. He spelled out the demands of justice in terms of voting, education, public accommodations, housing and jobs and this was to be achieved on earth, in our history, now. In his "Dream Speech" he reminded America of the "fierce urgency of *now.*"

> *Now* is the time to make real the promises of Democracy. *Now* is the time to rise from the dark and desolate valley of segregation to the sunlit path of racial justice. *Now* is the time to open the doors of opportunity to all of God's children. *Now* is the time to lift our nation from the quicksands of racial injustice to the solid rock of brotherhood.[86]

Here is reflected the social gospel's concern to transform the present social order and approximate a society determined by the will of God. For King, as for Rauschenbusch before him, "religion demands social expression."

3. *Love*

Another significant aspect of the biblical base for the beloved community is the Christian concept of love-*agape*. As we have seen, *agape* as understood by King is "understanding, redeeming good will for all men" and "love in action."[87] *Agape* is a community creating force. It is necessary for *agape* to result in community. It will insist on community. It is of its nature to create binding human relationships among men–making them neighbors and friends.

King claims that "*agape* is love seeking to preserve and create community." Its inherent unselfishness allows mutuality to be a priority, rather than individualism. This type of love will go to any length to restore community.[88] By the same token, hate destroys community and depersonalizes men, for "creation is so designed that my personality can only be fulfilled in the context of community."[89] King points to the social character of God. God and community are inseparable–there is something in the universe that seeks to perpetuate community. If man perverts or destroys community, he is resisting the whole of creation. For King, the Crucifixion-Resurrection-Pentecost symbols of Christianity naturally issue in the foundation of qualitative human community.

> The cross is the eternal expression of the length to which God will go in order to restore broken community. The resurrection is a symbol of God's triumph over all the forces that seek to block community. The Holy Spirit is the continuing community creating reality that moves through history.[90]

The beloved community is a community of love, formed by love, and issuing in love relationships. *Agape* can establish positive human community and not simply desegregation.

Harvey Cox is right when he suggests that King's dream is a contemporary embodiment of the Hebrew term *shalom*. The love, joy, peace, hope, social harmony, human reciprocity, and exalted justice which *shalom* describes is the character of the messianic era. It is an era of reconciliation, in which barriers and divisions between men are dissolved; an era of freedom in which we are delivered from past bondage to a future of responsibility for the world; an era of hope in which we expect to see a continuing renewal of God's world.[91] Cox points accurately to the biblical flavor of King's dream of the beloved community and supports King's own self-understanding as a Christian thinker primarily and a social philosopher secondly, but also a man who saw religion and social issues inextricably bound together.

It is for this reason that one wonders at the remark of Arnold Schuchter in *White Power and Black Freedom*. He makes a distinction between the "religious" character of the beloved community and "integration." He says that King, in calling for the creation of the beloved community in America, was "expressing more than a religious point of view."

> The "beloved community" and in the broadest sense of the term, "integration," means access to social justice, human dignity, equality, and freedom in American society.[92]

Schuchter is right to relate integration to beloved community, but certainly wrong, from King's point of view, to suggest that all that integration stands for should be separate from his religious basis for justice, love, peace, and brotherhood.

F. *Kingdom and Church in King*

The centrality of community for King is directly related to his ethical concern. As Rauschenbusch said, an interest in the Kingdom of God is inseparable from an interest in ethics. Rauschenbusch tended to depreciate the church and identify it with ritual and ceremony. He was concerned to have the church instrumental to the realization of the Kingdom of God and not be the end of faith. Whenever this position was reversed, when the church and the Kingdom were synonymous or when the church usurped the Kingdom's place as the end, interest in ethics waned, the revolutionary stance of the church lapsed, and the church appeared as a cultural echo.

King, in essence, agreed with this position. As his sermon, "Paul's Letter to the American Christians," and his "Letter from Birmingham Jail" suggest, the church is always under the judgment of God's will. "If any earthly institution or custom conflicts with God's will, it is your Christian duty to oppose it."[93] The test of the church's true nature was its unity and ethical concern. King's ideal church would have been one without denominational and racial divisions and one involved in alleviating the needs of humanity.[94]

King's idea of the beloved community is somewhere in between Rauschenbusch's concept of the Kingdom of God and his understanding of the institutional church. The former is interested primarily in righteousness and the latter in worship. Whereas King's beloved community would allow a place for both worship and righteousness. The church must remember that it is "the conscience of the state" and "that worship at its best is a social expression in which people from all levels of life come together to affirm their oneness and unity under God."[95]

G.   Means to Achieve the Beloved Community

As we suggested in the chapters on social gospel and nonviolence, King strongly believed that nonviolence was the only effective way to create the beloved community. In his earliest interpretation of the Montgomery boycott[96] he was insisting that the purpose of the boycott was reconciliation and redemption; "the end is the creation of the beloved community."

Nonviolence was espoused because it has the capacity to recreate a fragmented community and to restore human relationships to a level of trust and to establish a community at peace with itself.[97] King observed that history proved the counterproductive nature of violence. He noted that communities which adopted hatred and violence as methods of change or as avenues to unity have eventually brought destruction upon themselves.[98] In even stronger language, King denounces violence as immoral because it's source is hatred and not love.

It destroys community and makes brotherhood impossible. It leaves society in monologue rather than dialogue. Violence ends by defeating itself. It creates bitterness in the survivors and brutality in the destroyers.[99]

King's trip to India in 1959 convinced him of the power of nonviolent love to create community. There he saw the relationship between Indian and Britisher relatively free of hostility and tension. This was "marvelous" to King and underscored nonviolence as the methodology for oppressed people to achieve social change and liberation. What he experienced in India was the kind of situation between white and black King was hoping to create by using a nonviolent strategy in the South.

After the victory in Montgomery seemed a certainty, and the Supreme Court ruling was finally handed down, King reminded his people that they could not be "satisfied with a court victory" over their white brothers. Since they had walked with such dignity in nonviolence for a year, a violent, vengeful thought or act would mean they had walked in vain.[100] In another article reviewing the Montgomery success, King exhorted his followers

We must act in such a way as to make possible a coming together of white people and colored people on the basis of a real harmony of interests and understanding. We seek an integration based on mutual respect. We have worked and suffered for non-segregated buses, but we want this to be a step towards equality, not a step away from it.[101]

The insisting on one's own rights is too narrow a basis for brotherhood. Nor can one alleviate tension by thinking of oneself as less than man or more than man. In returning to nonsegregated buses, King asked his people to destroy the superior-inferior relationship.

Instead of accepting the division of mankind, it is our duty to act in the manner best designed to establish man's oneness. If we go back in this spirit, our mental attitude will be one that must in the long run bring about reconciliation.[102]

For King, there was a victory in Montgomery. But it was not simply the victory of black people over white oppression. It was a victory of truth over falsehood and justice over injustice. It was a victory for the "unity of mankind." It is again obvious that King did not wish to invert the social pyramid and have blacks in a supremacist, oppressive role dominating the entire community. That sort of reversal or "triumph" would not allow people to live together in peace and equality.

That would only result in transferring those now on the bottom to the top. But, if we can live up to nonviolence in thought and deed, there will emerge an interracial society based on freedom for all.[103]

King allowed that some significant political change has been brought about by violence, e.g., the American Revolution. But he is quick to assert that the Negro revolution is seeking integration, not independence. Usually those fighting for independence have as their goal the eradication of the oppressor. "But here in America, we've got to live together. We've got to find a way to reconcile ourselves to living in community, one group with the other."[104] And this is done most effectively by nonviolent love.

There are two significant aspects of King's thought which are implied by this discussion. They both relate directly to his contention that nonviolence is the only method to reestablish the broken community or to create the beloved community. These are 1) relation of means to ends and 2) the nature and place of love. They have been discussed at length in the chapter on nonviolence.

1. *Means and Ends*

For King there is a direct interrelationship between means and ends. It is not so much that "the end justifies the means" but that "the end determines the means." It was inconceivable for King that moral ends could be achieved by immoral means. Since for King the "end represents the means in process and the ideal in the making," and "the end is pre-existent in the means," there would be a radical lack of consistency for him to attempt to establish the beloved community on any other basis than love and nonviolence. Here King is supported by Rauschenbusch's concern that the method used to achieve the transformed community be love and nonviolence, and Gandhi's stress on the inviolable connection between means and ends as illustrated by the relationship of the seed to the tree. There is an internal consistency between King's unyielding social strategy, his personal life style (nonviolent means), and his ultimate objective, the realization of the beloved community.

2. Love as Means

Agape presupposes and creates community. It is "mankind's most potent weapon for personal and social transformation."[105] It is so because it is the "supreme unifying principle of life."[106] This love, which we have seen is not sentimental or affectionate, but an all-embracing, redemptive good will for all people, can create a beloved community by transcending barriers, divisions, and all that would separate men. It can create a world-wide fellowship by lifting our concern beyond our tribe, race, class, and nation. Since love is the essence of God, it would appear that God is concerned that community exist.[107] Love can turn enemies into friends; move a protest to reconciliation; transform inhumanity to justice.[108] As we struggle against evil systems, we must do so with love in our hearts. It enables people to continue in the movement with "wise restraint and calm reasonableness."[109]

Since King was not interested in substituting one tyranny for another, one supremacy for another, and since he believed the God who is love is interested in the freedom of the whole human race, not merely segments of it, he recommends to his people the way of love. Hatred, violence, and retaliation belong to the old age. If we attempt to usher in the new era with such methods, the new age will be a duplication of the old one. King challenged his hearers and readers to have at the center of their lives as they enter the new age the Christian virtues of love, mercy, and forgiveness.[110] Man is never to relinquish his privilege and obligation to love. "While abhorring segregation, we shall love the segregationist. This is the only way to create the beloved community."[111]

H. The Metaphysical Base for the Beloved Community

King's affirmation that each man has inherent worth and dignity had its philosophical roots in the metaphysics of personalism. Personality is the "key to reality,"[112] and of highest value. Hence, the nature of ultimate reality, the essence of the Supreme Being (God) is personal. All reality participates in that reality. Yet there is a logical relationship between the personal and the social. We noted how Brightman stressed the social character of personalism. "The World of persons is a social world."[113] The inevitable expression of a group of persons is community. For the social nature of personality is ultimately grounded in the nature of the Divine Personality. The God who is love is naturally seeking companionship. He is the "Great Socius." So

Christian community, a "world of values," the beloved community, is at the same time the reflection of God's seeking fellowship and the goal of the individual. The ideal human community would reflect the universe, which is a "society of interacting selves and persons," and do so in the name of *agape* and *logos*, the basal elements of the universe's structure.[114]

1. *Metaphysical Unity*

For personalism, all reality is one and therefore unified. All of life, natural, physical, and human, is an expression of the energy which flows from the One. The monism inherent in personalism found its way into King, who noted a "creative force working for universal wholeness."[115] This "force" would be the moral law or love which, while affirming the value of human personality, is always creating community. The beloved community is an historical expression of the metaphysical and the moral foundations of reality. The unity of the metaphysical and the ethical in personalism makes possible serious thinking about man's life together.We can best reflect the unity of all being by being in unity as persons.

2. *Perfectibility of Human Community*

As we saw, Brightman held that there were unlimited possibilities open to man. His stance was melioristic, i.e., man was capable of improving himself. The "universe is always susceptible of improvement."[116] Since good is finally victorious over evil and value triumphant over disvalue, man, by aligning himself with this positive notion, will continue to improve himself. Of a piece with meliorism, the movement towards perfection is typified by cooperation. The meaning of religion for Brightman is "devotion to personal values" or mutual cooperation of men.

> This world of shared values can reach such a level of cooperation that man is liberated from his selfishness and is empowered to give himself to his neighbor. On this level of cooperation the Kingdom of God is realized–where "all races and creeds can meet, learn, and respect each other in religious liberty."[117]

With King's appropriation of the central themes of the social gospel and personalism into his own ethical thought, he embodied what Walter Muelder called "social personalism."[118] King would agree with Muelder's comment that "the ideal social possibility of the Kingdom of God is the full actualization of personal and group relationships in love."[119] In his attempt to combine the personal and the social, to include the metaphysical value of the human person with the biblical vision of the righteous community, King's own dream emerges as the beloved community.

I. *The Historical Possibility of the Beloved Community*

One of the issues perennially raised concerning ideal communities is whether they can be realized in history or whether they appear only at the end of history. Reinhold Niebuhr's understanding of the Kingdom of God is that it appears at the behest of God at the end of history. History does not have the moral power nor do men have the necessary resources to create the Kingdom. The liberal children of light dismissed this apocalyptic note in the biblical vision. They thought that the Kingdom of God would be found eventually in history as history gradually evolved.

But for Niebuhr, the Kingdom of God is "impossible of realization" and will come finally by the gracious act of God.[120] The dream of perpetual peace and brotherhood among men is one which will never be fully realized.[121] Niebuhr castigates the idealistic illusions of universalists who assume:

> that the logic which inheres in the universal character of the moral imperative and in the global interdependence of a technical civilization would naturally and inevitably bring the political institution of mankind into conformity with it.[122]

It is for this reason that realist Niebuhr claimed that the avowing of ideals would not destroy evil. But for Niebuhr, the symbol of the Kingdom of God is important to retain. It is "relevant to every moment of history as an ideal possibility and as a principle of judgment upon present realities."[123] The ambiguity in man's motivation, his inevitable egoism, his inability to transcend himself and his society's needs in a truly selfless way, will always prevent men from completely realizing the dream of brotherhood and equality among all people. There will be tension between the world and the Kingdom of God until the end of history.

Martin Luther King, on the other hand, had more faith in the vitalities of history. Although his own optimism about man and history bequeathed to him by the social gospel was, to an appreciable degree, neutralized by his study of Niebuhr, he maintained a confidence in man's ability to produce a better society, even the ideal society. King's basic understanding of man's relationship to the Kingdom of God could be viewed within the framework of Rauschenbusch's understanding that although God initiates the Kingdom, man's response is necessary to see it to fruition. It is out of this context that King said, "We are striving for the removal of all barriers that divide and alienate mankind, whether racial, economic, or psychological."[124]

King felt that if Negro leadership could be true to the principles of nonviolence, could continue to distinguish between unjust systems and people and, with the help of the 1954 Supreme Court decision, "we shall be able to bring into new being a new nation where men will live together as brothers; a nation where all men will respect the dignity and worth of the human personality."[125] King felt that there were forces at work to assure the realization of integration, but he reminded his readers that they cannot rely automatically on time and must work to help that day arrive.[126] His "hope and dream" was that color would cease to be a judgmental factor in human relationships.

> Indeed, it is the keystone of my faith in the future that we will someday achieve a thoroughly integrated society. I believe that before the turn of the century, if trends continue to move and develop as presently, we will have moved a long, long way toward such a society.[127]

King, however, was realistic enough to know that the "Kingdom of God as a universal reality is *not yet*."[128] He learned from Niebuhr that sin exists on every level of man's existence and by virtue of the nature of man and the demonic forces in history, the destruction of one tyranny often issues in the surfacing of another. King, in his typically dialectical fashion, wanted to avoid a "superficial optimism" and a "crippling pessimism." He knew that there was a tentative character about all progress in human affairs, but "Within limits real social progress may be made."

> Although man's moral pilgrimage may never reach a destination point on earth, his never-ceasing strivings may bring him ever closer to the city of righteousness. And though the Kingdom of God may remain *not yet* as a universal reality in history . . . in the present it may exist in such isolated forms as in judgment, in personal devotion, and in some group life.[129]

King's reaction to the Hippie movement elucidates his notion of "judgment." The Hippies, like their seventeenth- and eighteenth-century antecedents, the sectarian utopian communities, are resisting the established order of things. But they will not survive because they are fundamentally escapist. They are important and necessary, in King's view, "to their contemporaries because their dreams of social justice and human value continues as a dream of mankind."[130]

Perhaps here King betrays his self-understanding about his dream and its role in history. It is needed to inspire men, as well as to qualify all their attempts at true human community. But it nevertheless remains a dream, to be striven for with all our human energy on the one hand, and, on the other, never be totally realized in history.

Conclusions

The concluding summary statements will be presented in propositional form.

1. Martin Luther King, Jr., intellectually, must be understood against the background of American liberal theological thought, especially as it was expressed in the social gospel and personalism.

2. He was introduced to the intellectual basis of theological liberalism by George W. Davis at Crozer Seminary. The liberal themes present in Davis's theological orientation, e.g., God present in the historical process, the moral foundations of reality, the value of the human person, life as social, and the ethical nature of faith, remained an integral part of King's thought.

3. King was primarily concerned with the social dimension of life and was interested in changing social structures.

4. To this end, he developed, with the aid of the social gospel and Walter Rauschenbusch, a theological rationale for the Christian church's role as a change agent in society.

5. The optimism in Rauschenbusch concerning man's nature is corrected in King's mind by the realism of Reinhold Niebuhr, even though Rauschenbusch remains the dominant influence on King's thought.

6. Rauschenbusch's main emphases–the prophetic roots of Christianity, the necessary relation of the church to social issues, the gospel for the whole man, the Christian faith has ethically transforming power for society, the Kingdom of God as a Christianized social life and a community of righteousness–all were instrumental in King's theological formulations.

7. King was heir to a long tradition of protest in America which in the 1940s and 1950s provided him with a time of opportunity to involve the black man in a renewed effort to achieve his civil rights.

8. Nonviolence, which was central to King's activity, was *one* of the intellectual strands of his thought.

9. Gandhi's adherence to *Satyagraha*, *Ahimsa* and his loyalty to Truth reinforced King's own understanding of Jesus's teaching on nonviolence and *agape*. The latter was the essential content of his Christian nonviolence.

10. King was greatly helped by Richard Gregg's articulation of "moral jui-jitsu."

11. For King, a law was unjust when it violated human personality. This was the justification for his acts of civil disobedience.

12. Nonviolence was the strategy King employed to change social systems and to eliminate public discrimination of minority peoples. And although his tactics changed in terms of their degree of confrontation, i.e., from passive resistance in Montgomery to nonviolent direct action in Birmingham and Selma to the planned massive disruption of entire cities in Chicago and Washington, D.C., King never deviated from the principle of nonviolence.

13. King's understanding of nonviolence as a pure ideal was irrevocably qualified by Reinhold Niebuhr's criticism of pacifism in *Moral Man and Immoral Society*. As a result of his contact with Niebuhr, King became more realistic about human nature, i.e., the egoistic impulse of man pervades every level of human thought and activity.

14. Niebuhr's contention that *agape* and the Kingdom of God were not simple historical possibilities did not radically affect King's hope that the beloved community would materialize.

15. King did not turn Niebuhrianism upside down, as James Sellers asserts, by making justice the goal and love the instrument of social change. With his concern that the end determines the means, the beloved community would have to be sought through loving means. There is a sense in which King reveals a "love-monism."

16. From Niebuhr, King learned to appreciate the place of power in social groups and the historicity of reason, i.e., we tend to reason from self-interest.

17. Personalism, with its emphasis on personality as the key to reality, provided King with a philosophical base to attack segregation. Segregation denies the value of the human person.

18. Personalism further buttressed King's strong belief in the moral order of the universe. The universe, history, and God are on the side of justice.

19. King's theological and philosophical conviction that beyond the contradictions of this life was ultimate resolution (the unity of virtue and fulfillment), was articulated for him by the idealistic theism of personalism.

20. Although King was greatly influenced by the dialectical method of Hegel, he never adopted the content of Hegelian philosophy.

21. The motivating force, the predominant concern in King's life, was the realization of the beloved community. This community would transcend the barriers of race, religion, and national and social position. This community reflects the Judeo-Christian understanding of the messianic era and the Kingdom of God.

22. The dream of the beloved community was found in his earliest writings and his preoccupation with it continued through his final articles and addresses.

23. King's dream was a religious version of the secular dream of democracy and yet was not completely identified with the American dream.

24. The theological basis for the beloved community was Rauschenbusch's understanding of the Kingdom of God. The method by which the community will be achieved is nonviolence–a method provided by Gandhi. The content of life in the community was supplied by the Christian idea of *agape* and the sacredness of human personality espoused by personalism. Niebuhr's criticism of liberal optimism qualified King's belief that the community would be realized in history.

25. Nevertheless, King remained a liberal in mind and heart. He continued to believe in the goodness of man, the possibilities of history, the power of the rational, the importance of integration, the futility of adopting extreme positions, and the necessity of reconciling all divisions in human life.

Notes

PREFACE–1989

1. Reprinted 1986 by University Press of America.
2. See Cone's article "Martin Luther King, Jr., Black Theology–Black Church" in *Theology Today*, January 1984, pp. 409-420, and his article "The Theology of Martin Luther King, Jr." in the *Union Seminary Quarterly Review*, Vol. XL, No. 4, pp.21-39, especially the long footnote No. 2 on p. 36.
3. *Martin Luther King, Jr.: The Making of a Mind*, New York: Orbis, 1982.
4. Ansbro, p. 320, Note 176.
5. See David Garrow's *Bearing the Cross: Martin Luther King, Jr. and the Southern Christian Leadership Conference*, New York: William Morrow and Co., 1986, pp. 111-112.
6. See index entry under King, Martin Luther, Jr.–adaptations of the writings of others.
7. Downing, Frederick L., *To See the Promised Land: The Faith Pilgrimage of Martin Luther King, Jr.*, Macon, Georgia: Mercer University Press, 1986.

CHAPTER ONE

1. Martin Luther King, Jr., "Karl Barth's Conception of God," Graduate term paper in Boston Collection.
2. _____, "How Modern Christians Should Think of Man," Graduate term paper in Boston Collection.
3. _____, *Strength to Love*, New York: Pocket Books, Inc., 1964 (Hereafter referred to as STL), p. 165.
4. Kenneth Cauthen, *The Impact of American Religious Liberalism*, New York: Harper and Row, 1962 (Hereafter referred to as Cauthen).
5. Henry P. Van Dusen, *The Vindication of Liberal Theology*, New York: Charles Scribner's Sons, 1963 (Hereafter referred to as Van Dusen).
6. Lloyd J. Averill, *American Theology in the Liberal Tradition*, Philadelphia: The Westminster Press, 1967 (Hereafter referred to as Averill).
7. This list is culled from his book, *The Impact of American Religious Liberalism* (Chapter 2, "Types of American Liberalism") and from a summary article he wrote for *The Christian Century*, August 8, 1962, entitled "Religious Liberalism Evaluated," pp. 955-58.
8. See Van Dusen, Chapter 2 and p. 151 for an excellent summary.

9. Van Dusen, p. 24. See also his reference to Henry Sloane Coffin's definition: "We are first and foremost evangelicals–evangelicals to the core of our spiritual beings. . . . And we are liberals–not liberals in the sense that we cultivate freedom for its own sake, but for the gospel's sake. We are liberals on behalf of our evangelicalism" cited in Van Dusen, p. 38.

10. Cauthen, pp. 33-35.

11. In a letter to George W. Davis from Martin Luther King, Jr., dated December 1, 1953. Used by permission of Mrs. Davis. At this time, King was a graduate student at Boston University.

12. Lawrence D. Reddick, *Crusader Without Violence*, New York: Harper and Brothers, 1959, p. 79. This reference is also quoted in Lenwood G. Davis, *I Have a Dream: The Life and Times of Martin Luther King, Jr.*, Chicago: Adams Press, 1969, p. 24.

13. David L. Lewis, *King: A Critical Biography*, New York: Praeger Publishers, 1970, pp. 29, 34.

14. Kenneth L. Smith, "The Intellectual Sources of the Thought of Martin Luther King, Jr.," unpublished manuscript p. 17. (Hereafter referred to as Smith). Dr. Smith, formerly professor of ethics at Crozer Seminary, prepared an excellent paper on King's Crozer days. It was written in the fall of 1969 and it was in this paper that the writer was introduced to the significant role Davis played in King's intellectual development and to it he is indebted for much of the technical information about Davis's work at Crozer. Dr. Smith is now at Colgate-Rochester Divinity School, Bexley Hall, Crozer in Rochester, New York. Crozer moved there from Chester, Pennsylvania in 1970.

15. The sources for this material are Smith, Crozer catalogues, and King's Crozer transcript.

16. Smith, p. 18.

17. Smith, p. 19.

18. Smith, p. 23.

19. Davis changed to Harold DeWolf's *A Theology of the Living Church* when it appeared in 1953, but in DeWolf Davis was still adhering to an evangelical liberal position.

20. Smith, p. 24.

21. Cauthen, p. 42.

22. Smith, p. 23.

23. William Newton Clarke, *An Outline of Christian Theology*, New York: Charles Scribner's Sons, 1916, p. 1 (Hereafter referred to as Clarke).

24. *Ibid.*, p. 20.

25. *Ibid.*, p. 8. King reflects this openness in *Where Do We Go From Here: Chaos or Community?*, New York: Harper and Row, 1967 (Hereafter referred to as WDWGFH), pp. 190-91. 26.Clarke, p. 13.

27. *Ibid.*, p. 150. This "something" King refers to many times.

28. *Ibid.*, see discussion on pp. 66-68.

29. *Ibid.*, p. 55.

30. Martin Luther King, Jr., *Stride Toward Freedom*, New York: Perennial Library, 1964, p. 73 (Hereafter referred to as STF). The book was first published

in 1958 and is King's account of the Montgomery bus boycott. It was originally planned to be titled "A Moment in History." The writer discovered this in a letter dated October 13, 1957 in the Boston Collection. It was part of a series of letters discussing the Harper's contract.

31. The second version was written for *The Christian Century* Series, "How My Mind Has Changed," (April 13, 1960) and reprinted as the last chapter in STL. See STL, p. 168. It is possible King may have heard the name of Rauschenbusch at Morehouse. Dr. Benjamin Mays, the college president, was very interested in the social gospel. However, Dr. Mays does not recall talking to King about Rauschenbusch, nor did Mays teach King at Morehouse. Mays surmises that King might have heard references to Rauschenbusch in the many chapel talks he gave. This was discussed with Dr. Mays by the writer in his Atlanta home on May 28, 1970.

32. *The Crozer Quarterly*, January 1943, p. 62.

33. STF, p. 78.

34. Smith, p. 26. We shall have occasion to refer to several of these books as we discuss King and nonviolence.

35. George W. Davis, "Liberalism and a Theology of Depth," *Crozer Quarterly*, July 1951, p. 205 (Hereafter referred to as "Theology of Depth.")

36. The only known published writings of Davis are four articles in *The Crozer Quarterly* and one article in *Theology Today*.

37. "Theology of Depth," p. 193.

38. *Ibid.*, p. 193.

39. *Ibid.*, p. 195.

40. *Ibid.*, p. 198.

41. *Ibid.*, p. 202.

42. *Ibid.*, p. 202.

43. *Ibid.*, p. 206.

44. *Ibid.*, p. 209.

45. David spends about three times as much space on "moral foundations" as he does on "Jesus" as a depth phenomenon. As we shall see later, this emphasis on the moral order is a central affirmation of King.

46. George W. Davis, "God and History," *Crozer Quarterly*, January 1943 (Hereafter referred to as "God and History.").

47. *Ibid.*, p. 26.

48. *Ibid.*, p. 28.

49. "Theology of Depth," p. 201. This is actually a quotation from a statement by the Federal Council of Churches Commission on a Just and Durable Peace, which he uses in support of his convictions that there is a moral order in the universe.

50. "God and History," p. 22.

51. "Theology of Depth," p. 204.

52. "God and History," p. 19.

53. *Ibid.*

54. "Theology of Depth," p. 207.

55. *Ibid.*, p. 208.

56. Further, in a paper for DeWolf at Boston, analyzing a theological journal (King chose *The Crozer Quarterly*) and apparently referring to this Davis article, King said, "Yet Dr. Davis is right in affirming that liberalism has all too often been overly concerned with the surface and sub-surface phenomena of the Christian faith to the total exclusion of the depth phenomena. Neo-orthodox theologians have reminded us, on every hand, of liberalism's appalling failure at this point. Reinhold Niebuhr, probably more than any other thinker in America, has stressed the need of a 'dimension of depth' transcending nature, transcending history, if ethical action here and now is to be sustained by a faith that touches absolute bottom." Report for Seminar in Systematic Theology 1951-52 in Boston Collection.

57. "God and History," p. 25. See also "For it (Jesus's religion) established in a world unaware of the value of personality an idea of the infinite worth of every human soul to God, no matter how degraded it might happen to be in the eyes of men." George W. Davis, "The Ethical Basis of Salvation," *Crozer Quarterly*, July 1939, p. 180-81.

58. "God and History," p. 25.

59. *Ibid.*, p. 23.

60. *Ibid.*, p. 28. 30.

61. *Ibid.*, p. 31.

62. *Ibid.*, p. 27-28.

63. *Ibid.*, p. 29.

64. *Ibid.*, p. 31.

65. *Ibid.*, p. 35-36. Cf. The last chapter in King's WDWGFH entitled, "The World House."

66. "Theology of Depth," p. 205.

67. See Martin Luther King, Jr., "Showdown for Nonviolence," *Look*, April 16, 1968.

68. George W. Davis, "The Ethical Basis of Salvation," *The Crozer Quarterly*, July 1939, p. 181.

69. *Ibid.*, p. 181-82. King was also strongly convinced that the Sermon on the Mount was a model for Christian behavior.

70. *Ibid.*, p. 189.

CHAPTER TWO

1. *Types of Modern Theology*, p. 11, London, Nisbet & Co. Ltd., 1954 (Hereafter referred to as Mackintosh).

2. See Mackintosh, p. 12.

3. King was reinforced by this tradition not only from Rauschenbusch himself, but from the texts used in Davis's theology courses, especially the Ritschlian strain in William Adams Brown and the dependence of William Newton Clarke on Schleiermacher.

4. Van Dusen, p. 40.

5. Albrecht Ritschl, *The Christian Doctrine of Justification and Reconciliation*, p. 11, English translation by H.R. Mackintosh and A.B. Macaulay, Clifton, New Jersey: Reference Book Publishers, Inc., 1966 (Hereafter referred to as Ritschl).

6. Mackintosh, p. 144.

7. Averill, p. 43.

8. Averill, p. 85. It is important to note that for Rauschenbusch and King the latter kind of "experience" is the one supported by them.

9. Averill, p. 43.

10. "The Value and Use of History," *Foundations*, July-September, 1969, p. 264.

11. Averill, p. 43.

12. Ritschl, p. 13. See also p. 12.

13. *Theology of the Social Gospel*, New York: The Macmillan Co., 1918, p. 155 (Hereafter referred to as TSG).

14. TSG, p. 47.

15. Bernard M.G. Reardon, *Religious Thought in the Nineteenth Century*, Cambridge: The University Press, 1966, p. 138 (Hereafter referred to as Reardon).

16. Reardon, p. 126.

17. E.g., "Jesus has the value of God for us." See Ritschl's discussion on pp. 385ff., especially pp. 392-93.

18. Averill notes that Harnack is the author most quoted in Rauschenbusch's books. This is true, but Schleiermacher and Ritschl run a very close second.

19. TSG, p. 293.

20. TSG, p. 125.

21. Quoted in TSG, p. 94.

22. TSG, pp. 138-39.

23. TSG, pp. 27-28.

24. Robert T. Handy, ed., *The Social Gospel in America 1870-1920*, New York: Oxford University Press, 1966, p. 15 (Hereafter referred to as Handy).

25. New Haven: Yale University Press, 1940, p. 12 (Hereafter referred to as Hopkins).

26. The following is a summary of Handy, pp. 10-11 and Hopkins, p. 123 and pp. 300ff.

27. Hopkins, p. 125.

28. Samuel Harris in Hopkins, p. 21.

29. Hopkins, p. 190.

30. Handy, p. 11.

31. William Dwight Porter Bliss in Hopkins, p. 182.

32. Hopkins, p. 209 or as P.S. Moxom pointed out in a sermon, "the salvation of society is the salvation of the individual extended throughout his relationships," cited in Hopkins, p. 129.

33. Handy, pp. 5-6.

34. Hopkins, p. 318.

35. Hopkins, pp. 215-16.

36. Reinhold Niebuhr, *An Interpretation of Christian Ethics*, New York: Meridian Books, 1956, p. 8.

37. Handy, p. 255.

38. STF, p. 73. See also STL, p. 168.

39. New York: The Macmillan Co., 1918.

40. Robert D. Cross, ed., New York: Harper Torch Books, 1964 (Hereafter referred to as CSC).

41. *Christianizing the Social Order*, his other book of real size, is a spelling out of themes already found in CSC.

42. CSC, p. 286.

43. CSC, p. xxi.

44. CSC, p. 220.

45. CSC, p. 83.

46. CSC, p. 51.

47. TSG, p. 51.

48. TSG, p. 5.

49. CSC, p. 343.

50. TSG, p. 25.

51. CSC, p. 162.

52. See CSC, pp. 169-70.

53. TSG, p. 175.

54. TSG, p. 174-75.

55. TSG, p. 177.

56. TSG, p. 186.

57. TSG, p. 186-87. Here is one theological root of King's dream of the beloved community.

58. TSG, p. 98-99.

59. See TSG, p. 187.

60. TSG, p. 99, see also p. 47.

61. TSG, p. 48.

62. TSG, p. 50.

63. TSG, p. 46.

64. TSG, p. 54.

65. TSG, p. 47.

66. TSG, p. 47.

67. TSG, p. 55.

68. TSG, p. 47.

69. TSG, p. 47.

70. TSG, pp. 46-47.

71. TSG, p. 48.

72. TSG, p. 50.

73. TSG, p. 48.

74. TSG, p. 48.

75. TSG, p. 57.

76. See discussion in TSG, pp. 57-61.

77. TSG, p. 79.

78. TSG, p. 81. Cf. Rauschenbusch's long quotation from Schleiermacher's *The Christian Faith* on pp. 71ff. in TSG in which Schleiermacher discusses in detail his understanding of the "universal racial sin of humanity.".

79. TSG, p. 97.

80. TSG, p. 99.

81. TSG, p. 5.

82. TSG, p. 5.

83. TSG, p. 95.

84. TSG, p. 117. Also note here the danger often ascribed to Rauschenbusch–the temptation to identify the Kingdom of God with the existing order, e.g., altruism of business and political democracy.

85. "Jesus was the successor of the Old Testament prophets." Walter Rauschenbusch, *The Righteousness of the Kingdom*, New York: Abingdon Press, 1968, p. 70. Max Stackhouse has edited this volume and has also written an excellent introduction to it. (Hereafter referred to as RF.)

86. CSC, p. 3.

87. CSC, p. 98. Cf. James 1:9-11.

88. Cf. Stackhouse in RK, p. 55, in which he discusses the difference between synoptic and Pauline thought and claims that the former contains the essential revolutionary seeds of Christianity.

89. TSG, p. 195.

90. CSC, p. 90.

91. See TSG, p. 195.

92. TSG, p. 195. This free church Baptist tradition is also mirrored in King's life and thought.

93. CSC, p. 361.

94. CSC, p. 7.

95. TSG, p. 102.

96. CSC, p. 176. Also "Every forward step in the historical evolution of religion has been marked by a closer union of religion and ethics and by the elimination of non-ethical religious performances. This union of religion and ethics reached its highest perfection in the life and mind of Jesus." Cited in TSG, p. 14. It is Rauschenbusch's conclusion that undue interest in sacraments and ritual paralyzed the morally transforming power of early Christianity and numbed its ethical passion. See CSC, p. 177.

97. Cf. Ritschl's deep suspicion of mysticism also.

98. TSG, p. 104.

99. TSG, p. 194.

100. CSC, p. 338.

101. See CSC, p. 338.

102. TSG, p. 106.

103. TSG, p. 20.

104. TSG, p. 20.

105. CSC, p. 8.

106. CSC, p. 11.

107. CSC, pp. 249ff.

108. CSC, pp. 279ff.

109. CSC, pp. 42-43.

110. CSC, p. 12.

111. CSC, p. 11.

112. CSC, p. 10.

113. See CSC, pp. 17-18.

114. King often made this statement which was really a paraphrase of a comment made by former Chief Justice Warren.

115. CSC, p. 40.

116. CSC, pp. 40-41.

117. CSC, pp. 38-39.

118. CSC, p. 205.

119. TSG, p. 279.

120. TSG, p. 108.

121. King uses more than a dozen times the passage from Amos 5:24. In the last chapter of *The Trumpet of Conscience*, he quotes from four prophets in a most moving fashion.

122. STF, pp. 186-87.

123. STF, p. 25.

124. Statement to Judge Loe in Boston Collection.

125. CSC, p. 51.

126. Martin Luther King, Jr., *Where Do We Go From Here: Chaos or Community?*, New York: Harper & Row, 1967, pp. 187–88 (Hereafter referred to as WDWGFH).

127. STL, p. 14.

128. RK, p. 28.

129. RK, p. 28.

130. RK, p. 30.

131. RK, p. 57.

132. TSG, p. 221. Cf. The similarity of this statement to G.W. Davis's article, "God and History" in *Crozer Quarterly*.

133. TSG, pp. 223-24. Cf. Also TSG, p. 146.

134. TSG, p. 190.

135. TSG, p. 191.

136. CSC, p. xxiii.

137. CSC, p. 45.

138. Cited in *Foundations*, pp. 270-71.

139. *Ibid.*, p. 271.

140. STL, p. 78.

141. *Why We Can't Wait*, New York: Harper & Row, 1964, p. 1. (Hereafter referred to as WWCW). He could have said the "forces of history" or the *Zeitgeist*, the spirit of the times, against which it is difficult to protest.

142. STF, p. 140.

143. King's concept of the "moral law" will be discussed at length later (see pp. 197-199).

144. CSC, p. 342.

145. CSC, p. xi in the Introduction.

146. CSC, p. 198.

147. CSC, p. 149.

148. CSC, pp. 149-50.
149. CSC, p. 151.
150. CSC, p. 151.
151. CSC, p. 151.
152. CSC, p. 246.
153. TSG, p. 75.
154. CSC, p. 349.
155. CSC, p. 349.
156. CSC, p. 349.
157. CSC, p. 48.
158. CSC, pp. 48-49.
159. CSC, p. 367.
160. CSC, p. 364.
161. CSC, pp. 365-66.
162. CSC, pp. 106-107.
163. CSC, p. 107.
164. TSG, p. 128.
165. STF, p. 182.
166. *Playboy* Interview, "Martin Luther King," January 1965, p. 118. Reprinted in *The Best From Playboy Number Three*. Page numbers are from the latter.
167. WDWGFH, p. 96.
168. STF, p. 185, see also STL, p. 160.
169. *Martin Luther King, Jr., Pastor and Revolutionary*, MLKS E6905, SCLC Audio Library, New York.
170. WDWGFH, p. 96.
171. STL, p. 119.
172. STL, p. 120.
173. WDWGFH, p. 96.
174. WDWGFH, p. 96.
175. *Ibid*.
176. STF, p. 185, see also STL, p. 120.
177. STF, p. 184, see also STL, p. 160.
178. STF, p. 185, see also STL, pp. 160-61.
179. STL, pp. 56-57.
180. WWCW, p. 96.
181. WWCW, p. 96. Also see Rauschenbusch "(The Church) does its best work when it is the party in opposition, poor but vociferous," as cited in CSC, p. 188.
182. STL, p. 57.
183. "Current Crisis in Race Relations," *The New South*, March 1958, p. 11.
184. "Who is Their God?" in *Nation*, October 13, 1962, p. 210.
185. WWCW, p. 96. This entire section of the "Letter From Birmingham Jail" is excellent for King's understanding of church's relation to society.
186. "Current Crisis in Race Relations," pp. 11-12.
187. STF, p. 31.
188. WWCW, p. 135.
189. STF, p. 10.

190. STF, p. 15.
191. See STF, pp. 16, 17, 26.
192. STL, p. 119.
193. WWCW, p. 95.
194. STF, p. 97.
195. STF, p. 98. King holds out for wholeness, but does not theologize further, e.g., he does not discuss the relation of Incarnation to ethical involvement.
196. STF, p. 20.
197. STF, p. 21. "Religion at its best realizes that the soul is crushed as long as the body is tortured with hunger pangs and harrowed with the need for shelter," as cited in STL, pp. 63-64.
198. STF, pp. 20-21.
199. STL, p. 70.
200. STL, p. 70.
201. STL, p. 90.
202. STL, p. 149.
203. STL, p. 149.
204. STF, p. 21, also see STL, pp. 118-19.
205. WWCW, p. 65.
206. STL, pp. 108-109.
207. "We are still Walking," *Liberation*, December 1956, p. 9. See also WWCW, pp. 24-25, "Negro ministers, with a growing awareness that the true witness of a Christian life is the projection of a social gospel, had accepted leadership in the fight for racial justice.".
208. WDWGFH, pp. 188-98.
209. TSG, p. 131. See also TSG, p. 144. This was precisely the purpose of TSG.
210. CSC, p. 185.
211. CSC, p. 29.
212. CSC, p. 170.
213. TSG, p. 189. Cf. also in CSC, "The churches of the first generation were not churches in our sense of the word. They were not communities for the performance of a common worship, so much as communities with a common life. They were social communities with a religious basis," p. 119.
214. RK, p. 80.
215. RK, pp. 110-11.
216. TSG, pp. 139-40.
217. TSG, p. 139.
218. TSG, p. 141.
219. CSC, p. 210. Cf. King's stress on a "New Era" emerging with the dawn of the civil rights movement. "Facing the Challenge of a New Age," *Fellowship*, February 1957.
220. RK, pp. 87-88. Cf. TSG, p. 140.
221. TSG, pp. 133-34.
222. CSC, p. 67.
223. TSG, p. 140.
224. TSG, p. 134.

225. TSG, p. 137.
226. TSG, p. 137.
227. TSG, p. 143.
228. CSC, p. 185.
229. CSC, p. 181.
230. TSG, p. 136.
231. TSG, p. 136.
232. TSG, pp. 129-30.
233. TSG, p. 145.
234. "Trustees are apt to regard themselves as the practical owners of the funds they have long administered," CSC, p. 183.
235. CSC, p. 71.
236. RK, p. 87.
237. CSC, p. xxiii. Cf. "The coming of the Kingdom of God will be the regeneration of the super-personal life of the race, and will work out a special expression of what was contained in the personality of Christ," as cited in TSG, p. 116. It was this trust in Rauschenbusch which eventually found expression in King and gave partial content to his dream of the beloved community.
238. CSC, p. 143.
239. CSC, p. 65.
240. Cf. King's concern for a new Atlanta and a new Memphis in last address, "A View from the Mountaintop, Dr. King's Last Message," *Renewal*, April 1969, p. 4.
241. TSG, p. 142.
242. TSG, p. 155.
243. TSG, pp. 158-59.
244. CSC, p. 71. What Rauschenbusch means by righteousness is what King means by justice.
245. TSG, pp. 142ff. Earlier in TSG he had defined the Kingdom as a "realm of love," p. 54.
246. TSG, p. 143.
247. TSG, p. 55.
248. TSG, p. 238.
249. TSG, pp. 186-87.
250. CSC, p. 73. Also cf. an earlier statement, "Jesus . . . extended the limits of the Kingdom. For the idea of God's nation he substituted the idea of God's humanity," as cited in RK, p. 98. Cf. also "The Jewish hope became a human hope with universal scope." Cited in CSC, p. 65.
251. CSC, p. 116.
252. CSC, p. 114.
253. CSC, p. 118.
254. TSG, p. 224. The above references are obvious evidence of the affinity between King's dream of the beloved community and Rauschenbusch.
255. CSC, p. 64.

256.CSC, p. 67. Also "Love with Jesus was not a flickering and wayward emotion, but the highest and most steadfast energy of a will bent on creating fellowship." Cited in CSC, p. 68. See also STF, p. 87.

257. CSC, p. 68. Cf. King's STL, pp. 46-49.

258. TSG, p. 165.

259. TSG, p. 141.

260. *Ibid.* See also RK, p. 35.

261. CSC, p. 309.

262. CSC, p. 420.

CHAPTER THREE

1. Thomas Merton, *Faith and Violence*, Notre Dame, Indiana: University of Notre Dame Press, 1968, pp. 130-31.

2. For example, Staughton Lynd, ed., *Nonviolence in America: A Documentary History*, New York: The Bobbs-Merrill Co., 1966, "Pilgrimage to Nonviolence," pp. 379-96; "Letter From Birmingham Jail," pp. 461-81 and Hugo Adams Bedau, ed., *Civil Disobedience: Theory and Practice*, New York: Pegasus, 1969, "Letter From Birmingham City Jail," pp. 72-89.

3. *Playboy* Interview, p. 120.

4. See Lerone Bennett, Jr., *Before the Mayflower*, Revised Edition, Baltimore: Penguin Books, 1966, p. 306.

5. Part of this interview is in Louis Fischer, ed., *The Essential Gandhi*, New York: Vintage Books, 1963, p. 337.

6. Reinhold Niebuhr, *Moral Man and Immoral Society*, New York: Charles Scribner's Sons, 1932, p. 252 (Hereafter referred to as MM).

7. "A Short Biography of W.L. Garrison," Vladimir Tchertkoff in Tolstoy's *Writings on Civil Disobedience and Nonviolence*, New York: New American Library, 1967, pp. 281-86.

8. Lerone Bennett, *What Manner of Man*, Third Revised Edition, Chicago: Johnson Publishing Co., 1966, p. 4. This reference is also in *The Essential Gandhi*, p. 322.

9. *The Essential Gandhi*, pp. 321-22.

10. See STF, p. 81.

11. From an interview with Dr. Muelder, October 30, 1969. It is known that King did apply to and was accepted by the University of Edinburgh. A letter to this effect is in the Boston Collection.

12. Howard Thurman, *Jesus and the Disinherited*, New York: Abingdon, 1949, p. 100.

13. Mohandas K. Gandhi, *An Autobiography*, Boston: Beacon Press, 1957, p. 153 (Hereafter referred to as *Autobiography*).

14. See STF, p. 7.

15. Bedau, p. 63.

16. On November 10, 1955, Dr. Wofford delivered a lecture at Hampton Institute entitled, "Gandhi the Civil Rights Lawyer." The lecture was sent to the

writer by Dr. Wofford, who is now president of the State University of New York at Old Westbury. Incidentally, there is a remarkable similarity in wording between King (STF, pp. 192-93, 196 and WWCW, p. 85) and Wofford's article, "Nonviolence and the Law: The Law Needs Help" in Bedau, pp. 64-65. An earlier version of this article was given as an address to the Montgomery Improvement Association's Institute on Nonviolence and Social Change. Wofford's article appeared first as an address at Howard University in October 1957. King was present at the MIA meeting, Wofford relates in a letter to the writer (dated May 13, 1970). His version of the similarity of language is as follows: "King may have had the 1957 talk in hand while doing the first draft of *Stride*. It is even possible that I personally added a few of the lines because I worked with him directly on the manuscript, editing some of the sections on civil disobedience. . . ." Of course, King does express gratitude to Wofford for his help in the preface of STF, p. x.

17. STF, p. 77. Also note that Muste, in a letter to King, October 30, 1958, inviting him to a Peace Conference in Evanston, said, "Men like John Bennett are coming closer to our position and some of them incidentally will be participants in the Evanston Conference." Cited in the Boston Collection. This is probably not an accurate evaluation of King, but Muste's wishful thinking. Bennett and King were probably closer to each other than either was to Muste.

18. See list in Chapter 2.

19. STF, p. 78.

20. STF, pp. 78-79.

21. STF, p. 79. This summary statement betrays reliance on Paul Ramsey, *Basic Christian Ethics*, New York: Charles Scribner's Sons, 1950, Chapter 7 especially.

22. *Autobiography*, p. 158.

23. Quoted in Joan V. Bondurant, *Conquest of Violence: The Gandhian Philosophy of Conflict*, Revised Edition, Berkeley and Los Angeles: University of California Press, 1967, p. 161 (Hereafter referred to as Bondurant).

24. Bondurant, p. 163.

25. Quoted in Louis Fischer, *The Life of Mahatma Gandhi*, Toronto: Collier Books, 1969, p. 120 (Hereafter referred to as Fischer).

26. Fischer, p. 110.

27. STF, p. 83.

28. STF, p. 66. Cf. The reference "little brown saint" and "a little brown man in India" in Speech Before NAACP Legal and Educational Fund May 17, 1956 (Boston Collection) is from a book he read at Crozer titled, *That Little Brown Man From India*. See list of Gandhi books in Chapter I.

29. STF, p. 67.

30. This was the second anniversary of the Supreme Court Decision to desegregate schools. King often made major speeches on this day.

31. Boston Collection, pp. 7-8. Much of the above is contained in an article titled, "Walk For Freedom" in *Fellowship*, May 1956, but in the article, obviously written a month or more before publication, there is no mention of Gandhi by name or his movement. King describes the boycott in terms of love, passive resistance, nonviolent protest, with prayer central to this "spiritual movement." King in an address to the National Conference of Religion and Race in 1963 said,

"I am happy to say that the nonviolent movement in America has come not from secular forces but from the heart of the Negro church. . . . The great principles of love and justice which stand at the center of the nonviolent movement are deeply rooted in our Judeo-Christian heritage." Mathew Ahmann, ed., *Race: Challenge to Religion*, Chicago: Regnery, 1963, p. 165.

32. "My Trip to India," Boston Collection, p. 5.

33. STF, pp. 188ff.

34. C.F. Andrews, *Mahatma Gandhi's Ideas*, New York: The Macmillan Co., 1930, p. 60.

35. Fischer, p. 37.

36. *Autobiography*, p. 205.

37. *Bhagavad Gita*, a new translation by P. Lal, Calcutta: Writers Workshop, 1965, p. 4.

38. Quoted in George Hendrick, "The Influence of Thoreau's 'Civil Disobedience' on Gandhi's Satyagraha," *The New England Quarterly*, December, 1956, p. 468.

39. *Autobiography*, p. 69.

40. John Ruskin, *Unto This Last*, Everyman's Library, New York: E.P. Dutton & Co., 1932, pp. 145-46 (Hereafter referred to as Ruskin).

41. Ruskin, pp. 126ff.

42. Ruskin, pp. 157ff.

43. *Autobiography*, p. 299.

44. *Autobiography*, p. 137.

45. From *The Kingdom of God*, quoted in Tolstoy's *Writings on Civil Disobedience and Nonviolence*, p. 253.

46. Quoted in Fischer, p. 103.

47. *Autobiography*, p. 160.

48. M.K. Gandhi, *Nonviolent Resistance*, New York: Schocken Books, 1968, p. 3 (Hereafter referred to as NVR).

49. See Bedau, p. 16.

50. Henry David Thoreau, *Walden or, Life in the Woods and On the Duty of Civil Disobedience*, New York: Signet Classics, 1962, p. 230 (Hereafter referred to as Thoreau).

51. Fischer, p. 94.

52. Quoted in Fischer, pp. 93-94.

53. *Autobiography*, p. 68.

54. *Autobiography*, p. 35.

55. Thomas Merton, ed., *Gandhi on Nonviolence*, New York: New Directions Publishing Corp., 1965, p. 4.

56. See Lynd, p. xvii.

57. NVR, p. iv. Cf. also *Satyagraha* is always superior to armed resistance. This can only be effectively proved by demonstration, not by argument. It is the weapon that adorns the strong. It can never adorn the weak. By weak is meant the weak in mind and spirit, not in body. (NVR, p. 381.).

58. Bondurant, p. 108.

59. NVR, pp. 251-52.

60. NVR, p. 364.

61. NVR, p. 364. Cf. also a Tamil proverb, "God is the only Help of the helpless." "The grand theory of *Satyagraha* is built upon a belief in that Truth." (NVR, p. 189.).

62. *Autobiography*, p. xiii. Cf. also p. 167, "I was confirmed in my opinion that religion and morality were synonymous.".

63. *Autobiography*, p. xii.

64. NVR, p. 38.

65. *Ibid.*

66. Quoted in Bondurant, p. 19. Cf. also from the *Gita*, "The untrue never is; the True never isn't. The knower of truth knows this," p. 6.

67. *Autobiography*, pp. xiii-xiv.

68. When King used the phrase, "Soul Force," he may have had in mind two meanings: the Gandhian sense of Truth and the contemporary black understanding of "soul" as something that comes from deep within the person, not necessarily connected with Truth.

69. NVR, p. 3. Cf. also "Untruth itself is violence," in M.K. Gandhi, *The Law of Love*, Second Edition, Bombay: Bharatiya Vidya Bhavan, 1962, p. 90.

70. Bondurant, p. 31.

71. The major issues to be negotiated in Birmingham were all based on a fundamental appeal to human dignity and equality. (WWCW, p. 109.).

72. NVR, p. 19.

73. NVR, p. 42.

74. NVR, pp. 41-42.

75. NVR, p. 161.

76. See NVR, p. 161.

77. NVR, p. 221.

78. Quoted in Creighton Lacy, *The Conscience of India*, New York: Holt, Rinehart & Winston, 1965, p. 147. Cf. King, "When I speak of love, I am speaking of that force which all the great religions have seen as the supreme unifying principle of life. Love is the key that unlocks the door which leads to ultimate reality. This Hindu-Moslem-Christian-Jewish-Buddhist belief about ultimate reality is beautifully summed up in the First Epistle of Saint John: 'Let us love one another: for love is of God.'" (WDWGFH, p. 190.).

79. *Autobiography*, p. 28. Cf. I. Cor. 13.

80. NVR, p. 221.

81. NVR, p. 15.

82. Bondurant, p. 24.

83. *Nonviolence: A Christian Interpretation*, New York: Schocken Books, 1966, p. 25 (Hereafter referred to as Miller).

84. Miller, p. 26.

85. Miller, p. 25.

86. Lacy, p. 139.

87. Lacy, p. 141.

88. Lacy, p. 141.

89. Bondurant, p. 112. Remember King's observation that Gandhi helped him to see that love was applicable to social systems.

90. NVR, p. 77. See also the details for *Satyagraha* discipline on page 79 and note the reflection of the Sermon on the Mount here.

91. NVR, p. 298.

92. *Autobiography*, p. 505.

93. NVR, p. 176.

94. NVR, p. 170.

95. NVR, p. 146.

96. STF, p. 36.

97. NVR, p. 117.

98. NVR, p. 162.

99. NVR, p. 165.

100. NVR, p. 161.

101. NVR, p. 165.

102. NVR, p. 116.

103. NVR, p. 168.

104. Cf. King, as he reflected on the Montgomery boycott, "What we were really doing was withdrawing our cooperation from an evil system, rather than merely withdrawing our economic support from the bus company." (STF, p. 36.).

105. NVR, p. 169.

106. "All civil disobedience is a part of *Satyagraha*, but all *Satyagraha* is not civil disobedience." (NVR, p. 69.).

107. See NVR, p. 63.

108. NVR, p. 172. Cf. King, "If he (the Negro) has to go to jail for the cause of freedom, let him enter it in the fashion Gandhi urged his countrymen, 'as the bridegroom enters the bride's chamber'–that is, with a little trepidation but with great expectation." (STF, p. 197.).

109. Quoted in Fischer, p. 434. Also see C.F. Andrews, p. 368. Cf. King, "So it was that, to the Negro, going to jail was no longer a disgrace but a badge of honor." (WWCW, p. 19.) This is reminiscent of Thoreau's "Under a government which imprisons any unjustly the true place for a just man is also a prison." (Thoreau, p. 230), which found a true home in Gandhi and King.

110. NVR, p. 174.

111. NVR, p. 18.

112. See NVR, p. 174.

113. See *Autobiography*, p. 470. Also see NVR, p. 67.

114. See NVR, pp. 6-7.

115. See NVR, pp. 214-15.

116. See Bedau, p. 204.

117. See NVR, p. 175.

118. NVR, p. 110. King also did not believe that social change was automatic or inevitable. It had to be prompted.

119. Martin Luther King, Jr., *The Trumpet of Conscience*, New York: Harper & Row, 1968, p. 54 (Hereafter referred to as TC).

120. NVR, p. 222.

121. See *Playboy* Interview, p. 120.

122. See NVR, pp. 221-22.

123. Martin Luther King, Jr., "Nonviolence and Racial Justice" in *The Christian Century*, February 6, 1957, p. 164. Also ". . . legislation and court orders tend only to declare rights–they can never thoroughly deliver them." Martin Luther King, Jr., "Case Against Tokenism," *New York Times Magazine*, August 5, 1962, p. 52.

124. The discussion to follow is basically from STF, pp. 188-91. The same two or three points are found in the following articles, "Love, Law and Civil Disobedience," "Nonviolence and Racial Justice," and "The Current Crisis in Race Relations.".

125. STF, p. 189.

126. WWCW, pp. 131-32.

127. STF, p. 188.

128. STF, p. 189.

129. STF, p. 189.

130. WWCW, p. 131.

131. See STF, p. 190.

132. STF, p. 83.

133. STF, p. 83.

134. NVR, p. 132.

135. NVR, p. 132.

136. NVR, p. 133.

137. NVR, p. 134.

138. King sees "self-defense" as justifiable in an individual sense, i.e., defending one's home or life when attacked, but tactically unwise, e.g., to carry a gun during a nonviolent demonstration. (Cf. WDWGFH, pp. 27, 55.).

139. Richard B. Gregg, *The Power of Nonviolence*, Second Revised Edition, New York: Schocken Books, 1959, p. 50 (Hereafter referred to as Gregg).

140. NVR, p. 34.

141. STF, p. 84.

142. NVR, p. 51.

143. Gregg, p. 75.

144. STF, p. 84; italics mine.

145. Martin Luther King, Jr., "After Segregation: What?" prepared for *Coronet*, but never published. (In Boston Collection, p. 5.).

146. STF, p. 84.

147. *Ibid*.

148. See "Case Against Tokenism," *New York Times Magazine*, p. 52.

149. STF, p. 193.

150. NVR, p. 147.

151. NVR, p. 149.

152. Gregg, p. 43.

153. Gregg, p. 44.

154. Gregg, p. 45.

155. Cf. STL, p. 45ff.

156. WWCW, pp. 107-108.

157. Gregg, p. 45.

158. Gregg, p. 46.

159. *Ibid.*
160. Gregg, p. 51.
161. NVR, p. 375.
162. NVR, p. 202.
163. *My Trip to India* in Boston Collection, p. 6.
164. *Playboy* Interview, p. 120.
165. TC, p. 5.
166. STF, p. 84.
167. Gregg, p. 51.
168. STF, p. 84.
169. NVR, p. 77.
170. STF, p. 85.
171. NVR, p. 194.
172. A.J. Muste, *Non-Violence in an Aggressive World*, New York: Harper & Brothers, 1940, p. 19.
173. NVR, p. 33.
174. NVR, p. 181.
175. NVR, p. 194.
176. NVR, p. 119.
177. NVR, p. 17.
178. NVR, p. 271.
179. STF, p. 193.
180. STF, p. 193.
181. STF, p. 194, see also STL, pp. 48-49.
182. STL, p. 101. Cf. also STF, p. 200 and WDWGFH, pp. 46-47.
183. STF, p. 85.
184. STF, p. 86.
185. NVR, p. 161.
186. NVR, p. 221.
187. Gregg, p. 49.
188. The other was John Bennett's *Christian Ethics and Social Policy*.
189. Smith's unpublished paper, p. 47. Also a required written assignment in the course was to contrast critically A.C. Knudson's *The Principles of Christian Ethics* (representing the liberal approach) and Reinhold Niebuhr's *An Interpretation of Christian Ethics* (the neo-orthodox approach).
190. STF, p. 86.
191. In STF he says, "There are three words for love in the Greek New Testament" (86). He apparently means "in the Greek language." He corrects this in a later version in LLCD, but the same error occurs in Martin Luther King, Jr., *Strength to Love*, p. 44. The word *eros* does not appear in the New Testament.
192. *Ibid.*
193. Anders Nygren, *Agape and Eros*, translated by Philip S. Watson, Philadelphia: Westminster Press, 1953, p. 170 (Hereafter referred to as Nygren).
194. See discussion in Nygren, pp. 175-81.
195. *Ibid.*
196. *Ibid.*

197. Nygren, pp. 75-81.
198. *Ibid*. Obviously, King means "therefore."
199. Ramsey, p. 92.
200. Ramsey, p. 95.
201. Ramsey, p. 94.
202. *Ibid*.
203. STF, p. 86.
204. Ramsey, p. 96.
205. STF, p. 86.
206. Ramsey, pp. 98-99.
207. STF, pp. 86-87.
208. STF, p. 87.
209. Ramsey, p. 92.
210. See King, STL, p. 21.
211. Nygren, p. 91.
212. Cf. Nygren, p. 78 and Ramsey, p. 94.
213. STF, p. 87.
214. Ramsey, p. 238.
215. Cf. Ramsey, pp. 241-42.
216. STF, p. 88.
217. NVR, p. 41.
218. NVR, p. 155.
219. Gregg, p. 71.
220. Gregg, p. 49.
221. STF, p. 88.
222. *Ibid*.
223. NVR, p. 383.
224. Quoted in Lacy, p. 139.
225. WDWGFH, p. 77.
226. "Love, Law and Civil Disobedience," in *The New South*, December, 1961, p. 10 (Hereafter referred to as LLCD).
227. In an original manuscript in the Boston Collection, these two chapters follow one another. Their outline and content suggest that this is quite logical.
228. Here is a list of the articles, "Nonviolence and Racial Justice," *Christian Century*, February 6, 1957; "Out of the Long Night of Segregation," *Presbyterian Outlook*, February 10, 1958; "Out of Segregation's Long Night," *The Churchman*, February, 1958; "Out of the Long Night of Segregation," *Advance*, February 28, 1958; "The Power of Nonviolence," *Intercollection*, May, 1958; "An Experiment in Love," *Jubilee*, September, 1958. Note the Gandhian allusion in the last title. Also in the last of the aforementioned articles there is the complete list of points King made in STF.
229. It was given to the annual meeting of the Fellowship of the Concerned in Atlanta and appeared in the December issue of *New South*.
230. LLCD, p. 4.
231. LLCD, pp. 4-5.
232. "The Case Against Tokenism," p. 12.

233. STL, p. 161.
234. *Playboy* Interview, p. 123.
235. *Ibid.*
236. STL, p. 63.
237. WDWGFH, p. 183.
238. "The Case Against Tokenism," p. 12.
239. Gandhi in NVR, p. 16.
240. *Faith and Violence*, p. 23.
241. *Faith and Violence*, p. 23.
242. STF, p. 193.
243. Gregg, p. 62.
244. WDWGFH, p. 130.
245. See NVR, p. 358.
246. Lacy, pp. 150-51.
247. Lacy, pp. 150-51.
248. STF, p. 36.
249. WWCW, pp. 98-99. Cf. Gandhi, "There can be no *Satyagraha* in an unjust cause." (NVR, p. 56.).
250. WWCW, p. 99.
251. NVR, p. 10.
252. LLCD, p. 5.
253. LLCD, p. 6.
254. LLCD, p. 6.
255. LLCD, p. 7.
256. NVR, p. 386.
257. LLCD, p. 7.
258. STF, p. 188. Also cf. Gandhi, "Non-cooperation with evil is as much a duty as cooperation with good." (NVR, p. 165).
259. See STF, p. 73.
260. Thoreau, p. 229.
261. Thoreau, p. 229, 231.
262. STF, p. 36.
263. STF, p. 73.
264. See Bedau, p. 19 and Lynd, p. xxvii.
265. Reddick, p. 17. Italics are Reddick's.
266. Quoted by Bedau, p. 20.
267. STF, p. 98.
268. STF, p. 37.
269. Thoreau, p. 230.
270. See *Summa Theologica* Part II, Question 91, Article 2, also Question 96, Article 6.
271. Haig Bosmajian, "The Letter From Birmingham Jail," in C. Eric Lincoln, ed., *Martin Luther King, Jr.: A Profile*, American Profiles Series, New York: Hill & Wang, 1970, p. 137.
272. Thoreau, p. 230.
273. STF, p. 129.

274. WWCW, p. 19.

275. Thoreau, p. 223.

276. Kenneth B. Clark, *The Negro Protest, James Baldwin, Malcolm X, Martin Luther King, Jr. talk with Kenneth B. Clark*, Boston: Beacon Press, 1963, p. 39.

277. Address to NAACP May 17, 1956, "Walk For Freedom," *Fellowship*, May 1956. Cf. also in his last article in *Look*, "Showdown for Nonviolence," April 16, 1968, King calls violence "not only morally repugnant (but) pragmatically barren.".

278. "Experiment in Love," in *Jubilee*, September, 1958, p. 14. See also STF, p. 194.

279. See WWCW, p. 168.

280. In an unpublished and untitled manuscript in the Boston Collection, pp. 6-7. The only designation given the article is that it apparently was written for *Challenge*, but did not appear in that journal. Cf. also "But every one who accepts nonviolence whether as an article of faith or policy would assist the mass movement." (NVR, p. 225, also p. 303.).

281. See *Playboy* Interview, p. 118.

282. *Saturday Review*, "Behind the Selma March," April 3, 1965, p. 57.

283. Address to Montgomery Improvement Association, December 3, 1959. Cf. also Gandhi in South Africa being asked to remove his turban in court; not that he wanted to, but, "I wanted to reserve my strength for fighting bigger battles." (*Autobiography*, p. 147.) He noted also that the insistence on truth had taught him to appreciate the "beauty of compromise." The spirit of compromise was an "essential part of *Satyagraha*." (*Ibid.*, p. 148.).

284. WWCW, p. 24.

285. TC, p. 14.

286. WDWGFH, p. 139.

287. See WDWGFH, pp. 130-31 and "The Last Steep Ascent" in *Nation*, March 14, 1966.

288. WDWGFH, pp. 20-21.

289. TC, pp. 14-15.

290. TC, p. 15. King did not endorse deception or clandestine behavior–no "guerilla romanticism." But the call to a new mass form of civil disobedience would syphon off the deep rage boiling in the ghetto.

291. "Showdown for Nonviolence," April 16, 1968, p. 25.

292. WDWGFH, p. 21.

293. See TC, pp. 59-60.

294. STF, p. 117.

295. STF, p. 120.

296. STF, pp. 135-37.

297. STF, pp. 148-49.

298. STF, pp. 144-45.

299. STF, p. 160.

300. Boston Collection.

301. Boston Collection.

302. "Showdown for Nonviolence," p. 25.

CHAPTER FOUR

1. Mary Frances Thelen, *Man as Sinner in Contemporary American Realistic Theology*, New York: King's Crown Press, 1946, p. 1.

2. *Realistic Theology*, New York: Harper and Brothers, 1934, p. 12.

3. *Ibid.*

4. William Hordern, *A Layman's Guide to Protestant Theology*, New York: The Macmillan Co., 1955, p. 145.

5. "In my opinion adequate spiritual guidance can come only through a more radical political orientation and more conservative religious convictions than are comprehended in the culture of our era." Reinhold Niebuhr, *Reflections on the End of an Era*, New York: Charles Scribner's Sons, 1934, p. ix (Hereafter referred to as REE).

6. *Stride Toward Freedom*, Perennial Library, New York: Harper and Row, 1964, p. 79 (Hereafter referred to as STF).

7. Reinhold Niebuhr, *Leaves From a Notebook of a Tamed Cynic*, New York: Richard Smith, Inc., 1930, p. 59.

8. New York: Charles Scribner's Sons, 1937, p. ix (Hereafter referred to as BT).

9. BT, p. 63.

10. BT, p. 65.

11. BT, p. 109.

12. BT, p. 189.

13. See discussion in BT, p. 222.

14. Reinhold Niebuhr, *An Interpretation of Christian Ethics*, New York: Living Age Books, Meridian Books, 1956, p. 111 (Hereafter referred to as ICE).

15. *Discerning the Signs of the Times*, New York: Charles Scribner's Sons, 1946, p. 12.

16. BT, p. 190.

17. BT, p. 28.

18. *The Nature and Destiny of Man*, Vol I, New York: Charles Scribner's Sons, 1953, p. 150 (Hereafter referred to as NDM).

19. *Faith and History*, p. 121.

20. ICE, p. 75.

21. BT, p. 189.

22. NDM, I, p. 255.

23. *Love and Justice Selections from the Shorter Writings of Reinhold Niebuhr*, Edited by D.B. Robertson, New York: Meridian Books, The World Publishing Co., 1967, p. 128 (Hereafter referred to as LJ).

24. LJ, p. 130.

25. ICE, p. 110.

26. BT, p. 181.

27. LJ, p. 37.

28. *The Children of Light and the Children of Darkness*, New York: Charles Scribner's Sons, 1944, p. 111. See also pp. 59-60 (Hereafter referred to as CLCD).

29. King reflects this realism. "Will Negroes generally find it as easy to give up their own prejudices as it now is to demand their rights of others? Will the same forthrightness be shown in admitting whites to Negro clubs, fraternities and other voluntary associations that is now being shown in pressing for admittance to restaurants and theatres?" Martin Luther King, Jr., "After Segregation: What?" in Boston Collection, pp. 3-4 and "Let me make it clear that I don't think white men have a monopoly on sin and greed." Martin Luther King, Jr., "A Testament of Hope," *Playboy*, January 1969, p. 231.

30. NDM, I, p. 223.

31. BT, p. 103.

32. NDM, I, p. 226, see also p. 225.

33. STF, pp. 80-81. Of course, these are typical of liberal caricatures of Barth and the dialectical school of theology. The application of an American standard (Fundamentalism) to continental biblical theology is inappropriate. Most of those theologians were never affected by the liberal-fundamentalist controversy primarily experienced in America. And the first chapter of Barth's *Dogmatics in Outline* would clarify the charge of "anti-rationalism.".

34. STF, p. 81. See also *Strength to Love*, pp. 78, 165-66. On page 166 in STL, King says, "I realized that liberalism had been all too sentimental concerning human nature . . ."–a phrase he obtained from Niebuhr.

35. STL, p. 167.

36. STF, p. 82.

37. Especially in *Moral Man and Immoral Society*, New York: Charles Scribner's Sons, 1932, pp. 70-78 (Hereafter referred to as MM). Note also that King's doctoral advisor at Boston, L. Harold DeWolf, has some significant criticism of Niebuhr. It justifiably centers around the charge that the idealism Niebuhr is attacking is also a caricature and a one-sided interpretation of Paul. See his *A Theology of the Living Church*, Second Revised Edition, New York: Harper & Row, 1960, p. 184, and *The Case for Theology in Liberal Perspective*, Philadelphia: Westminster, 1959, pp. 38-50.

38. See REE, pp. 261-62.

39. CLCD, p. 59.

40. *Ibid*.

41. LJ, p. 53.

42. LJ, p. 53. In the foreword to the 1959 edition of CLCD, Niebuhr reaffirms his thesis of the original edition, which was that a free society prospers best in an atmosphere which encourages neither a "too pessimistic nor too optimistic view of human nature." A free society requires some confidence in the ability of men to reach tentative and tolerable adjustments between their competing interests and to arrive at some common notions of justice which transcend all partial interests" (CLCD, p. xii). It is necessary to go beyond a consistent pessimism and a consistent optimism because of the inherent dangers in both, namely political absolutism and political chaos. Modern democracy requires a more "realistic philosophical and religious basis . . ." "Man's capacity for justice makes democracy possible; but man's inclination to injustice makes democracy necessary" (CLCD, p. xxiii).

261

43. Gordon Harland, *The Thought of Reinhold Niebuhr*, New York: Oxford University Press, 1960, p. 46.

44. Paul's Letter to American Christians," Boston Collection, p. 2. See also STL, pp. 163-64.

45. STL, p. 107.

46. STL, p. 110.

47. STL, p. 111.

48. See above discussion in Chapter 3.

49. LLCD, p. 6.

50. *Ibid.*

51. LLCD, p. 7.

52. CLCD, pp. 71-72.

53. MM, p. 44.

54. MM, p. 117.

55. STL, p. 166. Karl Barth and other neo-orthodox theologians would hardly disagree with this. One wonders how King could have called Barth anti-rational. Some possible reasons are: 1) it was a liberal shibboleth, 2) it indicates that King was not a logical or systematic thinker, or 3) it reveals the several strong intellectual currents flowing in his mind had not been synthesized.

56. WDWGFH, p. 88.

57. CLCD, p. 144.

58. STF, p. 100.

59. WDWGFH, p. 128.

60. "My Trip to India," in Boston Collection, p. 12.

61. WDWGFH, p. 151.

62. "Reinhold Niebuhr's Ethical Dualism," in the Boston Collection, pp. 13-14.

63. *Ibid.*, p. 14.

64. *Ibid.* Actually, King first met this criticism of Niebuhr in another personalist, Albert Knudson, who made somewhat the same observation as Muelder. "In the later history of the church a long list of distinguished names might be cited in support of the view that a relative sinlessness, a sinlessness not inconsistent with growth, is possible on earth" (*The Principles of Christian Ethics*, New York: Abingdon, 1943, p. 150). An assignment in Kenneth Smith's ethics course, which King took as a senior at Crozer, was to compare Niebuhr's ICE and Knudson's book on ethics. (See Smith, p. 47.).

65. STF, p. 79, STL, p. 111, WDWGFH, p. 143, *Why We Can't Wait*, p. 82 (Hereafter referred to as WWCD), and *Playboy* Interview, p. 128.

66. MM, p. xi.

67. See MM, pp. 9 and 28.

68. STL, p. 111.

69. MM, p. xxiii. See also p. 31.

70. MM, p. 4.

71. MM, p. 121.

72. MM, p. 164.

73. MM, p. 34.

74. MM, p. 176.

75. MM, pp. 176-77.
76. MM, p. 177.
77. MM, p. xii.
78. MM, p. 165.
79. MM, p. 33.
80. MM, p. 234.
81. MM, p. 252.
82. MM, p. 252.
83. MM, p. 253.
84. The Montgomery boycott was an expression of this.
85. WDWGFH, p. 143.
86. MM, p. 254.
87. WDWGFH, p. 138.
88. WWCW, p. 123.
89. WDWGFH, p. 75.
90. From the article Martin Luther King, Jr., "The Un-Christian Christian" in *The White Problem in America*, by the editors of *Ebony*, Chicago: Johnson Publishing Co., Inc., 1966, p. 61. It also appeared in *Ebony* in August 1965.
91. *Playboy* Interview, p. 128. Virtually the same statement appears in "Letter From Birmingham Jail," although there he concludes with the observation, "We know through painful experience that freedom is never voluntarily given by the oppressor; it must be demanded by the oppressed" (WWCW, p. 82). Cf. also ". . freedom is not given, it is won" (WDWGFH, p. 19).
92. See STL, p. 170.
93. "Nonviolence and Racial Justice," in *The Christian Century*, February 6, 1957, p. 166.
94. STL, p. 38.
95. WDWGFH, p. 118.
96. WDWGFH, p. 129.
97. See "Honoring Du Bois," *Freedomways*, Spring 1968.
98. From "The Right to Vote" in *New York Times Magazine*, March 14, 1965, p. 95.
99. "Love, Law and Civil Disobedience," *The New South*, December 1961, p. 6.
100. LJ, p. 9.
101. NDM, II, p. 256.
102. Brunner tends to be dualistic, seeing the norm of love applying to personal relationships and the norm of justice applying to the realm of social systems and the orders of life. See Emil Brunner, translated by Olive Wyon, *The Divine Imperative*, Philadelphia: The Westminster Press, 1947, p. 328. Brunner attempts to alter this in a later book. "That does not mean that justice and law are two independent principles. Such a dualism would be insupportable to Christian thought. It is rather that justice is a manifestation of love. Justice is that love which is applies to order" (*Christianity and Civilization*, Vol. I, New York: Charles Scribner's Sons, 1947, p. 116). Notwithstanding this, Brunner does not emphasize the dialectical character of the relation as Niebuhr does. Brunner does not stress the approximation of love

in justice, whereas Niebuhr talks of the indeterminate approximation of love in justice.

103. NDM, II, p. 246. See also NDM, I, p. 285.

104. See Chapter 4 of ICE.

105. LJ, pp. 32-33.

106. LJ, p. 38.

107. MM, p. 57.

108. ICE, p. 163.

109. LJ, p. 28. Also note: "There seems nothing in the Christian ethic about prudence, and prudence is what is demanded in such critical situations as this one. But a genuine charity is the father of prudence" (LJ, p. 154). Niebuhr is here speaking of the problem of desegregating public schools.

110. Another alternative for some was a kind of cynicism and defeatism which resulted in little social achievement because of the knowledge that love simply would not work.

111. LJ, p. 25.

112. LJ, p. 112.

113. LJ, pp. 111-12.

114. LJ, p. 300.

115. *Ibid.*

116. CCP, pp. 26-27.

117. LJ, p. 43.

118. LJ, p. 28.

119. Reinhold Niebuhr, *Christianity and Crisis*, "The Montgomery Savagery," June 12, 1961, p. 103.

120. WDWGFH, pp. 89-90.

121. WDWGFH, p. 90.

122. *Ibid.*, for an elaboration of this, see "Honoring Dr. Du Bois," *Freedomways*, Spring, 1968, pp. 110-11.

123. Essentially the same discussion is found in STL, pp. 28-29, STF, pp. 175-76, "The Challenge of the New Age," *Phylon*, April 1957, p. 32, "The American Dream," *Negro History Bulletin*, May 1968, p. 14, "The Case Against Tokenism," *New York Times Magazine*, August 5, 1962, p. 49.

124. "The American Dream," *Negro History Bulletin*, May 1968, p. 14.

125. STL, p. 28. King said, "The law may not change the heart, but it can restrain the heartless" ("The Case Against Tokenism," *New York Times Magazine*, August 5, 1962, p. 49 and "The Ethical Demands of Integration," Methodist Student Movement, Nashville, 1964, p. 9 (Hereafter referred to as "Ethical Demands"), but no credit is given Niebuhr.

126. WDWGFH, p. 90.

127. *Playboy*, "A Testament of Hope," January 1969, p. 231.

128. WDWGFH, p. 37.

129. New York: Oxford University Press, 1960, p. 11. This book was first printed in 1954, while King was writing his dissertation on Tillich and Wieman. There is no credit given Tillich by King.

130. January 1962 (Hereafter referred to as Sellers).

131. Sellers, p. 425.
132. Sellers, p. 427.
133. Sellers, p. 429.
134. "Walk For Freedom," *Fellowship*, May 1956, p. 5.
135. "Facing the Challenge of a New Age," *Phylon*, April 1957, p. 30.
136. ICE, p. 9.
137. See above discussion on nonviolence in Chapter 3.
138. Martin Luther King, Jr., "Our Struggle," *Liberation*, April 1956.
139. Kenneth Smith suggests there is a relation between this "love monism" and a "Jesus monism" in King's thought. Smith, p. 55.
140. First appeared in *Religion and Labor*, May 1963.
141. "Ethical Demands," p. 4.
142. "Ethical Demands," p. 9. Also note: It is this context that the official slogan of the Montgomery Improvement Association, "Justice without Violence," must be understood.
143. Sellers, p. 431.
144. *e.g.*, STF, pp. 86-88.
145. Note especially STL, pp. 48-49.
146. STL was published in 1963, but all the sermons had been preached in Dexter Avenue Baptist in Montgomery or in Ebenezer Baptist in Atlanta and several of them had been preached many times over during King's innumerable speaking engagements throughout the country. Some had appeared in religious journals.
147. Sellers, p. 428.
148. STL, p. 163. See also WDWGFH, pp. 190-91. In the original sermon in the Boston Collection, King goes on to say that love is the greatest virtue.
149. MM, pp. 2542–55.
150. Reinhold Niebuhr, *Christianity and Power Politics*, New York: Charles Scribner's Sons, 1940, p. 28 (Hereafter referred to as CPP).
151. New York: Charles Scribner's Sons, 1965, pp. 86-87. A Mennonite theologian, John Yoder, responds, "Slavery may be 'worse than war' in the sense that it is more unpleasant for me; but in war the sin is mine, in slavery it is not." *Reinhold Niebuhr and Christian Pacifism*, Washington: The Church Peace Mission, 1966, p. 17.
152. LJ, p. 252.
153. LJ, p. 250. See also p. 34. King finally realized this in his confrontation with the urban north in America.
154. CPP, p. 18. See also p. 2.
155. CPP, p. 10.
156. ICE, p. 166.
157. CCP, p. 10.
158. This criticism is not completely fair to Gregg, who has a very important exception in that book. Cf. "Courageous violence, to try to prevent or stop a wrong, is better than cowardly acquiescence. Cowardice is more harmful morally than violence. The inner attitude is more important than the outer act. . . ." (Gregg, p. 50) which agrees with Niebuhr's "nothing is intrinsically immoral except ill-will and nothing intrinsically good except goodwill" (MM, p. 170). Cf. also

Gandhi, "I do believe that where there is only a choice between cowardice and violence I would advise violence . . . I would rather have India resort to arms in order to defend her honor then she should in a cowardly manner become or remain a helpless witness to her own dishonor" (NVR, p. 132).

159. MM, p. 172.
160. MM, pp. 172, 179.
161. LJ, p. 257.
162. CPP, pp. 5-6.
163. BT, p. 197.
164. ICE, p. 169.
165. STF, pp. 79-80.
166. *Ibid.*, p. 80.
167. STF, p. 80.
168. STF, p. 80.
169. *The New Testament Basis of Pacifism and the Relevance of an Impossible Ideal, An answer to the views of Reinhold Niebuhr*, Nyack, New York: Fellowship Publications, 1968, pp. 154-55.
170. STF, p. 81 and STL, p. 171.
171. STF, p. 81.
172. STL, p. 81.
173. STL, p. 171.
174. An address given in Los Angeles, February 25, 1967, "The Casualties of the War in Vietnam," in a pamphlet published by Clergy and Laymen Concerned about Vietnam.
175. *Op. cit.*, pp. 5-8.
176. The four primary sources of his views on Vietnam are "The Casualties of the War in Vietnam," "Beyond Vietnam" (in Clergy and Laymen Concerned pamphlet), "Declaration of Independence from the War in Vietnam," Michael Hamilton, ed., *The Vietnam War: Christian Perspectives*, Grand Rapids: Erdsmans, 1969 and "Conscience and the Vietnam War" in *Trumpet of Conscience*, p. 21ff. The latter three are quite similar in content with the last one an abbreviated form of all three. Also in his last major book, WDWGFH, he becomes increasingly concerned about Vietnam. See pp. 35ff, 86, 133, 182ff.
177. TC, p. 24.
178. STF, p. 77.
179. "Who is their God?" in *Nation*, October 3, 1962, p. 210.
180. STL, p. 171.
181. *Op. cit.*, *Love and Justice*, p. 20.
182. LJ, p. 20.
183. "The Casualties of the War in Vietnam," p. 3.
184. Cf. Discussion above on Sellers' criticism of King's perversion of Niebuhr.
185. When the *Playboy* interviewer asks King the meaning of "militant nonviolence," a label King uses to describe his position, he replied, "I mean to say that a strong man must be militant as well as moderate. He must be a realist as well as an idealist" (p. 120).
186. Letter to the writer from Niebuhr dated September 22, 1969.

187. ICE, p. 166.
188. CLCD, p. 5.
189. CLCD, p. 50.
190. CLCD, p. 154. Cf. Title of King's book, *Where Do We Go From Here: Chaos or Community?*.
191. See discussion in MM, pp. 60-61.
192. MM, pp. 71-72.
193. BT, p. 53.
194. MM, p. 21.
195. CCP, p. 20.
196. CLCD, p. 188.
197. ICE, p. 23.
198. CPP, p. 21.
199. MM, p. 82.
200. MM, p. 82.
201. CLCD, p. 163.
202. See NDM, II, pp. 290-91.
203. BT, p. 285.
204. See BT, pp. 285-86.
205. CLCD, p. 187.

CHAPTER FIVE

1. STF, p. 82.

2. *Bostonia*, p. 7, Spring 1957. Also, however, to a Baptist group, he once paid high praise to Morehouse and Crozer, both Baptist schools. "I gained my major influence from these two institutions–Morehouse and Crozer–and I feel greatly indebted to them. They gave me the basic truths I now believe . . . the world view which I hope to have . . . the idea of the oneness of humanity and the dignity and worth of all human personality" (*Crusader*, April 1957, p. 7). One would suspect he was attempting to gratify respective constituencies, but he probably was sincere in both cases.

3. Rudolf Hermann Lotze, *Microcosmus: An Essay Concerning Man and His Relation of the World*, Translated by Elizabeth Hamilton and E.E. Constance Jones, Volumes I and II, Edinburgh: T.&T. Clark, 1885, pp. 626-89 (Hereafter referred to as Lotze).

4. Lotze, Vol. II, p. 351. Then there follows a strong defense of Idealism, pp. 351ff.

5. R.T. Flewelling, *Personalism and the Problems of Philosophy*, New York: The Methodist Book Concern, 1915, p. 98 (Hereafter referred to as Flewelling).

6. Borden Parker Bowne, *Personalism*, New York: Houghton Mifflin Co., 1908, p. 303. Cf. also, "The practical trustworthiness of life can be learned only from experience and verified only in experience" (*Ibid.*, p. 305). (Hereafter referred to as *Personalism.*).

7. Albert C. Knudson, *The Philosophy of Personalism*, New York: The Abingdon Press, 1969, p. 173 (Hereafter referred to as Knudson).

8. Lotze, Vol. I, p. 416.

9. Flewelling, *op. cit.*, p. 102.

10. Lotze, Vol. II, p. 724.

11. Lotze, Vol. II, p. 723-24.

12. Lotze, Vol. II, p. 672.

13. B.M.G. Reardon, *Religious Thought in the Nineteenth Century*, Cambridge: University Press, 1966, p. 126 (Hereafter referred to as Reardon).

14. Lotze, Vol. II, pp. 671-72. Cf. Also Bowne, who later said that determinations of theistic thought fall into two classes, metaphysical and ethical. "The former aim to tell what God is by virtue of his position as first cause, and the second relate to his character. Or the former refer to the divine nature, the latter to the divine will" (Borden Parker Bowne, *Philosophy of Theism*, New York: Harper and Brothers, 1887, pp. 139-40). All personalist philosophers and/or theologians have had a decided interest in ethics. E.g., Bowne, *The Principles of Ethics*, Brightman, *Moral Laws*, Knudson, *The Principles of Christian Ethics*, Bertocci, *The Human Venture in Sex, Love, and Marriage*, and DeWolf is now writing a book on Christian ethics as a sequel to his *Theology of the Living Church*. All of these men, reflecting Lotze's inseparability of metaphysics and ethics and the ultimate worth of the person, strive to grapple seriously with the ethical life. The assumption also that God is the ideal personality, implying love and will, enables these men to emphasize the ethical aspect of ultimate reality, as well as the metaphysical. One can see how King's Christian's convictions would be open to this world-view.

15. Knudson, p. 85.

16. Reardon, p. 125.

17. Flewelling, p. 20.

18. Knudson, pp. 85-86.

19. Knudson, p. 76.

20. *Personalism*, p. 268. See his definitive chapter, "The Personal World.".

21. Flewelling, p. 106.

22. *Personalism*, p. 158.

23. Edgar Sheffield Brightman, *An Introduction to Philosophy*, Revised by Robert N. Beck, New York: Holt, Rinehart and Winston, 1963, p. 336 (Hereafter referred to as IP). This was first published in 1925 and revised in 1951. See also p. 346. This theme is again strongly expressed in *Nature and Values*. ". . . personalism will be taken to mean the belief that the universe is a society of conscious beings, that the energy which physicists describe is God's will in action, and that there is no wholly unconscious or impersonal being. Everything that is, is a conscious mind or some phase or aspect of a conscious mind. To speak religiously, the universe consists of God and his family. Nature is divine experience" (Edgar Sheffield Brightman, *Nature and Values*, Nashville: Abingdon-Cokesbury Press, 1945, p. 114 (Hereafter referred to as NV).

24. NV, pp. 139-39. Cf. King, "Behind the harsh appearances of the world there is a benign power" (STL, p. 173).

25. NV, p. 59.

26. NV, p. 60. King strongly identified with this idealist position. He said we have "spiritual experiences that cannot be explained in materialistic terms," and we never see "the love and faith of individuals" whose sacrifice made possible the construction of cathedrals, for instance, which we do see. "As you presently gaze at the pulpit and witness me preaching this sermon, you may immediately conclude that you see Martin Luther King. But then you are reminded that you see only my body, which in itself can neither reason nor think. You can never see the *me* that makes me me, and I can never see the you that makes you you. That invisible something we call personality is beyond our physical gaze. Plato was right when he said that the visible is a shadow cast by the invisible" (STL, pp. 91-92). King wrote a term paper for the course on Plato he took at Harvard. In the paper, he attempted to determine what Plato meant by God and gods. The discussion was limited to the *Timeaus* and *Laws*.

27. NV, p. 115.

28. NV, pp. 116-18.

29. NV, p. 140.

30. *Personalism*, p. 325.

31. *Ibid*., p. 263.

32. This was the text used by King for the course in personalism taught by DeWolf. Every student was to have mastered the content of this work.

33. Knudson, p. 67.

34. NV, p. 114.

35. NV, p. 148.

36. *Personalism*, p. 197.

37. Knudson, p. 62.

38. Knudson, p. 80. This would have been the major appeal to and influence in the thought of Martin Luther King, Jr.

39. *Philosophy of Theism*, p. 257.

40. *Ibid*., p. 249.

41. *Personalism*, p. 302.

42. Knudson, p. 254.

43. NV, p. 137.

44. Lotze, Vol. I, p. 707.

45. Lotze, Vol. I, p. 708.

46. *Ibid*., p. 688.

47. Knudson, p. 237.

48. NV, p. 113. King uses virtually the same language in his definition in STF, p. 82.

49. IP, p. 330.

50. *Personalism*, pp. 277-78. See also IP, p. 314.

51. NV, p. 57. Actually this book is an attempt to explore exhaustively this "perhaps.".

52. IP, p. 330. Also the same distinction is made in a footnote in NV, p. 115.

53. See *Philosophy of Theism*, p. 128.

54. Knudson, p. 83.

55. Edgar Sheffield Brightman, *Moral Laws*, New York: Abingdon Press, 1933, p. 242 (Hereafter referred to as *Moral Laws*).

56. See the discussion in NV, pp. 149-52.

57. NV, pp. 160-63.

58. NV, pp. 163-65.

59. NV, p. 140.

60. *Personalism*, p. 266.

61. Edgar Sheffield Brightman, *A Philosophy of Religion*, New York: Prentice-Hall, Inc., 1940, p. 226 (Hereafter referred to as PR).

62. IP, pp. 278-79.

63. PR, p. 226.

64. *Personalism*, pp. 266-67. King quotes a part of this passage in his dissertation as he discusses Wieman and Tillich on the "supra-personal" character of God. Both of these men see an element of limitation in applying personality to God. Using this Bowne passage as his argument, King concludes, "the conception of God as personal, therefore, does not imply limitation of any kind" (Martin Luther King, Jr., "A Comparison of the Conception of God in the thought of Henry Nelson Wieman and Paul Tillich," doctoral dissertation, Boston University, p. 270, see discussion on pp. 268-70). King disavowed Brightman's idea of the "finite God." In fact, the notion of theistic finitism is virtually unique to Brightman among personalist philosophers. Knudson and DeWolf both hold that God is both good and powerful (see especially *A Theology of the Living Church* by DeWolf, pp. 108, 134-37). King adopted this position in his dissertation (p. 298). A philosopher of religion like Brightman might conclude that God's power is relatively finite while his will for good is infinite, but theologians grounded in Biblical faith would naturally affirm the "almightiness" of God. For Brightman's discussion of "Finite God," see PR, chapters IX and X.

65. See IP, pp. 279-80.

66. IP, p. 279.

67. *Ibid.*, p. 280.

68. See IP, p. 343.

69. NV, p. 72.

70. NV, p. 63.

71. NV, p. 74.

72. NV, p. 75.

73. NV, p. 74.

74. NV, p. 23.

75. NV, p. 73.

76. PR, p. 88.

77. *Ibid.*

78. PR, p. 89.

79. PR, pp. 134-35.

80. PR, p. 135. See also p. 240.

81. *Ibid.*, p. 343.

82. *Ibid.*, p. 230. See also IP, p. 279.

83. *Moral Laws*, p. 286.

84. *Moral Laws*, p. 45.

85. Walter G. Muelder, *Moral Law in Christian Social Ethics*, Richmond: John Knox Press, 1966, p. 146 (Hereafter referred to as *Moral Law in Christian Social Ethics*).

86. Lotze, Vol. II, p. 675.

87. *Philosophy of Theism*, p. 214.

88. *Philosophy of Theism*, p. 220-21.

89. Knudson, p. 307.

90. *Ibid.*, p. 55.

91. *Ibid.*

92. *Philosophy of Theism*, pp. 214-15.

93. *Moral Laws*, p. 264.

94. *Moral Laws*, p. 276.

95. NV, p. 64.

96. NV, p. 117.

97. NV, p. 117.

98. Albert C. Knudson, *The Principles of Christian Ethics*, New York: Abingdon Press, 1943, p. 214 (Hereafter referred to as *The Principles of Christian Ethics*).

99. IP, p. 353. There may be some significance in the fact that these are the last words of the book. Muelder says that Brightman's early orientation in personalism was individualistic, with an interest primarily in virtue and the good, but that he became increasingly socially sensitive in his later years. Muelder modestly claims that this was due, in part, to his own influence on Brightman (in an interview with the writer on October 30, 1969). But Brightman does not espouse a social gospel of the Rauschenbusch variety, much less was he an activist. The climax of this social-mindedness of Brightman was during King's student days at Boston University.

100. *The Principles of Christian Ethics*, p. 118.

101. NV, p. 117.

102. NV, p. 117.

103. NV, p. 117.

104. IP, p. 352.

105. *The Principles of Christian Ethics*, p. 238.

106. PR, pp. 276-77.

107. PR, p. 435, italics his.

108. NV, p. 165.

109. NV, p. 165.

110. NV, p. 166.

111. NV, p. 166. Two chapters in this book are titled, "One World: Naturalism," and "One World: Personalism.".

112. WDWGFH, p. 97.

113. *Ibid.*, p. 97, italics are mine.

114. The discussion of WDWGFH, word for word, appeared first in "The Ethical Demands of Integration," Methodist Student Movement Study Paper, Nashville, in 1964 (Hereafter referred to as "Ethical Demands"). I am relying, for the moment, on the material in WDWGFH.

115. *Ibid.*

116. *Ibid.*, p. 180.
117. "A Realistic Look at Progress of Race Relations," in the Boston Collection, p. 3.
118. WDWGFH, p. 99.
119. "Ethical Demands," p. 7.
120. *Ibid.*, p. 99.
121. *Ibid.*, p. 97.
122. *Ibid.*, p. 97.
123. *Ibid.*, p. 100.
124. *Ibid.*, p. 97.
125. *Ibid.*, p. 97.
126. See STF, p. 75.
127. "Ethical Demands," p. 5.
128. "The Case Against Tokenism," *New York Times Magazine*, August 5, 1962, p. 49.
129. WDWGFH, p. 180.
130. TC, p. 72.
131. STL, p. 79.
132. See STL, p. 79.
133. STL, p. 115. Cf. PR, pp. 134-35.
134. STL, p. 115.
135. STL, pp. 172-73.
136. STL, p. 172 and STF, p. 88.
137. Martin Luther King, Jr., "The Man Who Was a Fool," *The Pulpit*, June 1961, TC, p. 75, WDWGFH, p. 180.
138. STF, p. 88, "Love, Law and Civil Disobedience," p. 10, STF, p. 51.
139. STL, pp. 74 and 127.
140. See STL, p. 142
141. Martin Luther King, Jr., "The Montgomery Story," in the Boston Collection, pp. 8-9.
142. The address was first given in December 1956 and was printed in *Phylon*, April 1957. The same themes appeared in the original sermon, "The Death of Evil on the Seashore," which was preached May 17, 1956 in St. John the Divine Cathedral in New York. For a more organized presentation of these same ideas, see STL, p. 71.
143. STL, p. 128, also p. 116.
144. WDWGFH, p. 180.
145. "Paul's Letter to American Christians," in the Boston Collection, p. 3.
146. "Love, Law and Civil Disobedience," *The New South*, December 1961, p. 7.
147. "A View of the Dawn," *Interracial Review*, May 1957, p. 9.
148. STL, p. 160.
149. "The Montgomery Story" in the Boston Collection, p. 12.
150. "The Power of Nonviolence," *Intercollegian*, May 1958, p. 9.
151. STF, p. 88.

152. See the fine article, "On Jesus, Pharoahs, and the Chosen People: Martin Luther King as Biblical Interpreter and Humanist," by James H. Smylie in *Interpretation*, January 1970, pp. 74-91, in which King's understanding of the Exodus as an "archetypal experience" is examined.

153. STL, pp. 71-81.

154. STL, p. 73.

155. STL, pp. 77-78.

156. STF, p. 51.

157. Prayer Pilgrimage Speech in D.C. May 17, 1957, in the Boston Collection, p. 4. In his lecture notes from Systematic Theology I at Boston, King has, "Only on the basis of personality in God and man can fellowship be possible. Aristotle's God is a self-knowing God but not an other loving God. Fellowship demands a will and feeling between the parties involved in the fellowship" (Boston Collection).

158. WWCW, p. 26.

159. We mentioned earlier in the chapter on nonviolence that a basic element in nonviolent resistance "is that it is based on the conviction that the universe is on the side of justice" (STF, p. 88).

160. "Love, Law and Civil Disobedience," p. 10. King frequently would call the roll of poets who believed in the ultimate triumph of good over evil, as supporting evidence. E.g., "There is something in this universe that justifies Carlyle in saying no lie can live forever. We shall overcome because there is something in this universe which justified William Cullen Bryant in saying truth crushed to earth shall rise again" (LLCD, pp. 10-11), or "Something in this universe justified Shakespeare in saying, 'There's a divinity that shapes our ends, rough-hew them how we will,' and Lowell in saying, 'Though the cause of Evil prosper, Yet 'tis Truth alone is strong,' and Tennyson is saying, 'I can but trust that good shall fall, At last–far off–at last, to all, and every winter change to spring'" (STL, p. 74).

161. STL, p. 127. In "A Realistic View of Progress of Race Relations," he said, "until walls of injustice are crushed by the battering rams of historical necessity," (Boston Collection, p. 3).

162. STL, p. 127.

163. STL, p. 60.

164. STL, p. 104.

165. *Personalism*, p. 110.

166. *Ibid.*, p. 157.

167. *Ibid.*, p. 160.

168. PR, pp. 251-52. See entire discussion on pp. 251-59.

169. *Ibid.*, p. 276.

170. Especially in "Philosophy of History" audited at the University of Pennsylvania 1949-50 and "Seminar in History of Philosophy" at Boston 1952-53.

171. Brightman became ill the first semester and did not return to teach. Bertocci finished the Seminar in Brightman's absence.

172. Published as "Facing the Challenge of a New Age," *Phylon*, April 1957, p. 25.

173. *Ibid.*, p. 25.

174. Annual address by President Martin Luther King, Jr. on the Fourth Anniversary of the MIA, Boston Collection, p. 15.

175. STF, p. 29.

176. WWCW, p. 91.

177. STF, p. 173.

178. "A Realistic Look of Progress of Race Relations," p. 2.

179. See "A View of the Dawn," *Interracial Review*, May 1957, pp. 82-83.

180. Bertocci revealed this in an interview with the writer. The main text for the Seminar was G.W.F. Hegel, *The Phenomenology of Mind*, translated by J.B. Baillie, Second Edition, New York: George Allen and Unwin, 1961. The dialectical relationship of lordship to servant is on pp. 234-40.

181. STF, p. 46.

182. WWCW, p. 142.

183. STF, p. 188.

184. "Facing the Challenge of a New Age," p. 33.

185. STF, p. 18.

186. "A Testament of Hope," *Playboy*, January 1969, p. 231.

187. Other illustrations of this method at work in King's writings are: ". . . the truth about man is found neither in the thesis of pessimistic materialism nor the antithesis of optimistic humanism, but in a higher synthesis. Man is neither villain nor hero; he is rather both villain and hero" (STL, p. 107). "The Kingdom of God is neither the thesis of individual enterprise nor the antithesis of collective enterprise, but a synthesis which reconciles the truth of both" (STL, p. 121). "The Renaissance was too optimistic, and the Reformation too pessimistic . . . for neither God nor man will individually bring the world's salvation. Rather, both man and God, made one in a marvelous unity of purpose" (STL, pp. 148, 152). Other examples are in STL, pp. 58, 78, 146-54, 166, and in STF, pp. 188, 191. Since most of these references are found in his sermons, he must have found it a useful homiletical device.

188. See STF, p. 82.

CHAPTER SIX

1. *Fellowship*, December 1956, p. 9.

2. *Phylon*, April 1957, p. 30.

3. STF, p. 196. See also STL, p. 28.

4. STL, p. 48.

5. "Ethical Demands," p. 7.

6. *Playboy*, p. 125.

7. *Playboy*, p. 128.

8. WDWGFH, p. 171.

9. TC, p. 68.

10. TSG, pp. 186-87.

11. See especially chapter 4, "The Realm of Grace," *The Problem of Christianity*, Josiah Royce, Chicago: University of Chicago Press, 1968, pp. 121ff.

12. TSG, pp. 126-27.

13. "Ethical Demands," p. 7.

14. *Negro History Bulletin*, May 1968, p. 22.

15. See "Facing the Challenge of a New Age," p. 28, and WWCW, p. 168.

16. STL, p. 66, TC, p. 69.

17. STL, p. 65, and WDWGFH, p. 181.

18. STL, p. 88.

19. WWCW, p. 79. See also discussion on p. 65 and in STF, p. 177.

20. See WWCW, pp 65-66.

21. WDWGFH, p. 181. Also note "In the final analysis, I must not ignore the wounded man on life's Jericho Road, because he is a part of me and I am a part of him. His agony diminishes me, and his salvation enlarges me" (STL, p. 29). See also STF, p. 88.

22. See WDWGFH, p. 65-66.

23. WWCW, p. 168.

24. Francis L. Broderick, August Meier, ed., *Negro Protest Thought in the Twentieth Century*, The American Heritage Series, New York: The Bobbs-Merrill Co., 1965, p. 373 (Hereafter referred to as *Negro Protest Thought*).

25. "Ethical Demands," pp. 3-4.

26. "After Desegregation: What?" in Boston Collection, p. 3.

27. *Playboy* Interview, p. 128.

28. "Ethical Demands," p. 4.

29. From an untitled manuscript in Boston Collection, p. 8.

30. Prayer Pilgrimage Address in May 1957 in Boston Collection, pp. 3-4.

31. "After Desegregation: What?" in Boston Collection, p. 5.

32. These references are from the "I Have a Dream" Speech in *Negro Protest Thought*, pp. 403-405. King often uses the figure of the races joining hands. Besides the above, see STF, p. 178.

33. "Honoring Dr. Dubois," *Freedomways*, Spring 1968, pp. 110-11.

34. "Paul's Letter to the American Churches," in Boston Collection, p. 2.

35. See WDWGFH, pp. 164-65.

36. *The Black Politician*, July 1969, p. 4.

37. Harvey Cox, *On Not Leaving It To The Snake*, New York: The Macmillan Co., 1967, p. 133.

38. STF, p. 68.

39. WDWGFH, p. 9. See also "The Right to Vote" in *New York Times Magazine*, March 14, 1965, p. 96, where much the same observation is made about the Selma campaign.

40. "The Case Against Tokenism," in *New York Times Magazine*, August 5, 1962, p. 49.

41. "Facing the Challenge of a New Age," *Phylon*, April 1957, p. 25.

42. *Ibid.*, p. 34.

43. *Ibid.*, p. 34.

44. Article entitled "The Rising Tide of Racial Consciousness.".

45. *Ibid.*, These are the very lines of the address.

46. "The American Dream," *Negro History Bulletin*, May 1968, pp. 10-15.

47. *Ibid.*, p. 15.

48. *Ibid.*, p. 15.

49. From the Album, "The Great March to Freedom," by Gordy, No. 906.

50. *Martin Luther King, Jr.*, p. 156.

51. *King: A Critical Biography*, p. 227.

52. *Negro Protest Thought*, p. 401.

53. *My Life with Martin Luther King, Jr.*, p. 236.

54. *Negro Protest Thought*, p. 405.

55. *Ibid.*, p. 403.

56. *Ibid.*, p. 403.

57. In conversation on January 23, 1971.

58. *Negro History Bulletin*, May 1968, p. 21.

59. TC, p. 76. These words are from a Christian sermon delivered at Ebenezer Baptist Church at Atlanta on Christmas Eve 1967.

60. *Ibid.*, p. 78. Note this reference from Job which concluded the address given in December 1956, "Facing the Challenge of a New Age," *Phylon*, April 1957, p. 34.

61. From *The Black Politician*, July 1969, in "A Contrast: The Last Major Political Speeches of Martin Luther King and Eldridge Cleaver," p. 30. King said the subject of his speech, delivered to the California Democratic Council, was "The Other America." This title reflects Michael Harrington's book by the same name about America's poor and we should note the inclusion in the last paragraph of this version of the dream "all ethnic groups." Earlier in the address he refers to the Mexican-American, Puerto Rican American, American Indians, and Appalachian whites when discussing plans for the Poor People's Campaign.

62. MM, p. 61.

63. MM, p. 60.

64. *Negro History Bulletin*, May 1968, p. 10.

65. *Ibid.*, p. 10.

66. "The Time For Freedom Has Come," in *New York Times Magazine*, September 10, 1961, p. 119. Hugo Adam Bedau offered his *Civil Disobedience: Theory and Practice* in memory of King, "who labored in the tradition of these words" and then Bedau quotes the Preamble to the Constitution. Bedau sensed the affinity King had for those lofty goals of our American democracy.

67. STL, p. 13.

68. "A Testament of Hope," *Playboy*, January 1969, p. 234.

69. Sherwood Eddy, *The Kingdom of God and the American Dream*, New York: Harper, 1941.

70. Paul Tillich, *On the Boundary*, New York: Charles Scribner's Sons, 1966, p. 96.

71. Reinhold Niebuhr, *Beyond Tragedy*, New York: Charles Scribner's Sons, 1937, p. 85.

72. "Ethical Demands," p. 3.

73. James Cone, *Black Theology and Black Power*, New York: The Seabury Press, 1969, p. 108.

74. "For All: A Non-Segregated Society," in the Boston Collection.

75. STL, p. 23.

76. For an excellent discussion on how King saw the Bible used as a legitimation of slavery and segregation, see STL pp. 35-38.

77. STF, p. 182.

78. MM, pp. 71-72.

79. TC, pp. 77-78.

80. I am identifying the passages from the prophets. This is Amos 5:24.

81. Micah 6:8.

82. Isaiah 2:4.

83. Isaiah 11:6.

84. Micah 4:4.

85. Isaiah 40:3-5.

86. *Negro Protest Thought*, p. 402.

87. STF, pp. 86-87.

88. STF, p. 87. Cf. Paul Ramsey, *Basic Christian Ethics*, New York: Charles Scribner's Sons, 1950, pp. 241-42. Ramsey states that *agape* can create community, but only self-interest can preserve it. King, betraying his liberal optimism, once said, "Love, *agape*, is the only cement that can hold this broken community together" (STF, p. 88).

89. STF, p. 87.

90. STF, p. 87.

91. Harvey Cox, *God's Revolution and Man's Responsibility*, Valley Forge: The Judson Press, 1965, pp. 58-69. Rauschenbusch also claimed that the purpose of Christianity was "to transform human society into the Kingdom of God by regenerating all human relations and reconstituting them in accordance with the will of God" (p. xxiii in introduction to *Christianity and the Social Crisis*). King's beloved community is a transformed and regenerated human society.

92. Schuchter, *op. cit.*, p. 569.

93. STL, p. 158.

94. STL, p. 159. See also STF, p. 182ff. and WWCW, pp. 95-96.

95. STL, pp. 57-58.

96. "Facing the Challenge of a New Age," pp. 29-30.

97. See STF, p. 193; "The Case Against Tokenism," *New York Times Magazine*, August 5, 1962, p. 52.

98. See STL, p. 48.

99. STF, p. 189.

100. See address to Montgomery Improvement Association, December 20, 1956, in the Boston Collection.

101. "We Are Still Walking," *Liberation*, December 1956, p. 1.

102. *Ibid.*, p. 2.

103. Martin Luther King, Jr., "Our Struggle," *Liberation*, April 1956.

104. *Playboy* Interview, January 1965, p. 125.

105. STL, p. 29 and WDWGFH, p. 101.

106. WDWGFH, p. 190.

107. *Ibid.*, pp. 190-91.

108. Cf. STF, pp. 148-49.

109. Martin Luther King, Jr., "The Power of Nonviolence," in *Intercollegian*, May 1958, p. 9.

110. See "Facing the Challenge of the New Age," p. 29.

111. STL, p. 48.

112. Albert C. Knudson, *The Philosophy of Personalism*, New York: The Abingdon Press, 1927, p. 237.

113. NV, p. 64. "For personalism, social categories are ultimate. . . . The structure of experience is social" (NV, p. 117).

114. See above discussion in chapter on Personalism.

115. STF, p. 88.

116. Edgar Sheffield Brightman, *A Philosophy of Religion*, New York: Prentice-Hall, 1940, pp. 276-77.

117. NV, p. 165.

118. Walter G. Muelder, *Moral Law in Christian Social Ethics*, Richmond, Virginia: John Knox Press, 1966, p. 29. See entire Chapter 2.

119. *Ibid.*, p. 16.

120. MM, p. 82.

121. MM, p. 21.

122. CLCD, pp. 162-63.

123. BT, p. 285.

124. Martin Luther King, Jr., "We Are Still Walking," *Liberation*, December 1956, p. 9.

125. Martin Luther King, Jr., "A View of the Dawn," *Interracial Review*, May 1947, p. 85.

126. "The Future of Integration," Boston Collection, p. 9.

127. *Playboy* Interview, p. 128.

128. STL, p. 78.

129. *Ibid.*

130. TC, p. 42.

Bibliography

I. MARTIN LUTHER KING, JR.

A. Book-Length Writings by King

King, Martin Luther, Jr., "A Comparison of the Conceptions of God in the Thinking of Paul Tillich and Henry Nelson Wieman." Ph.D Dissertation, Boston University, 1955.
–*Stride Toward Freedom:The Montgomery Story*. New York: Harper and Row, 1958.
–*The Measure of Man*. Philadelphia: Christian Education Press, 1959.
–*Strength to Love*. New York: Harper and Row, 1963.
–*Why We Can't Wait*. New York: Harper and Row, 1964.
–*The Trumpet of Conscience*. New York: Harper and Row, 1967.
–*A Martin Luther King Treasury*. Negro Heritage Library. New York: M.W. Lads, 1964.

B. Posthumous Editions of King's Writings

King, Martin Luther, Jr., *The Measure of a Man* (with a biographical sketch by Truman Douglass). Boston: Pilgrim Press, 1968.
–*The Trumpet of Conscience* (with a Foreword by Coretta Scott King). New York: Harper and Row, 1968.
Ezekial, Nissim, ed. *A Martin Luther King Reader*. Bombay: Popular Prakashan, 1968.
Hoskins, Lotte, ed. *I Have a Dream*. New York: Grosset and Dunlop, 1968.
The Wisdom of Martin Luther King. Edited by Bill Adler Books, 1968.

C. Chapters in Books

–"I Have a Dream." Leinwand, Gerald, ed. *The Negro in the City*. New York: Washington Square Press, 1968.

–"I Have a Dream." *Nonviolence and the United States Civil Rights Struggle*. Geneva: Secretariat on Racial and Ethnic Relations, 1964.

–"I Have a Dream." Saunders, Doris. *The Day They Marched*. Chicago: Johnson Publishing, 1963.

–"I Have a Dream." Franklin, John Hope; Starr, Isidore, eds. *The Negro in Twentieth Century America*. New York: Vintage Books (Random House), 1967.

–"I Have a Dream." Chambers, Bradford, ed. *Chronicles of Black Protest*. New York: New American Library, 1968.

–"Pilgrimage to Nonviolence." Weinberg, Arthur and Lila, ed. *Instead of Violence*. Boston: Beacon Press, 1968.

–"Pilgrimage to Nonviolence." Lynd, Staughton, ed. *Nonviolence in America: A Documentary History*. New York: Bobbs-Merrill, 1966.

–"Letter From Birmingham Jail." Bedau, Hugo Adam, ed. *Civil Disobedience: Theory and Practice*. New York: Pegasus Publishing Co., 1969.

–"Letter From Birmingham Jail." Lynd, Staughton, ed. *Nonviolence in America: A Documentary History*. New York: Bobbs-Merrill, 1966.

–"Letter From Birmingham Jail." Raines, Robert, ed. *Creative Brooding*. New York: Macmillan Co., 1968.

–"Letter From Birmingham Jail." Weston, Alan F., ed. *Freedom Now: The Civil Rights Struggle in America*. New York: Basic Books, 1964.

–"Letter From Birmingham Jail." Daniel, Bradford, ed. *Black, White, and Gray: Twenty-One Points of View on The Race Question*. New York: Sheed and Ward, 1964.

–"Letter From Birmingham Jail." Franklin, John Hope; Starr, Isidore, eds. *The Negro in Twentieth Century America*. New York: Vintage Books (Random House), 1967.

–"Letter From Birmingham Jail." Gustafson, James; Laney, James T., ed. *On Being Responsible*. London: SCM Press, 1968.

–"The Day of Days, December 5." Chambers, Bradford, ed. *Chronicles of Black Protest*. New York: New American Library, 1968.

–"Nonviolence and Racial Justice." Fey, Harold E., Frakes, Margaret, ed. *The Christian Century Reader*. New York: Association Press, 1962 (reprint from *Christian Century*, June 5, 1957).

–"Love in Action." Davies, Alfred T., ed. *The Pulpit Speaks on Race*. New York: Abingdon, 1965 (reprint from *Strength to Love*).

–"Declaration of Independence from the War in Vietnam." Hamilton, Michael, ed. *The Vietnam War: Christian Perspectives*. Grand Rapids: Erdmans Publishing, 1967.

–"Martin Luther King Talks with Kenneth B. Clark." *The Negro Protest*. Clark, Kenneth B., ed. Boston: Beacon Press, 1963.

–"Sensitive Companionship." Potthoff, Harvey H. *The Inner Life*. Nashville: Graded Press, 1969 (from *Strength to Love*, pp. 143-44).

–"The Un-Christian Christian." Editors of *Ebony*. *The White Problem in America*. Chicago: Johnson Publishing, 1966.

–"Introduction." Huie, William Bradford. *Three Lives For Mississippi*. New York: New American Library, 1964.

–"Foreward." Gregg, Richard. *The Power of Nonviolence*. New York: Schocken Books, 2nd ed., 1959.

–"Introduction." Clayton, Edward T. *The Negro Politician: His Success and Failure*. Chicago: Johnson Publishing Co., Inc., 1964.

D. Articles in Periodicals

1956

–"Our Struggle." *Liberation*, April 1956.
–"Walk for Freedom." *Fellowship*. May 1956.
–"We Are Still Walking." *Liberation*. December 1956.

1957

–"Nonviolence and Racial Justice." *The Christian Century*. February 6, 1957.
–"Facing the Challenge of a New Age." *Fellowship*. February 1957.
–"Facing the Challenge of a New Age." *Phylon*. April 1957.
–"A View of the Dawn." *Interracial Review*. May 1957.

–"The Most Durable Power." *The Christian Century*. June 5, 1957.
–"Advice for Living" (a regular column in *Ebony*). September, October, December, 1957.

1958

–"Out of the Long Night of Segregation." *Presbyterian Outlook*. February 10, 1958.
–"Out of the Long Night of Segregation." *Advance*. February 28, 1958.
–"Out of Segregation's Long Night." *The Churchman*. February 1958.
–"The Current Crisis in Race Relations." *The New South*. March 1958.
–"Who Speaks for the South." *Liberation*. March 1958.
–"The Ethics of Love." *Religious Digest*. April 1958.
–"The Power of Nonviolence." *Intercollegian*. May 1958.
–"An Experiment in Love." *Jubilee*. September 1958.
–"Advice for Living." *Ebony*. January, February, March, April, May, July, August, September, November, December 1958.

1959

–"The Future of Integration." *Crises in Modern America*. H. John Heinz III, ed. Yale University. April 1959.
–"My Trip to the Land of Gandhi." *Ebony*. July 1959.
–"The Social Organization of Nonviolence." *Liberation*. October 1959.

1960

–"Pilgrimage to Nonviolence." *The Christian Century*. April 13, 1960.
–"Meet the Press Interview." April 17, 1960.
–"Suffering and Faith." *The Christian Century*. April 27, 1960.
–"The Burning Truth About the South." *The Progressive*. May 1960.
King, Martin Luther, Jr. "The Rising Tide of Racial Consciousness." *The YWCA Magazine*. December 1960.
–"Is Violence Necessary to Combat Injustice?" *The Southern Patriot*. January 1960.

1961

-"Equality Now: The President Has The Power." *The Nation.* February 4, 1961.

-"The Man Who Was a Fool." *The Pulpit.* June 1961.

-"Time for Freedom Has Come." *The New York Times Magazine.* September 10, 1961.

-"Love, Law and Civil Disobedience." *The New South.* December 1961.

1962

-"Fumbling on the New Frontier." *The Nation.* March 3, 1962.

-"Case Against Tokenism." *The New York Times Magazine.* August 5, 1962.

-"Who is Their God?" *The Nation.* October 13, 1962.

-"The Luminous Promise." *The Progressive.* December 1962.

1963

-"Bold Design for a New South." *The Nation.* March 30, 1963.

-"The Ethical Demands of Integration." *Religion and Labor.* May 1963.

-"Letter from Birmingham Jail." *The Christian Century.* June 12, 1963.

-"Emancipation-1963." *Renewal.* June 1963.

-"Letter from Birmingham Jail." *Liberation.* June 1963.

-"Letter from Birmingham Jail." *Interracial Review.* July 1963.

-"Letter from Birmingham Jail." *Ebony* (excerpts). August 1963.

-"In a Word: Now." *The New York Times Magazine.* September 29, 1963.

1964

-"Hammer of Civil Rights." *The Nation.* March 9, 1964.

-"Why We Can't Wait." *Life.* May 15, 1964 (excerpts from book).

-"Why We Can't Wait." *Saturday Review.* May 30, 1964 (excerpts from book).

-"Negroes are not Moving Too Fast." *Saturday Evening Post*. November 7, 1964.

-"The Sword that Heals." *The Critic*. June-July 1964 (excerpts from *Why We Can't Wait*, chapter 2).

1965

-"Interview with Martin Luther King." *Playboy*. January 1965.

-"Dreams of a Brighter Tomorrow." *Ebony*. March 1965.

-"Civil Right No. 1." *The New York Times Magazine*. March 14, 1965.

-"Let Justice Roll Down." *The Nation*. March 15, 1965.

-"Behind the Selma March." *Saturday Review*. April 3, 1965.

-"Unchristian Christian." *Ebony*. August 1965.

-"Next Stop: The North." *Saturday Review*. November 13, 1965.

1966

-"The Last Steep Ascent." *The Nation*. March 14, 1966.

-"Nonviolence: The Only Road to Freedom." *Ebony*. October 1966.

-"Gift of Love." *McCall's*. December 1966.

1967

-"Interview: Dr. Martin Luther King, Jr." *The New York Times*, April 2, 1967.

-"The Casualties of the War in Vietnam." *Speak on the War in Vietnam*. Clergy and Laymen Concerned About Vietnam. April 1967.

-"Martin Luther King Defines Black Power." *The New York Times Magazine*. June 11, 1967.

1968

-*The Catholic Worker* (excerpts from *Where Do We Go From Here?*). April 1968.

–"Never Let Them Rest." *Liberation*. April 1968 (reprint of "The Social Organization of Nonviolence." *Liberation*. October 1959).
–"Showdown for Nonviolence." *Look*. April 16, 1968.
–"The American Dream." *Negro History Bulletin*. May 1968.
–"America's Racial Crisis." *Current*. May 1968.
–"Honoring Dr. Dubois." *Freedomways*. Spring 1968.
–"Dark Yesterdays, Bright Tomorrows." *Reader's Digest*. June 1968.
–"Say That I Was a Drum Major." *Reader's Digest*. June 1968.
–"Moving to Another Mountain." *Wesleyan Alumnus*. Spring 1968.

1969

–"A Testament of Hope." *Playboy*. January 1989.
–"A View from the Mountaintop." *Renewal*. April 1969.
–"The Last Major Political Speeches of: Martin Luther King and Eldridge Cleaver." *The Black Politician*. July 1969.

E. Nobel Speeches

–"The Acceptance."–Speech accepting the Nobel Peace Prize (December 10, 1964) in *Dear Dr. King*. New York: Buckingham Enterprises, Inc. 1968.
–"The Lecture"–Dr. Martin Luther King's Nobel Lecture delivered in the Aula of the Oslo University, Norway (December 11, 1964) in *Dear Dr. King*, *op. cit.*

F. Films and Filmstrips

"I Have a Dream," 35 minute black and white film on life and work of Martin Luther King (16mm) from Mr. Vincent Deforest, SCLC, 427 Whittier St. N.W., Washington, D.C. 20012.
"Martin Luther King," a filmed interview, 30 minutes in length (16mm) black and white produced by BBC-TV and available from Peter M. Robeck and Co., Inc., 230 Park Avenue, New York 10017, (212-691-2930).

"The Reverend Martin Luther King, Jr.," a sound filmstrip (A244-3), Society for Visual Education, Inc., 1325 Diversey Parkway, Chicago, Illinois 60614.

G. Record Albums

–We Shall Overcome! Documentary of the March on Washington. Broadside Records, BR-592.
–The Great March on Washington. Gordy, 908.
– . . . Free At Last. Gordy, 929.
–The Great March to Freedom. Detroit, June 23, 1964. Gordy, 906.
–Martin Luther King, Jr., Pastor . . . Revolutionary. mlks, E 6905.
–I've Been to the Mountaintop. mlks, 6914.
–A Knock at Midnight. Creed.
–Why I Oppose the War in Vietnam. Motown, Detroit.
–Remaining Awake Through a Great Revolution. May 8, 1964, Nashboro (Rec. Co.).
–Dr. Martin Luther King, Jr. at Zion Hill. Pica Productions, DTL, 831.
–The American Dream. Dooto Records. Los Angeles, DTL, 841.
–We Shall Overcome: Songs of Freedom Rides and Sit-ins.

H. Unpublished Material in the Boston Collection

1. Term Papers Written During Graduate Work at Boston University

–An Exposition of the First Triad of Categories of the Hegelian Logic–Being, Non-Being, Becoming.
–The Transition from Sense-Certainty to Sense in Hegel's Analysis of Consciousness.
–The Transition from Sense-Perception to Understanding Objective Spirit.
–A Conception and Impression of Religion Drawn from Dr. Brightman's Book Entitled, *A Philosophy of Religion.*
–Religion's Answer to The Problem of Evil.
–Karl Barth's Conception of God.
–A Comparison and Evaluation of the Philosophical Views Set Forth in J.M.E. McTaggart's *Some Dogmas of Religion* and William E. Hocking's

The Meaning of God in Human Experience with those Set Forth in Edgar S. Brightman's Course on "Philosophy of Religion."
–The Personalism of J.M.E. McTaggart Under Criticism.
–Contemporary Continental Theology.
–Reinhold Niebuhr.
–Reinhold Niebuhr's Ethical Dualism.

2. Other unpublished manuscripts in the Boston Collection

–"The Montgomery Story." Address by Rev. Dr. Martin Luther King, Pastor of the Dexter Avenue Baptist Church and President of the Montgomery Improvement Association, Montgomery, Alabama, at 47th NAACP Annual Convention. Civic Auditorium, San Francisco, California. Wednesday, June 27, 1956.
–Statement of Martin Luther King, Jr., President of the Montgomery Improvement Association Before the National Democratic Platform and Resolutions Committee. August 11, 1956.
–Statement by the President of the Montgomery Improvement Association. The Rev. M.L. King, Jr. November 14, 1956.
–"A Realistic Look at the Question of Progress in the Area of Race Relations." Address delivered at the Second Anniversary of the NAACP Legal Defense and Educational Fund at the Waldorf Astoria Hotel. New York City. May 17, 1956.
–Statement by the President of the Montgomery Improvement Association. The Rev. M.L. King, Jr. December 20, 1956.
–"For All . . . A Non-Segregated Society." A message for Race Relations Sunday, February 10, 1957. Issued by The Executive Board of the Division of Christian Life and Work. The National Council of the Churches of Christ in the U.S.A.
–Address by Rev. Dr. Martin Luther King, Jr., Pastor. The Dexter Avenue Baptist Church. President of the Montgomery Improvement Association. Chairman, The Southern Leadership Conference. The Prayer Pilgrimage For Freedom at the Lincoln Memorial. Washington, D.C. May 17, 1957.
–Statement Presented by Martin Luther King, Jr. to Judge Eugene Loe. Friday, September 5, 1958. Montgomery, Alabama.
–Address by Dr. Martin Luther King, Jr. at National Bar Association. Milwaukee, Wisconsin. Thursday, August 20, 1959.

287

-"The Future of Integration." Speech Delivered by Dr. Martin Luther King, Jr. at The State University of Iowa. Wednesday, November 11, 1959. Iowa City, Iowa.

-Annual Address by President Martin Luther King, Jr., on the Fourth Anniversary of the Montgomery Improvement Association at the Bethel Baptist Church. December 3, 1959.

-Basic Points in Statement to be Presented to the American Baptist Convention on Reasons for Going to the Soviet Union.

-"After Segregation-What?"-Statement by Dr. Martin Luther King at Lawyers Advisory Committee Meeting. New York City, New York. May 8, 1961.

-An Address by Dr. Martin Luther King, Jr., President Southern Christian Leadership Conference at the "Pilgrimage for Democracy" in Atlanta, Georgia. Sunday, December 15, 1963.

-Statement Before the Platform Committee of the Republican National Convention. San Francisco, California. July 7, 1964, by Dr. Martin Luther King, Jr., President, Southern Christian Leadership Conference.

II. WRITINGS ABOUT MARTIN LUTHER KING, JR.

A. Articles

Boutelle, Paul; Novack, George; DeBerry, Clifton; and Hansen, Joseph. *Murder in Memphis*. New York: Merit Publishers, 1969.

Carberg, Warren. "The Story Behind the Victory." *Bostonia*. Spring, 1957.

Clayton, Helen J. "Martin Luther King: The Right Man at the Right Time." *The YWCA Magazine*. June 1968.

Curtis, C.J. "The Negro Contribution to American Theology: King." *Contemporary Protestant Thought*. Contemporary Theology Series. General editors: J. Frank Devine, Richard W. Rousseau. New York: The Bruce Publishing Co. 1970.

Deats, Paul, Jr. "King and Mondlane: Choice of Weapons." *Christian Advocate*. July 10, 1969.

Elder, John Dixon. "Martin Luther King and American Civil Religion." *Harvard Divinity Bulletin*. Spring 1968.

Fager, Charles E. "Dilemma for Dr. King." *The Christian Century*. March 16, 1966.

Good, Paul. "Bossism, Racism, and Dr. King." *The Intercollegian*. Fall 1966.

Griffin, John Howard. "Martin Luther King's Moment." *The Sign*. April 1963.

King, Coretta Scott. "The Legacy of Martin Luther King, Jr.: The Church in Action." *Theology Today*. July 1970.

Lincoln, C. Eric, ed. *Martin Luther King, Jr.: A Profile*. American Profiles. General editor: Aida DiPace Donald. New York: Hill and Wang. 1970.

Maguire, John David. "Martin Luther King and Vietnam." *Christianity and Crisis*. May 1, 1967.

McClendon, James William, Jr. "The Religion of Martin Luther King, Jr." Unpublished manuscript. Goucher College. 1971.

Negro History Bulletin. May 1968. (Entire Issue).

Quarles, Benjamin. "Martin Luther King in History." *The Negro History Bulletin*. May 1968.

Richardson, Herbert Warren. "Martin Luther King–Unsung Theologian." In *New Theology No. 6*, edited by Martin Marty and Dean Peerman. New York: The Macmillan Co. 1969.

Romero, Patricia W. "Martin Luther King and His Challenge to White America." *The Negro History Bulletin*. May 1968.

Schulz, William. "Martin Luther King's March on Washington." *Reader's Digest*. April 1968.

Smith, Donald H. "An Exegesis of Martin Luther King, Jr.'s Social Philosophy." *Phylon*. Spring 1970.

Smith, Kenneth L. "Martin Luther King, Jr.: Reflections on a Former Teacher." *Bulletin of Crozer Theological Seminary*. April 1965.

–"The Intellectual Sources of the Thought of Martin Luther King, Jr." Unpublished manuscript. Crozer Theological Seminary, 1969.

Smylie, James H. "On Jesus, Pharoahs, and the Chosen People: Martin Luther King as Biblical Interpreter and Humanist." *Interpretation*. January 1970.

Terrell, Robert. "Discarding the Dream." *Evergreen*. May 1970.

B. *Biographies*

Bartlett, Robert. "Martin Luther King, Jr." In *We, Too, Belong*, edited by Mary Turner. New York: Dell Publishing, 1969. This was originally in Robert Bartlett's *They Stand Invincible*. New York: Thomas Crowell, 1959.

Bennett, Lerone. *What Manner of Man*. Chicago: Johnson Publishing Co., 1964 and 1968.

Bleiweiss, Robert M., ed. *Marching to Freedom: The Life of Martin Luther King, Jr.* New York: New American Library, 1969.

Davis, L.G. *I Have a Dream*. Chicago: Adams Press, 1969.

Griffin, John Howard. "Martin Luther King" in *Thirteen for Christ*, edited by Melville Harcourt. New York: Sheed and Ward, 1963.

Holmes, Richard. "Ordeal of Martin Luther King." In *Listen, White Man, I'm Bleeding*. Edited by Phil Hirsch. New York: Pyramid Books, 1969.

King, Coretta Scott. *My Life With Martin Luther King, Jr.* New York: Holt, Rinehart, and Winston, 1969.

Lewis, David L. *King: A Critical Biography*. New York: Praeger   Publishers, 1970.

Lokos, Lionel. *House Divided: The Life and Legacy of Martin Luther King*. New Rochelle, New York: Arlington House, 1968.

Lomax, Louis. *To Kill a Black Man*. Los Angeles: Holloway House, 1968.

"Martin Luther King and the Montgomery Story" (in True Comic Book form). Fellowship. Nyack, New York. English and Spanish Editions. Spring 1957.

Miller, William Robert. *Martin Luther King, Jr.* New York: Weybright and Talley, 1968.

Poston, Ted. *Martin Luther King: Fighting Pastor. New York Post*. April 8-13, 1957.

Reddick, Lawrence. *Crusader Without Violence*. New York: Harper and Row, 1959.

Williams, John A. *The King God Didn't Save*. New York: Coward-McCown, Inc., 1970.

Uwen, Nathan. *Martin Luther King, Jr.* New York: New Dimensions Publishing Co., Inc., 1970.

C. General Background

Cruse, Harold. *The Crisis of the Negro Intellectual.* New York: William Morrow & Co., 1967.

Blair, Clay, Jr. *The Strange Case of James Earl Ray: The Man Who Murdered Martin Luther King.* New York: Grosset & Dunlop, Inc. Bantam Books, 1969.

Blaustein, Albert P.; Zangrando, Robert L., ed. *Civil Rights and the American Negro: A Documentary History.* New York: Washington Square Press, Inc., 1968.

Broderick, Francis L.; Meier, August, ed. *Negro Protest Thought in the Twentieth Century.* The American Heritage Series. New York: The Bobbs-Merrill Co., Inc., 1965.

Editors of *Ebony. The White Problem in America.* Chicago: Johnson Publishing Co., Inc., 1966.

Fager, Charles. *Uncertain Resurrection: The Poor People's Washington Campaign.* Grand Rapids: William B. Eerdmans Publishing Co., 1969.

Franklin, John Hope; Starr, Isidore, eds. *The Negro in Twentieth Century America: A Reader on the Struggle for Civil Rights.* New York: Random House, Vintage Books, 1967.

Huie, William Bradford. *He Slew the Dreamer: My Search for the Truth About James Earl Ray and the Murder of Martin Luther King.* New York: Delacorte Press, 1970.

Killian, Lewis M. *The Impossible Revolution?: Black Power and the American Dream.* New York: Random House, 1968.

Lomax, Louis E. *The Negro Revolt.* New York: The New American Library, A Signet Book, 1963.

Meier, August; Rudwick, Elliott, ed. *Black Protest in the Sixties.* A New York Times Book. Chicago: Quadrangle Books, 1970.

Muse, Benjamin. *The American Negro Revolution: From Nonviolence to Black Power.* Bloomington: Indiana University Press, 1968.

Quarles, Benjamin. *The Negro in the Making of America.* New York: Collier Books, 1964.

Rowan, Carl T. *Go South to Sorrow.* New York: Random House, 1957.

Schuchter, Arnold. *White Power/Black Freedom: Planning the Future of Urban America.* Boston: Beacon Press, 1968.

Weisberg, Harold. *Frame-Up: The Martin Luther King/James Earl Ray Case*. New York: Outerbridge & Dienstfrey, 1971.

Wolff, Miles. *Lunch at the Five and Ten: The Greenboro Sit-Ins*. New York: Stein and Day, 1970.

D. Posthumous Tributes to King

V. Illai, ed. *Indian Leaders on King*. Published by Inter-State Cultural League of India. New Delhi: Century Press, 1968.

Dear Dr. King. New York: Buckingham Enterprises, Inc., 1968.

Memorial–Martin Luther King. New York: Country Wide Publications, 1968.

I Have a Dream. New York: Time-Life Books, 1968.

Martin Luther King, Jr. Chicago: Johnson Publishing Co., 1968.

Jet. April 25, 1968.

Martin Luther King, Jr.: His Life–His Death. Fort Worth: Sepia Publishers, 1968.

Record Album, "Letter To My Dearest Friend," Ralph Abernathy, mlks.

III. A SELECTED BIBLIOGRAPHY OF KING'S INTELLECTUAL SOURCES

A. *American Religious Liberalism and the Social Gospel*

Barnes, Sherman B. "Walter Rauschenbusch as Historian." *Foundations*. July-September 1969.

Brown, William Adams. *Christian Theology in Outline*. New York: Charles Scribner's Sons, 1906.

Cauthen, Kenneth. *The Impact of American Religious Liberalism*. New York: Harper and Row, 1962.

Clarke, William Newton. *An Outline of Christian Theology*. New York: Charles Scribner's Sons, 1916.

Davis, George W. "The Ethical Basis of Christian Salvation." *Crozer Quarterly*. July 1939.

–"God and History." *Crozer Quarterly*. January 1943.

–"Theological Continuities in Crisis Theology." *Crozer Quarterly*. July 1950.

–"In Praise of Liberalism." *Theology Today*. January 1948.

–"Liberalism and a Theology of Depth." *Crozer Quarterly*. July 1951.

DeWolf, L. Harold. *The Case for Theology in Liberal Perspective*. Philadelphia: The Westminster Press, 1959.

Handy, Robert T., ed. *The Social Gospel in America, 1870-1920: Gladden-Ely-Rauschenbusch*. New York: Oxford University Press, 1966.

Hopkins, C. Howard. *The Rise of the Social Gospel in American Protestantism, 1865-1915*. Yale Studies in Religious Education XIV. New Haven: Yale University Press, 1940.

Mackintosh, Hugh Ross. *Types of Modern Theology: Schleiermacher to Barth*. London: Nisbet and Co. Ltd., 1954.

Nash, Arnold, ed. *Protestant Thought in the Twentieth Century*. New York: The Macmillan Co., 1951.

Niebuhr, Reinhold. "Walter Rauschenbusch in Historical Perspective." In *Faith and Politics*, edited by Ronald H. Stone. New York: George Braziller, 1968.

Rauschenbusch, Walter. *Christianity and the Social Crisis*. Edited by Robert D. Cross. New York: Harper and Row. Harper Torchbooks, 1964. It was first published in 1907.

–*Christianizing the Social Order*. New York: The Macmillan Co., 1912.

–*A Theology for the Social Gospel*. New York: The Macmillan Co., 1918.

–*Prayers of the Social Awakening*. Boston: The Pilgrim Press, 1910.

–*The Righteousness of the Kingdom*. Edited and Introduced by Max L. Stackhouse. New York: Abingdon Press, 1968.

–"The Value and Use of History." *Foundations*. July-September, 1969.

Reardon, Bernard M.G. *Religious Thought in the Nineteenth Century: Illustrated from Writers of the Period*. Cambridge: University Press, 1966.

Ritschl, Albrecht. *The Christian Doctrine of Justification and Reconciliation*. English translation by H.R. Mackintosh and A.B. Macauley. Clifton, New Jersey: Reference Book Publishers, 1966.

Roberts, David E., Van Dusen, Henry P., eds. *Liberal Theology, An Appraisal*. New York: Charles Scribner's Sons, 1942.

Schleiermacher, Friedrich. *The Christian Faith*. Edited by H.R. Mackintosh and J.S. Stewart. English translation of the Second German Edition. Edinburgh: T.&T. Clark, 1956.

Van Dusen, Henry P. *The Vindication of Liberal Theology: A Tract for the Times*. New York: Charles Scribner's Sons, 1963.

B. Nonviolence

Andrews, Charles Freer. *Mahatma Gandhi's Ideas*. New York: The Macmillan Co., 1930.

Bondurant, Joan V. *Conquest of Violence: The Gandhian Philosophy of Conflict*. Rev ed. Berkeley and Los Angeles: University of California Press, 1967.

Bedau, Hugo Adam, ed. *Civil Disobedience: Theory and Practice*. New York: Pegasus, 1967.

Douglass, James W. *The Nonviolent Cross: A Theology of Revolution and Peace*. London: Collier-Macmillan Ltd., 1968.

Ellul, Jacques. *Violence: Reflections from a Christian Perspective*. Translated by Cecelia Gaul Kings. New York: The Seabury Press, 1969.

Erikson, Erik H. *Gandhi's Truth: On the Origins of Militant Nonviolence*. New York: W.W. Norton and Co., 1969.

Fanon, Frantz. *The Wretched of the Earth*. Translated by Constance Farrington. New York: The Grove Press, Inc., 1968.

Fischer, Louis. *The Life of Mahatma Gandhi*. Toronto: Collier Books, 1962.
–ed. *The Essential Gandhi: His Life, Word, and Ideas. An Anthology*. New York: Random House, Vintage Books, 1963.

Fortas, Abe. *Concerning Dissent and Civil Disobedience*. New York: Signet Books, 1968.

Gandhi, M.K. *The Law of Love*. Pocket Gandhi Series No. 3. Edited and Published by Anand T. Hingorani. Bombay: Bharatiya Vidya Bhavan, 1962.

–*Nonviolent Resistance (Satyagraha)*. New York: Schocken Books, 1968.

–*An Autobiography: The Story of My Experiments With Truth*. Translated by Mahadev Desai. Boston: Beacon Press, 1957.

Gregg, Richard B. *The Power of Nonviolence*. 2d rev. ed. New York: Schocken Books, 1966.

Lacy, Creighton. *The Conscience of India: Moral Traditions in the Modern World*. New York: Holt, Rinehart and Winston, 1965.

Lynd, Staughton, ed. *Nonviolence in America: A Documentary History*. The American Heritage Series. New York: The Bobbs-Merrill Co., Inc., 1966.

Marty, Martin E., and Peerman, Dean G., ed. *New Theology No. 6*. London: Collier-Macmillan, Ltd., 1969.

Merton, Thomas. *Faith and Violence: Christian Teaching and Christian Practice*. Notre Dame, Indiana: University of Notre Dame Press, 1968.
–ed. *Gandhi on Nonviolence*. New York: A New Directions Paperback, 1965.

Miller, William Robert. *Nonviolence: A Christian Interpretation*. New York: Schocken Books, 1966.

Muste, A.J. *Nonviolence in an Aggressive World*. New York: Harper and Brothers, 1940.

–*Of Holy Disobedience*. Number 64. Wallingford, Pennsylvania: Pendle Hill, 1968.

Rolland, Romain. *Mahatma Gandhi*. Translated by Catherine D. Groth. New York: The Century Co., 1924.

Seifert, Harvey. *Conquest by Suffering: The Process and Prospects of Nonviolent Resistance*. Philadelphia: The Westminster Press, 1965.

Thoreau, Henry David. *Walden or Life in the Woods and On the Duty of Civil Disobedience*. New York: The New American Library, 1960.

C. Christian Realism

Harland, Gordon. *The Thought of Reinhold Niebuhr*. New York: Oxford University Press, 1960.

Horton, Walter M. *Realistic Theology*. New York: Harper and Brothers, 1934.

Kegley, Charles W., Bretall, Robert W., ed. *Reinhold Niebuhr: His Religious, Social, and Political Thought*. The Library of Living Theology, Vol. II. New York: The Macmillan Co., 1956.

Macgregor, G.H.C. *The New Testament Basis of Pacifism and The Relevance of an Impossible Ideal*. Nyack, New York: Fellowship Publications, 1954.

Niebuhr, Reinhold. *Moral Man and Immoral Society*. New York: Charles Scribner's Sons, 1932.

–*Reflections at the End of an Era*. New York: Charles Scribner's Sons, 1934.

–*Beyond Tragedy: Essays on the Christian Interpretation of History*. New York: Charles Scribner's Sons, 1937.

–*Christianity and Power Politics*. New York: Charles Scribner's Sons, 1940.

–*The Children of Light and The Children of Darkness: A Vindication of Democracy and a Critique of Its Traditional Defense*. New York: Charles Scribner's Sons, 1944.

–*Christian Realism and Political Problems*. New York: Charles Scribner's Sons, 1953.

–*The Nature and Destiny of Man: A Christian Interpretation*. Vol I. Human Nature, Vol II. Human Destiny. One Volume Edition. Gifford Lectures. New York: Charles Scribner's Sons, 1953.

–*An Interpretation of Christian Ethics*. New York: Meridian Books, 1956.

–*Essays in Applied Christianity*. Selected and Edited by D.B. Robertson. New York: Meridian Books, 1959.

–*Man's Nature and His Communities: Essays on the Dynamics and Enigmas of Man's Personal and Social Existence*. New York: Charles Scribner's Sons, 1965.

–*Love and Justice: Selections from the Shorter Writings of Reinhold Niebuhr*. Edited by D.B. Robertson. New York: The World Publishing Co., Meridian Books, 1967.

Niebuhr, Reinhold. *Faith and Politics: A Commentary on Religious, Social, and Political Thought in a Technological Age*. Edited by Ronald H. Stone. New York: George Braziller, 1968.

Sellers, James. "Love, Justice and the Nonviolent Movement." *Theology Today*, January 1962.

Thelen, Mary Frances. *Man as Sinner in Contemporary Realistic Theology*. New York: King's Crown Press, 1946.

Yoder, John. *Reihold Niebuhr and Christian Pacifism*. Washington, D.C.: The Church Peace Mission, 1966.

D. Personalism

Bowne, Borden Parker. *Philosophy of Theism*. New York: Harper and Brothers, 1887.

–*Personalism*. New York: Houghton Mifflin Co., 1908.

Brightman, Edgar Sheffield. *An Introduction to Philosophy*. Revised by Robert N. Beck. New York: Holt, Rinehart, and Winston, 1963. It was first published in 1925 and revised by Brightman in 1951.

–*Moral Laws*. New York: Abingdon Press, 1933.

–*A Philosophy of Religion*. New York: Prentice-Hall, 1940.

–*Nature and Values*. Nashville: Abingdon-Cokesbury, 1945.

DeWolf, L. Harold. *The Religious Revolt Against Reason*. New York: Harper and Brothers, 1949.

–*A Theology of the Living Church.* 2nd rev. ed. New York: Harper and Row, 1968. It was first published in 1953 and revised in 1960.

Flewelling, Ralph Tyler. *Personality and the Problems of Philosophy.* New York: The Methodist Book Concern, 1915.

Hegel, Georg W.F. *The Phenomenology of Mind.* 2nd ed. Translated by J.B. Baillie. New York: George Allen and Unwin, 1961.

Knudson, Albert C. *The Philosophy of Personalism.* New York: The Abingdon Press, 1943.

–*The Principles of Christian Ethics.* New York: Abingdon Press, 1943.

Lotze, Rudolph Hermann. *Microcosmus: An Essay Concerning Man and His Relation to the World.* Volumes I and II. Translated by Elizabeth Hamilton and E.E. Constance Jones. Edinburgh: T.&T. Clark, 1885.

Muelder, Walter G. *Moral Law in Christian Social Ethics.* Richmond: John Knox Press, 1966.

Index

Martin Luther King, Jr.

and the

Civil Rights Movement

DAVID J. GARROW, EDITOR